Y0-DYM-453

America's Economy problems and prospects

Timely Reports to Keep
Journalists, Scholars and the Public
Abreast of Developing Issues, Events and Trends

Editorial Research Reports
Published by Congressional Quarterly Inc.
1414 22nd Street, N.W.
Washington, D.C. 20037

About the Cover

The cover was designed by Staff Artist Belle Burkhart.

PRINTED IN THE UNITED STATES OF AMERICA
April 1983

Editor, Hoyt Gimlin
Managing Editor, Sandra Stencel
Editorial Assistants, Laurie De Maris, Elizabeth Furbush
Production Manager, I. D. Fuller
Assistant Production Manager, Maceo Mayo

Library of Congress Cataloging in Publication Data

Main entry under title:

Editorial research reports on America's economy problems
and prospects.

Bibliography: p.
Includes index.
1. United States — Economic conditions — 1981- —
Addresses, essays, lectures. 2. United States — Economic policy
— 1981-   — Addresses, essays, lectures.
I. Congressional Quarterly, Inc. II. Title: America's econ-
omy, problems and prospects.
HC106.8.E34   1983   330.973'0927   83-7290
ISBN 0-87187-256-0

Contents

Foreword

Out of the winter of America's economic discontent have come some rays of springtime prophecy that the recovery has begun. Economic forecasters tell us the signs point to the end of this country's longest and deepest recession since the Depression Thirties. Americans obviously want to believe the forecasters are correct even while remaining skeptical. After all, they heard similar prophecies a year ago.

Regardless of whether the end of the recession is drawing near, it will not soon be forgotten. Nor will all of its problems be easily dismissed. Unemployment still remains above 10 percent as these words are being written, and some of America's old-line industries may never recover fully. That is the considered opinion of experts, who are cited in these 10 Reports examining in detail such areas as America's employment outlook, small business difficulties, industrial technology, the dilemmas over Social Security funding, and a farm policy of dealing with agricultural overabundance at a time when charity-sponsored soup kitchens have returned to the urban scene. Among the hungry and homeless, the "new poor" have been added to the "hard-core poor."

Some New Deal-like solutions are in the offing. For instance, the House of Representatives has passed a federal jobs program that calls for the creation of an agency somewhat like FDR's Civilian Conservation Corps. And yet our economic seers tell us that these measures are but expedients — that the nation's economic health must be reclaimed in vigorous production and technological innovation. They speak of the coming "robot revolution" and other aspects of technology to keep this country competitive and prosperous.

Hoyt Gimlin
Editor

April 1983
Washington, D.C.

AMERICA'S EMPLOYMENT OUTLOOK

by

Robert Benenson

May 28
1 9 8 2

Editor's Note: After this Report was written, the American economy continued to sink into the deepest recession since the 1930s. Unemployment reached 10.8 percent of the work force in December before improving slightly in the early months of 1983. However, more than 11 million Americans were still looking for work. Among blacks, unemployment was nearly 20 percent; for black teen-agers it was approaching 50 percent.

Aside from unemployment, the year 1983 brought hope for recovery. There was a surge in the government's leading economic indicators, portending greater business activity and some restoration of consumer confidence. The "high-tech" revolution, long regarded as the fount of future economic growth was slowed but not halted by the recession. Even in the face of recession, engineers and many highly skilled technicians had few problems finding jobs.

President Reagan on March 11 sent Congress a detailed proposal for programs to relieve structural unemployment. Congress had meanwhile been pushing ahead with a multibillion-dollar jobs bill *(see p. 110)* which it soon passed. In separate action, the House on March 2 passed and sent to the Senate a bill authorizing $425 million in fiscal year 1984 to improve math, science and foreign language education.

AMERICA'S EMPLOYMENT OUTLOOK

AT A RECENT AFL-CIO conference in Washington, D.C., former Vice President Walter F. Mondale stated that the three biggest issues facing Americans today were "jobs, jobs and jobs." Later the same day, Sen. Edward M. Kennedy, D-Mass., told the unionists that the most important issues facing Americans were "jobs, jobs and more jobs." [1] This rhetorical replay may have been amusing, but there is nothing funny about the current employment situation in the United States. As the recession drags on, unemployment has reached a post-Depression high. The April unemployment rate of 9.4 percent, as measured by the federal government's Bureau of Labor Statistics, was the highest since 1941. Not since 1938 have as many as 10.3 million job-seekers been unable to find work.

These numbers do not tell the whole story: 5.8 million people are working only part time and 1.3 million are so-called "discouraged" workers, who have at least temporarily given up the job search. Certain segments of the population have been hit particularly hard. Black unemployment is 18.4 percent, black teen-age unemployment 48.1 percent, and Hispanic joblessness 12.5 percent. Unemployment in the goods-producing sector also is in double digits: construction, 19.4 percent; agriculture, 14.6 percent; and manufacturing, 11.3 percent. The impact has been harshest in the industrial Great Lakes and Midwest states and the timber-reliant Northwest states (see map, p. 6). The deep slump in the auto industry has put Michigan, with a 15 percent unemployment rate, on a near-depression footing.

According to a recent Gallup poll, unemployment has become Americans' greatest worry.[2] Of those surveyed, 44 percent called unemployment the country's greatest problem, followed by inflation at 24 percent. Eighty-five percent of the respondents said they would take a 10 percent pay cut to avoid a layoff and 77 percent said they would be unlikely to find a comparable job if they were laid off. For the first time in generations, a large majority of Americans appear pessimistic about financial and career growth, for themselves and for the work force at large.

---

[1] Mondale and Kennedy spoke on April 6, 1982, at the legislative conference of the AFL-CIO Building and Construction Trades Department.
[2] The poll was conducted April 2-5, 1982.

3

Changes in the labor market have been occurring at a rapid pace. There have been two lengthy recessions and a short one within the past seven years, and after each one the unemployment rate settled at a higher plateau *(see box, p. 5)*. Basic industries such as automobile and steel have been battered and shrunken by foreign competition, high interest rates and burdensome costs. Braniff Airlines has filed for bankruptcy and other companies, such as International Harvester, are in danger. The technological explosion of computers and robots seems to threaten thousands of workers *(see p. 7)*.

Many economists see this tableau as overly gloomy. The expected economic recovery, if combined with reduced interest rates, could release a pent-up demand for housing, cars and other durable goods, they say. Though employment levels in the basic industries may not return to pre-recession levels, these experts think growth in high-technology fields will result in a net gain of jobs and that the greater productivity provided by efficient new technologies will result in a general expansion of the economy.

Changed Nature of American Labor Market

The American labor market has undergone some astounding changes over the past few decades. According to the Bureau of Labor Statistics, nearly 110 million Americans were employed or actively sought work in April 1982, a figure larger than the entire U.S. population in 1920. The civilian labor force is more than twice that of 1940 (52.7 million) and is up from 82.7 million in 1970.

The primary factor behind this labor force growth was the postwar "baby boom." Around 4 million people were born each year from the late 1940s to the early 1960s, a birth rate of well over 20 per thousand.[3] Much of the economic growth in the postwar era can be attributed to this phenomenon: the need for housing, schools, services, durable and consumer goods. But virtually the entire baby boom generation is now in the labor force, at a time when the economy, burdened by inflation, high interest rates, high energy prices and foreign competition, is stagnant and prone to slumps.

Also expanding the size of the labor force was the great influx of women. While many of the women entering the work force were of the baby-boom generation, older women also sought work, often creating an inter-generational competition for entry-level positions. The reasons for the upsurge in female job seeking include higher education levels, the women's liberation movement and the removal of discriminatory barriers, later

---

[3] See "Baby Boom's New Echo," *E.R.R.*, 1981 Vol. I, pp. 469-488.

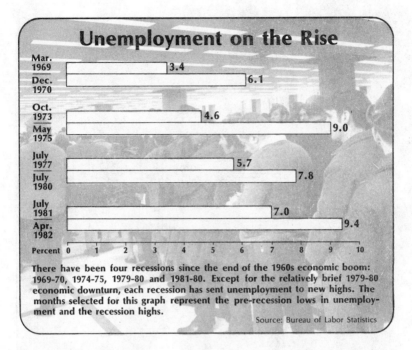

Unemployment on the Rise

	Percent
Mar. 1969	3.4
Dec. 1970	6.1
Oct. 1973	4.6
May 1975	9.0
July 1977	5.7
July 1980	7.8
July 1981	7.0
Apr. 1982	9.4

Percent 0 1 2 3 4 5 6 7 8 9 10

There have been four recessions since the end of the 1960s economic boom: 1969-70, 1974-75, 1979-80 and 1981-80. Except for the relatively brief 1979-80 economic downturn, each recession has sent unemployment to new highs. The months selected for this graph represent the pre-recession lows in unemployment and the recession highs.

Source: Bureau of Labor Statistics

marriage and childbearing, and the desire or need to supplement family income.[4]

President Reagan recently blamed high unemployment rates, in part, on the expansion of the work force. "Part of the unemployment is not as much recession as it is the great increase in the people going into the job market, and, ladies, I'm not picking on anyone, but because of the increase in women who are working today and two-worker families and so forth," Reagan said April 17.[5] But with many single and divorced women needing to support themselves, and many married women defending their families against inflation and layoffs of male "breadwinners," most women are in the work force out of necessity.

Competition for jobs and career advancement is expected to remain intense for those in the 25 to 44 age bracket. Some economists see reason for optimism in the lower birth rates of the 1960s and 1970s. The labor force, which grew by about 2.5 percent each year in the late 1970s, is expected to expand by only 1.5 percent by the late 1980s. Given a healthy national economy and normal retirement rates by older workers, these economists believe that there should be more jobs to go around and less competition for entry-level positions.

[4] See "Two-Income Families," *E.R.R.*, 1979 Vol. II, pp. 501-520, and "Equal Pay Fight," *E.R.R.*, 1981 Vol. I, pp. 209-228.
[5] Reagan was speaking to a group of editors and broadcasters from the Southeastern states at the White House.

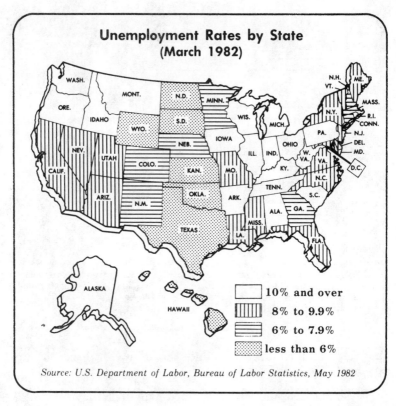

Unemployment Rates by State
(March 1982)

Source: U.S. Department of Labor, Bureau of Labor Statistics, May 1982

Legend:
- 10% and over
- 8% to 9.9%
- 6% to 7.9%
- less than 6%

These general statistics mean little to the person who is unemployed or who fears for his or her job. Many of these troubled people are members of the goods-producing sector: manufacturing, construction, agriculture. Although the proportion of Americans employed in production jobs has fallen precipitously, from over 80 percent in 1920 to under 33 percent today, many of the jobs in the booming information and service sectors are dependent on the goods-producers.

Blue-Collar Workers Hard Hit by Layoffs

The manufacturing and construction industries have been particularly hard hit by the economic vagaries of the past decade. Huge energy price increases, generous wage-and-benefit packages demanded and received by unionized workers, environmental and safety regulations, and, in some cases, lack of sound management added burdensome costs. Many manufacturers raised prices, making their goods less competitive against cheaper foreign imports. High interest rates resulting from big federal deficits and Carter and Reagan administration attempts to control inflation further crippled demand for big ticket items, such as cars and homes. In the auto industry alone, over 200,000 jobs have been lost since 1978.

Labor economists believe prospects for recovery in the

construction industry are fairly bright, if interest rates decline. Real estate and rental values have soared because of demands for housing by members of the baby-boom generation. This pent-up demand, along with needs for office space and factory modernization, could result in a healthy revival of the construction trades. "The construction industry is very cyclical . . . eventually construction will come back in terms of employment and employment growth," said Neal H. Rosenthal, director of the Bureau of Labor Statistics' Occupational Outlook Division.

The situation is more complicated in manufacturing. Continued foreign competition could hinder a full recovery in the "basic" industries, such as autos, steel and rubber. Industry leaders think they can become competitive again, but only by reducing labor costs and modernizing, in the fashion of the Japanese, and by introducing robots and other computer-controlled equipment into the factories.[6] Labor leaders admit that there will never be as many jobs in the basic industries as there were prior to the current recession. "Even if the auto companies make a complete comeback and exceed the production level of 1973, they would be doing it with fewer people," United Auto Workers President Douglas Fraser told *U.S. News & World Report*.[7]

Automation's Impact on Factory Employment

How many fewer people is what frightens blue-collar workers. Already robots have replaced workers, to a very limited degree, particularly in hazardous occupations, such as spray painting, welding, and handling hot or otherwise dangerous materials.[8] But as robots become more sophisticated and capable of performing complex jobs, many workers fear they will be replaced and relegated to the ranks of the "structurally unemployed."[9] A 1981 study by Carnegie-Mellon University said that by 1990 robots could displace 1 million workers in the automotive, electrical-equipment, machinery and fabricated-metals industries.[10]

There is much apocalyptic talk of "jobs that won't come back," of busy machines and idle hands. Many economists and industry experts dismiss this vision. For one thing, robot and computer technology, on a large scale, is expensive. Joseph

---

[6] See "Tensions in U.S.-Japanese Relations," *E.R.R.*, 1982 Vol. I, pp. 249-272, and "Rebuilding the Nation's Steel Industry," *E.R.R.*, 1982 Vol. I, pp. 169-188.
[7] *U.S. News & World Report*, May 3, 1982, p. 78.
[8] See "The Robot Revolution," *E.R.R.*, 1982 Vol. I, pp. 345-364.
[9] Structural unemployment "is defined as unemployment which cannot be cured by expansion of over-all monetary demand, but which is attributable to lack of proper skills, location, and attitudes among youth, the aged, the illiterate, minorities, the residents of depressed areas, and the technologically displaced." Source: Paul A. Samuelson, *Economics* (1967).
[10] Study cited by Joann S. Lublin in *The Wall Street Journal*, Oct. 26, 1981.

Engleberger, president of the robot-building Unimation Inc.,
estimated that replacement of just 5 percent of all of the blue-
collar jobs in the Western nations would cost $120 billion over
the next 40 years.[11] There is also the question of the destruction
of the value of existing capital. Few, if any, industries can afford
to plunge quickly into new technologies if they will render
thousands or millions of dollars worth of equipment and factories obsolete.

Some observers believe that the issue is not how many jobs
robots will cost, but how many they will save. ". . . The most
cogent response to those concerned with robots threatening jobs
is that, without robots, jobs in many industries will disappear
altogether," wrote Philip Lynch, the Australian minister for
industry and commerce. "Without the use of robots, a manufacturer will be unable to compete effectively." [12]

---

*"Even if the auto companies make a com-
plete comeback and exceed the production
level of 1973, they would be doing it with
fewer people."*

Douglas Fraser, president
of the United Auto Workers

Other economists predict that demand for workers in the
high-technology industries will soar. They point out that if
there are going to be a lot of robots and computers in factories,
workers will be needed to build, maintain and repair them. This
has been the historic pattern of American industry: new types of
business spring up to replace ones that are fading or obsolescent. "The economy basically will grow over the next decade,"
said Neal H. Rosenthal. "Some of the workers who are displaced
and are unable to get back into the industry they are in will be
able to get jobs in other industries."

Sar Levitan, a George Washington University economist and
chairman of the National Council on Employment Policy,
agrees.[13] "People are very flexible," Levitan said in a recent
interview. "You start a new industry, and you may think there

---

[11] Quoted in *Second Thoughts on Work* by Sar A. Levitan and Clifford M. Johnson, to be
published later this year.
[12] Writing in *The New York Times*, April 26, 1982.
[13] The National Council on Employment Policy, located in Washington, D.C., is a non-
profit research organization of labor scholars who study employment training programs,
discuss manpower issues and publish research results, books and policy statements.

will be a [labor] shortage, but when you have the demand, industry can train and can restructure jobs, and the people are absorbed." However, the transition is being complicated by the current recession. "It's going to be harder and slower and much more painful now, because we don't have a growth economy just sucking people out of declining industries," said Audrey Freedman, senior economist for the Conference Board.[14] Economists also point out that many workers tend to attach their identities to a certain job or trade and are unwilling to accept the fact that their jobs may be gone forever.

Retraining Workers for 'High-Tech' Jobs

Some observers believe that the United States urgently needs to retrain workers in aging industries for the "high technology" revolution that is expected to sweep America. "We have to retrain the millions whose current jobs can be kissed goodbye and who will be needed for new work," Pat Choate and Noel Epstein wrote in *The Washington Post* on May 9, 1982.[15] Legislation currently before Congress would devote part of a $3.9 billion jobs program to the retraining of workers displaced from the basic industries.[16] The Reagan administration has opposed this move, seeking instead a smaller training program aimed strictly at the chronically unemployed.

There are those who believe that the expected industrial changes will be so drastic that industry alone will not be able to handle the training task. Choate and Epstein suggested the establishment of "Individual Training Accounts." Employees and employers would each place $500 a year for six years into a trust fund, to be used for retraining if a worker's job disappeared. The money would be returned to the worker, plus interest, if not used by retirement.

The ruling assumption among many of those who advocate intensive retraining programs is that because the products of high technology are sophisticated and complicated, each of the jobs involved in their production will also be so. Sar Levitan rejects this concept. "The idea that the new technologies necessarily require higher skills and that anybody without a Ph.D. becomes obsolescent in the new age is simply exaggerated ...

[14] The Conference Board, based in New York City, conducts research and publishes studies on business and economics, operates an information service for members and distributes research data to the media and the public.

[15] Choate is senior policy analyst for economics at TRW, Inc.; Epstein is editor of the *Post's* Outlook Section.

[16] The Senate bill, introduced by Sens. Kennedy and Dan Quayle, R-Ind., was approved by the Senate Labor Subcommittee on Employment on April 22. A House bill, introduced by Rep. Augustus F. Hawkins, D-Calif., was reported by the House Education and Labor Committee on April 27. The main difference between the two bills is that the Senate bill gives a larger role to the states, while the House bill maintains the current structure that favors city and county governments.

because the new technologies create a great many jobs that require few skills," he said.

As an example, Levitan described the situation in the health care industry, which has expanded greatly over the past two decades. "The health industry obviously created the need for more doctors, more nurses, and some technical people, who are also skilled workers," Levitan said. "But it also created lots of jobs for pan-carriers, people to feed the patients in the hospital and whatever menial jobs there were."

The High-Technology Era

PRESIDENT Reagan caused a flap last January when he remarked at a news conference that the newspapers were full of help-wanted ads, because most of the jobs available were for highly skilled, highly trained workers, such as engineers, technicians and computer experts. A recent career supplement to *The Washington Post* was dominated by full- and half-page advertisements for such companies as Sperry, General Electric, American Satellite Co., MCI Telecommunications, and Planning Research Corporation seeking senior programmers, electronics engineers, microwave path engineers, software engineers and other technical workers.

Many college students are now bracing themselves for their first difficult plunge into the job market. But not engineering graduates. They are among the few students being aggressively recruited during the current recession. *Time* magazine reported recently that of the 65,000 men and women scheduled to graduate this year with B.S. degrees in engineering, 80 percent would begin work immediately. Average starting salaries reflected the demand, ranging between $21,000 and $30,000.[17]

The Bureau of Labor Statistics' 1982-83 "Occupational Outlook Handbook" projects faster-than-average growth in almost all engineering fields. Electrical engineering is the largest of the engineering occupations, employing 325,000 people who design and develop electrical and electronic equipment. As demand for computers, communications technology, advanced weaponry and business and consumer goods grows, electrical engineering is expected to boom. The drive for improved production methods is expected to enhance job possibilities for mechanical and industrial engineers. If President Reagan's proposed expansion of defense programs becomes a reality, aerospace engineering

---

[17] John S. DeMott, "Help Wanted: Engineers," *Time,* May 10, 1982, p. 88.

BLOOM COUNTY   by Berke Breathed

1982 Berke Breathed (distributed by The Washington Post Writers Group)

should prosper.[18] The search for domestic energy sources should increase demand for petroleum and mining engineers. Other engineering specialities expected to grow include agricultural, biomedical, ceramic, chemical, civil and metallurgical.

There is a great deal of overlap between the engineering and computer industries. Engineers utilize computers in many capacities, while electrical engineers design the silicon chips, microprocessors and other components that make today's and tomorrow's computer applications possible. The summer 1981 "Occupational Outlook Quarterly" published by BLS said that employment of computer and peripheral operators would more than double by 1990. The College Placement Council in Bethlehem, Pa., reported April 27 that graduating computer science majors were receiving average salary offers of $22,572.

In gross numbers, the greatest demand will be for computer programmers, the people who prepare the coded instructions that tell the computer what to do. There are expected to be 500,000 positions for programmers in 1990, up from 247,000 in 1978. Demand is also expected to be high for systems analysts, who develop customized plans for data processing and handling. Around 400,000 systems analysts will be needed by 1990, up from 182,000 in 1978. The greatest percentage growth in the computer field is projected to be in the area of computer service. With 5 million computer terminals expected to be installed by next year alone, the number of service technicians is expected to grow to at least 160,000 by 1990, a 154 percent increase over 1978.

Shortage of Qualified Technical Workers

The need for people trained in scientific and technical subjects is not limited to the engineering and computer fields. For example, as the population grows and ages, health care technicians will be in great demand. And as modern weaponry and equipment become more computerized, soldiers will need to be more technologically oriented.

---

[18] See "Defense Spending Debate," *E.R.R.*, 1982 Vol. I, pp. 273-292.

What's Hot and What's Not . . .

Accountants: Employment is expected to grow faster than average through the 1980s due to increasing pressure on businesses and government agencies to improve budgeting and accounting procedures.

Aerospace engineers: Employment of aerospace engineers is expected to grow faster than average as federal outlays on new military aircraft, missiles and other aerospace systems increase. Cutbacks in defense spending — like those that took place in 1969 and 1970 — can result in layoffs of aerospace engineers.

Architects: Architects are expected to face competition for jobs through the 1980s. Although employment of architects is expected to rise faster than average, the number of degrees granted in architecture is expected to continue growing as well.

Automobile mechanics: Job opportunities for automobile mechanics will be plentiful in the years ahead. Most persons who enter the occupation may expect steady work because changes in economic conditions have little effect on the automobile repair business.

Bartenders: Because many bartenders are students, or others who do not plan careers in this occupation, job turnover is relatively high.

Bricklayers: Employment of bricklayers is expected to grow faster than average. As population and business growth create a need for new homes, factories, offices and other structures, the demand for bricklayers will grow.

College and university faculty: It seems likely that enrollments will decline during the 1980s. As a result, job openings will result almost entirely from replacement needs.

Cooks and chefs: The demand for cooks and chefs will increase as the population grows and people dine out more. Higher personal incomes and more leisure time will allow people to go out for dinner more often. Also, with more women joining the work force, families may increasingly find dining out a welcome convenience.

Dentists: Dental school enrollments have grown in recent years, and the supply of new dentists is expected to be in balance with the number needed to fill openings created by growth of the occupation and by death or retirement from the profession.

Farmers: The number of farmers is expected to decline as farms become more expensive to buy and operate. The trend toward fewer and larger farms is expected to continue, reducing the number of jobs for farm operators.

Lawyers: Despite strong growth in the demand for lawyers, the sizable number of law school graduates entering the job market each year has created keen competition for jobs. Competition for jobs will remain intense.

Librarians: In some communities, declining enrollments and fiscal constraints are likely to result in staff cutbacks, with school librarians being transferred to classroom teaching. In other localities, however, population growth will spur demand of educational personnel, including librarians.

Machine tool operators: Employment is expected to increase about as fast as average. The use of faster and more versatile automatic machine tools and numerically controlled machine tools will result in greater output per worker and tend to limit employment demand.

Meteorologists: The number of applicants applying for jobs in this very small occupation is likely to exceed the number of job openings. Persons

... In the Job Market

with an advanced degree in meteorology should have the best job prospects.

Pharmacists: The employment outlook for pharmacists is expected to be favorable overall, but the anticipated surplus of pharmacy graduates in some localities seems likely to produce keen job competition in those places.

Police officers: Employment of police officers is expected to grow about as fast as average for all occupations through the 1980s as the nation's population and police protection needs increase. Employment growth will be tempered by increased use of civilian police department employees in traffic control, parking enforcement, administration and other routine non-hazardous areas of police work.

Programmers: Employment of programmers is expected to grow faster than average as computer usage expands, particularly in firms providing accounting, business management and computer programming services, and in organizations involved in research and development.

Retail sales persons: Employment of retail sales persons is expected to grow about as fast as the average for all occupations. The volume of sales will outpace employment increases, however, as self-service is extended to variety and other kinds of stores.

Secondary school teachers: Prospective secondary school teachers will face keen competition for jobs. If past trends continue, the supply of persons qualified to teach will greatly exceed requirements.

Social workers: Job prospects for social workers vary a great deal. Opportunities depend to some extent upon academic credentials, but geographical location is probably the most important consideration. Competition is keen in cities like Boston and New York and is likely to get worse as these localities cut back social service programs in response to budget pressures. At the same time, population growth in the Sun Belt states is spurring expansion of social service programs there.

Systems analysts: Employment of systems analysts is expected to grow much faster than the average for all occupations. The demand for systems analysts is expected to rise as computer capabilities are increased and as new applications are found for computer technology.

Typists: Very good job prospects are expected for typists in the years ahead. Even during slack economic periods, employment of typists is fairly stable because companies must process paperwork regardless of the level of business activity.

Veterinarians: Newly qualified vets will face increasing competition in establishing practices, for the number of veterinary school graduates rose sharply in the 1970s and is expected to continue growing. The considerable expense of establishing a practice has prompted more and more graduates to seek employment with established veterinarians.

Writers and editors: Each year, thousands of young people with college degrees in English, journalism, communications and the liberal arts seek writing and editing jobs. Many end up in other occupations because the number of people qualified to work as writers and editors greatly exceeds the number of positions available.

Source: Bureau of Labor Statistics, "Occupational Outlook Handbook," 1982-83 edition.

While labor economists project millions of job openings in technical fields, it does not necessarily follow that there will be enough trained, qualified people to fill them. There is a great deal of concern that the United States is lacking in its abilities to train students and workers in math, science and technical subjects. Some observers foresee a "knowledge gap" that could result in severe shortages of labor in vital technological fields.

According to the Communications Workers of America, "Top-flight designers, engineers and programmers will be in increasingly short supply as the industry grows." [19] A report prepared for California Gov. Edmund G. Brown Jr. stated that the electronics industry in that state would have 62,000 openings for electrical and computer scientists by 1987, but that only 14,000 qualified students would graduate from the state's universities during that period.[20]

To a degree, the high-technology fields are victims of their own prosperity. Professors with Ph.D.s in engineering or the computer sciences have been lured from the classroom into private industry by big salary offers. Even B.S. graduates are being offered salaries commensurate to what they would earn as teachers after two to five more years of schooling.

References have been made to the technological fields eating their own "seed corn." Defections of Ph.D.s and the reluctance of graduates to pursue teaching careers have cut down on the size and quality of faculties. Because of the lack of postgraduate ambition by American students, at least half of all graduate engineering students are foreigners, most of whom take their skills back to their homelands.[21] At the same time, undergraduate demand for technological training has expanded, resulting in larger class size and less individual instruction.

Quality of Teaching in Math and Sciences

There is also growing concern over the quality of mathematics and science teaching in the nation's elementary and secondary schools. Stanford University Professor Emeritus Paul DeHart Hurd told a National Convocation on Precollege Education in Mathematics and Science, sponsored by the National Academy of Sciences in Washington on May 12, that only one-third of all high school students take as much as three years of math and that half of all math and science teachers were "unqualified."

[19] Article prepared for a career supplement to *The Washington Post*, April 25, 1982.
[20] See "Help Wanted: Engineers," *Time*, May 10, 1982, p. 88.
[21] An immigration bill sponsored by Rep. Romano L. Mazzoli, D-Ky., and Sen. Alan K. Simpson, R-Wyo., would make it mandatory for these foreign graduates to return home. The bill, primarily aimed at stemming the tide of poor immigrants into this country, also contains a clause that would require all foreign students — not just those who are subsidized by their home governments — to return to their own countries for at least two years after graduation. Many academics and business executives oppose the bill.

Dr. Harry Lustig, dean for science at City College of New York, told *The New York Times* that no one qualified to teach high school science graduated in Connecticut last year and that 12 percent of all math teachers in New York City were not certified to teach that subject. The problem is akin to what is happening on the college level, since starting salaries for math teachers are $10,000 less than for computer programmers. "Anybody who can master enough math to be a math teacher certainly can master enough to be a computer programmer," Lustig said.[22]

The current state of math and science instruction is seen as threatening economic growth and national security. President Reagan, in a written message, told the National Academy of Sciences conference that problems in math and science teaching are "serious enough to compromise the nation's future ability to develop and advance our traditional industrial base to compete in international marketplaces." Many academics and commentators concur. "I see us becoming industrially a second-rate power," said Dr. Lustig. "I see us losing our lead in health research and basic science, in military science." Itek Corp. Chairman Robert P. Henderson wrote: "If this state of affairs is allowed to continue, high technology imports will increase, and the one bright spot in today's U.S. economy will go the way of automobiles, TV sets and shoes." [23]

In the late 1950s, following the Soviet launching of the first space satellite, American leaders rushed to bolster the nation's science and math teaching, funding university research and development projects, providing scholarships and otherwise encouraging young people to enter technological careers. Many people today advocate a similar "Sputnik-style" federal investment, but the Reagan administration opposes such an effort. "We disagree with those who say that the federal government should be ultimately responsible for this problem," presidential policy adviser Edwin L. Harper told the National Academy of Sciences meeting. Although President Reagan has voiced his concern about the problem, he has placed technical education programs on his budget chopping block, proposing to limit expenditures to $15 million, almost all of which would go toward higher education.

Private industry is partially responsible for the supposed crisis in science and math education, having coaxed away many present and future instructors with generous pay offers. Some corporations have begun to make amends. For example, the

---

[22] Quoted in *The New York Times*, April 6, 1982.
[23] Robert P. Henderson, "High Tech: Help Wanted," *Enterprise*, March 1982, p. 3. *Enterprise* is published by the National Association of Manufacturers.

Exxon Foundation has donated $15 million to help engineering schools get and keep faculty members, and Motorola gave $1.2 million to Arizona State University's engineering program. "Industry must be willing to invest in long-term educational goals, even if it means leaving some of the best engineering students and faculty in the university," wrote Henry Petroski, a Duke University associate professor of civil and environmental engineering.[24]

Although many universities are pressed by government aid cutbacks and declining overall enrollments, it is possible that the institutions will act to correct the situation on their own. Noting jokingly that schools might decide that an engineering professor is worth more than an economics professor, Sar Levitan said, "The marketplace can take care of itself."

White-Collar Work Force

DISCUSSIONS of future employment opportunities center on the plight of factory workers or the rosy future in high-technology fields. However, the largest single group of workers is made up not of technicians or laborers, but of white-collar workers. Clerical workers alone — secretaries, typists, book-keepers, clerks and so on — constitute the largest occupational group in the Bureau of Labor Statistics breakdown. In 1980, there were 18.9 million clerical workers in the United States. Although the anticipated percentage growth of 18-27 percent projected for 1990 is not as big as in some other fields, the total number of new clerical jobs, 3.5-5 million, is the largest of any occupation.

The era of technological innovation that is sweeping the laboratory and the factory is changing the face of the office as well. Self-correcting electronic word processors are replacing typewriters, whole inventories and filing systems are being placed in easily accessible computer systems, people and businesses are linked with each other and with all sorts of "information banks" by telephone lines, and the advent of portable personal computers has freed some people from the office routine altogether. The word "paperwork" may someday be obsolete, as businesses move toward the era of the "paperless office."

Many business executives are enthusiastic about advances in office technology. The elimination of reams of paper, smoother work-flow arrangements, and easy accessibility of information

---

[24] Writing in *The Washington Post*, Jan. 21, 1982.

lead businessmen to predict greater productivity, profits and growth. Some labor experts also see computerization as improving the quality of work life at the office. The most tedious tasks, such as typing letters or filing invoices, will be simplified and speeded by the labor-saving capabilities of the computer. The lack of "busy-work" could free clerical workers for more creative assignments.

As in the factory, though, there is a negative view. Labor officials are concerned that growth in information needs and the greater worker-monitoring capacity that computers afford will actually lead to the creation of more routine and stressful jobs. As workers communicate more with machines and less with people, feelings of isolation could grow. "Think of the alienation of the blue-collar assembly workers, and that's exactly what's being done, quite consciously, for 20 million Americans who work as clericals," said Karen Nussbaum of the Service Employees International Union.[25] There is also concern about the health effects of working with video terminals, such as eyestrain and stress.

Many office workers worry about being replaced by computers. Business officials, citing the need for more and different kinds of information and the expansion possibilities inherent in higher productivity, say that automation will not make clerical workers obsolete. Pessimists cite several European studies, including one that forecast a 30 percent job loss in France's banking and insurance industries.[26]

There is also the question of whether enough workers will be trained in the office skills of the computer age. "Within a few years, the ability to program and use computers may be as important as being able to read, write, type, drive, or use the telephone," *The Futurist* magazine noted in its August 1981 issue. Neal Rosenthal of the Bureau of Labor Statistics thinks these predictions may be unfounded. Noting that in his own office secretaries went from standard to electric typewriters to word processors, Rosenthal said: "Their skills are basically learned, at each conversion, in a couple of days. Their basic skills haven't changed, and they're operating fine without any additional types of training."

Some visionaries see the "office" becoming extinct. The advent of home computers and telecommunications networks, they say, will permit most, if not all, information employees to work at home. There are skeptics, though, who believe that

---

[25] Quoted in "The Paperless Office — How Workers Adapt," *U.S. News & World Report,* Feb. 22, 1982, pp. 77-78.
[26] See Colin Norman, *The God That Limps: Science and Technology in the Eighties* (1981), p. 135.

people work better in an office setting. "We egg each other on," said Conference Board economist Audrey Freedman. "We transmit a great deal that isn't in the rulebooks or the textbooks. We didn't bring it from school and we don't bring it from the personnel handbook and we don't get it from our bosses, either. We work with each other and interact."

Job Opportunities in the Services Sector

If one was to take a facetious look at the employment scene, big growth would be expected for two kinds of workers: economists, to figure out the nation's economic mess, and psychiatrists, to counsel the confused economists. In fact, growth is predicted to be fairly rapid in both fields, faster-than-average in economics and as-fast-as-average in psychology. But the number of people seeking these jobs will continue to outrun the number of available positions.

The same is true for many of the professional services. The legal profession provides a glaring example. In 1980, there were 535,000 lawyers chasing 416,000 jobs; by 1985, there are expected to be 639,000 lawyers and 500,000 jobs. The situation could get even worse, as the Reagan administration cuts back on government litigation and legal services for the poor.

The demand for health care services is expected to continue its growth, creating new positions throughout the industry. Nurses are in especially short supply. However, there has tended to be a geographic imbalance, with a glut of workers in big cities with high pay scales, and shortages in some smaller cities and rural areas.

Rising incomes and fear of inflation created a great demand in the 1970s for financial services: banking, accounting, tax advice, and investment counseling. These areas are expected to continue their growth in the 1980s. Similarly, affluence and expanded leisure time set off a boom in the personal-consumption services: retail salespersons, hotel and restaurant workers, hairstylists, amusement park and arena workers, exercise instructors, bartenders and many others. Assuming an economic recovery, labor analysts foresee continued growth in these areas.

A service area that is not expected to grow is the one most sensitive to population trends: education. The end of the "baby boom" reduced school enrollments and thousands of teachers have been laid off. A marginal increase in the birthrate in the last few years may boost enrollments, but the severe financial problems of many school systems are expected to hold down employment growth. Similarly, local fiscal woes are expected to restrain employment in public services that are in demand, such as police and fire protection and sanitation.

Structural Unemployment

F EW economists claim that every single American who desires work will be able to find it. Most economics textbooks say that this is not dangerous, that it is, in fact, necessary, since there must be a labor pool to replace workers who retire, die, take ill, are fired, or leave their jobs for whatever reasons. However, the level of "structural unemployment" has been climbing in recent years.

As late as 1978, the passage of the Humphrey-Hawkins Act expressed Congress' commitment to a "full employment" jobless rate of 4 percent. Yet most conservative and some liberal economists today have accepted a target of 6 percent unemployment. No matter what the theoretical level is, the actual level is expected to remain high for some time. The Business Council in Washington, D.C., recently predicted that unemployment would fall only as far as 8 percent by the end of 1983.[27]

Many economists say this level is too high. "I think that we were much too prompt to accept, as a matter of public policy, a full employment level of 6 percent," said Sar Levitan. "I think we could have achieved lower levels of unemployment if we had the proper public policy." To Levitan and other economists like him, proper public policy includes the traditional federal weapons against unemployment: job creation and job training.

In the late 1970s, as many as 750,000 people were employed in "public service" jobs under the Comprehensive Employment and Training Act (CETA). Conservatives complained that these jobs were costly, were generally of the make-work variety (park cleaning, for example), and often wound up in the hands of middle-class political appointees instead of the underprivileged for whom they were intended.

Despite the recession, the Reagan administration and Congress eliminated the jobs part of the CETA program last year. Some former CETA employees and others who might have taken advantage of the program are now collecting unemployment, welfare or food stamps. Noting that 1 percent unemployment adds $25 billion to $30 billion to the federal budget, Levitan said, "Now is the time to create jobs and target the jobs on areas and people who need them."

Modern job-training programs began in earnest 20 years ago with the passage of the Manpower Development and Training

---

[27] The Business Council is comprised of the chief executive officers of major corporations, who meet quarterly to discuss viewpoints and to explore public policy as it affects U.S. business interests.

Act (MDTA). The onset of urban riots resulted in the eclipse of job training by income transfer programs. "Starting in 1967, human development projects slowly got converted, right in front of your eyes, into transfer income systems and charity systems and pacification programs," said Audrey Freedman of the Conference Board, who worked as a government labor economist from the 1950s to the 1970s.

"I think that we were much too prompt to accept, as a matter of public policy, a full employment level of 6 percent."

Sar Levitan, chairman
of the National Council
on Employment Policy

MDTA was replaced in 1973 by CETA, which provided for a greater local role in job training. CETA's job training program was plagued by instances of fraud and waste, and was held up by conservatives as an example of a "big government" program gone wrong. Many economists countered that CETA was just hitting its stride after some much-needed reforms instituted by President Carter in 1978. The National Council on Employment Policy reported last year that the rate of "social returns" on CETA classroom training was 34 percent, and was 118 percent for on-the-job training.[28]

The training part of the CETA program expires this August. The job training program favored by the administration provides for $1.8 billion, less than half the amount in the bill working its way through Congress. The administration is also cutting back on aid to education. While much has been said about the problems in science and math instruction, many economists are even more concerned about the overall decline in education. The Adult Performance Level Project at the University of Texas estimates that 19 percent of all adults — 30.2 million people — are functionally incompetent, meaning that they lack the reading, writing and interpretive skills needed to cope with the minimal demands of everyday life. An additional 53.7 million people are "just getting by."[29]

---

[28] The "social returns" that NCEP related to CETA included greater employability and higher wages, reduced dependence on transfer payments, and higher tax revenues. See Sar A. Levitan and Garth L. Mangum, *The T in CETA: Local and National Perspectives* (1981), pp. 93-144.
[29] Estimates based on the 1980 census and the project's nationwide surveys.

At the same time, debt-ridden school systems are cutting back on personnel and programs. The impact of education cubacks is expected to fall most heavily on those at the bottom of the labor market: minorities and the poor. Many economists are concerned that growing numbers of Americans will be locked out of the job market or locked into low-paying, dead-end jobs. The creation of a permanent underclass of frustrated and angry people, they say, could have severe social consequences.

The Uncertainties of Economic Forecasting

The Bureau of Labor Statistics and other economists base their projections of future employment on reams of statistics on population, demographic and employment trends. Nonetheless, their predictions are not fail-safe. The economy, and the size of the job market, are contingent on many forces — government fiscal policy, balance of trade, OPEC oil pricing decisions, etc. — that are far from predictable.

Looking back 10 years, the United States had low interest rates, 3.3 percent inflation, 5.9 percent unemployment, a $23 billion federal budget deficit, and thriving auto and steel industries. Few, if any, economists in 1972 predicted all of the shocks — the enormous oil price increases, the surge of foreign imports, inflation and the decline of basic industries — that contributed

21

Calculating Unemployment

On the first Friday of each month, the Bureau of Labor Statistics (BLS) releases the official national unemployment statistics. The figures are extrapolated from the results of interviews conducted with 60,000 households across the country, with greater weight given to heavily industrialized areas.

The unemployment rate is the percentage of the labor force that is looking for work, but cannot find it. The "labor force" is the sum total of all workers, employed or unemployed. "Employed workers" are those who have worked at least one hour for pay in the week on which the survey interviews are based. "Unemployed workers" are defined as persons who have not worked at all in that week, but have sought work within the past four weeks. People who have not looked for work within the previous four weeks are called "discouraged workers," and are not counted as unemployed or as part of the labor force.

The government's method for calculating unemployment has been attacked, for differing reasons, by both liberals and conservatives. Labor organizations say the unemployment rate is underestimated, and that it should include both "discouraged workers" and those part-time workers who would resume full-time work if they could find it. If these workers were added, unemployment would soar to well over 10 percent.

Many conservatives claim that the unemployment rate is exaggerated. They say that programs instituted since the Great Depression, such as unemployment insurance, supplemental unemployment benefits and, in some cases, union- or employer-funded benefits, have taken much of the sting out of unemployment. These benefits, they say, have provided many unemployed workers with the leeway of rejecting undesirable employment in favor of waiting for better opportunities.

It is also stated that the growing number of two-income families has made rising unemployment less of a disaster. Some conservatives have even called for replacement of the unemployment index with a "distress" index, which would include only those workers who are in or are threatened by severe financial distress because of unemployment.

There is some dispute over the seasonal adjustments performed by BLS. The job market goes through several seasonal expansions and contractions each year. Retail stores hire many workers just for the Christmas-rush season. Many workers in outdoor occupations, such as construction or parks and recreation, are hired only for the "good weather" months.

President Reagan complained that the media played up April's record unemployment rate of 9.4 percent, but failed to mention that, in raw figures, employment rose by 400,000. But, BLS pointed out, employment normally rises considerably in April, and this year's increase was much smaller than usual.

to today's recessionary economy, high unemployment, exorbitant interest rates and incredible deficits.

Economic projections are based on assumptions. It is assumed that a multibillion-dollar defense buildup will create an enormous demand for engineers, computer specialists, skilled factory workers and others in the high-technology fields. However, this projected growth could be limited if Congress cuts defense spending increases in its battle against $100-billion-plus deficits. On the other hand, "public service" jobs that are being eliminated could make a comeback in the not-too-distant future, if the nation's urgent infrastructure needs are to be filled. It is estimated that $250 billion is needed to repair crumbling bridges, roads and water mains. Even a small percentage of this investment would result in thousands of jobs for unskilled laborers, as well as for skilled workers, such as civil engineers, landscape architects, and heavy machinery operators.

Perhaps the most unpredictable element in the employment picture is the length and depth of the current recession. A recovery is expected, but it is uncertain when it will occur. If interest rates remain in double digits, the recovery may be shallow and short-lived. As long as the economy stagnates, employment will be restrained, and many companies will defer the investment, innovation and research necessary to bring about the projected changes. Predictions of employment growth are cause for optimism, but until the recession ends, all bets are off.

Selected Bibliography

Books

Levitan, Sar A. and Garth L. Mangum, *The T in CETA: Local and National Perspectives,* The W. E. Upjohn Institute for Employment Research, 1981.

Norman, Colin, *The God That Limps: Science and Technology in the Eighties,* Norton, 1981.

Articles

Deakin, Doris, "Jobs of the '80s," *The Washingtonian,* May 1982.

DeMott, John S., "Help Wanted: Engineers," *Time,* May 10, 1982.

Hamrin, Robert D., "The Information Economy: Exploiting an Infinite Resource," *The Futurist,* August 1981.

Henderson, Richard P., "High Tech: Help Wanted," *Enterprise,* March 1982.

Murray, Thomas J., "Industry's New College Connection," *Dun's Review,* May 1981.

Reilly, Ann M., "What Is Full Employment?" *Dun's Review,* February 1979.

Sheler, Jeffery L. and Jeannye Thornton, "The Paperless Office — How Workers Adapt," *U.S. News & World Report,* Feb. 22, 1982.

Reports and Articles

Bureau of Labor Statistics, "Occupational Outlook Handbook," 1982-83 edition.

Editorial Research Reports: "The Robot Revolution," 1982 Vol. I, p. 347; "The Age of Computers," 1981, Vol. I, p. 105; "Shortage of Skills," 1965 Vol. II, p. 643.

Illustrations by Staff Artist Cheryl Rowe;
map (p. 6) by Staff Artist Robert Redding.

Small Business: Trouble on Main Street

by

Robert Benenson

**Jan. 28
1 9 8 3**

Editor's Note: President Reagan sent his second annual report on "The State of Small Business"* to Congress in March 1983. It portrays small businesses delaying capital expansion, cutting inventories and applying stricter business controls in an effort to survive. Many of them did not. There were 38 percent more business bankruptcies in 1982 than in 1981.

Construction, services, and the retail and wholesale trades — industries dominated by small businesses — accounted for about 65 percent of all bankruptcies. Many of these were attributed to high interest rates during the recession.

* "The State of Small Business: A Report of the President," transmitted to Congress March 1983; obtainable from the Superintendent of Documents, U.S. Government Printing Office, Washington, D.C. 20402.

SMALL BUSINESS:
TROUBLE ON MAIN STREET

WITHIN the next few weeks, President Reagan will send his annual report on "The State of Small Business" to Congress.[1] The report will likely be as full of praise as the one sent to Congress last March, when Reagan described small business as the provider of "much of the growth in jobs and innovation as well as being the supplier of services and deliverer of goods to virtually every farm, village, town and city in our nation." But the 1983 report will likely present a grayer portrait of the state of small business than last year's.

Business bankruptcies for 1982 totaled 65,657, up from 47,555 in 1981 and 43,374 in 1980, according to the Small Business Administration (SBA). Although there have been some highly publicized big business bankruptcies, such as Braniff Airlines, the fact that small businesses[2] make up the vast majority of all businesses (see p. 30) makes it safe to assume that they also make up the vast majority of business bankruptcies. The Dun & Bradstreet credit-rating service reported Jan. 20 that there were at least 25,343 business failures in 1982,[3] up 48.7 percent from 1981. The situation appeared to be getting worse rather than better; failures from the second half of the year were up 21 percent over the first half.

These numbers may just be the tip of the iceberg. The business failures that turn up in these figures are generally those that result in a loss to creditors. But most business failures result in no loss to creditors; business owners pay off their debts, liquidate their assets and close their doors. "We have some rough estimates that suggest maybe 10 to 15 firms cease operations for every one we would see in the Dun & Bradstreet number," said William C. Dunkelberg, chief economist for the National Federation of Independent Business (NFIB).[4]

---

[1] The report on small business will be sent to Congress in accordance with a provision in the 1980 authorization bill for Small Business Administration programs. It is being prepared by the SBA and the president's Council of Economic Advisers. As of Jan. 26, no date had been set for its release.

[2] Generally defined as those with less than 500 employees.

[3] In a bankruptcy case, a business can continue to function, operating under a court-ordered plan for business reorganization and debt settlement. A business failure means that the company ceased to operate.

[4] Dunkelberg, who is also a professor of economics at Purdue University, appeared on "The MacNeil-Lehrer Report," PBS-TV, June 4, 1982. The National Federation of Independent Business is a Washington-based research and advocacy group for small business.

Small-business failures are nothing unusual. Between 1969 and 1976, only 37 percent of businesses with under 20 employees survived more than four years, and only 9 percent lasted 10 years.[5] But it has not only been vulnerable young businesses that have been hard hit by the recession. SBA chief economist Thomas A. Gray, in a recent interview, described the situation in Fort Wayne, Ind., where firms "that had been viable, strong businesses for 75 years were going under like flies ... because the recession was so long and intense."

New Debate Over Economic Vulnerability

Many observers say that small businesses are particularly vulnerable to the vagaries of the economy. "The vast majority of small businesses do not have the capital resources that they can fall back on to tide them through a tough period," said Rep. Parren J. Mitchell, D-Md., chairman of the House Small Business Committee. Even before the recession, small businesses were burdened by inflation, which peaked at over 12 percent in 1980. Small businesses had to meet increased costs for labor, fuel, supplies and other items. Unlike large companies, which could spread price increases among a larger clientele, small businesses found it difficult to raise prices enough to meet increased costs without losing customers.

The resultant cash-flow problems increased the small business owner's need for capital. But inflation also reduced incentive to save, minimizing the resources of traditional sources of funds, such as friends and family. It also reduced the capital pool of financial institutions, which became more reluctant to lend to small businesses. Then came the tight money policies of the Federal Reserve, which sent interest rates as high as 25 percent for those businesses that were able to obtain loans. Even as the economy sputtered and inflation started to slide to its 1982 level of 3.9 percent, interest rates stayed high. "Normally when you start a strong downturn, you would expect interest rates to come down ... [but] they didn't go down in this recession," said Thomas Gray of the SBA.

Interest rates surpassed inflation as the most important small business problem in NFIB quarterly surveys of small business; poor sales followed close behind. Large businesses hit hard by the recession cut expenses by laying off employees, but small businesses had less flexibility. Since small businesses have fewer employees, each one is marginally more crucial to business operations than an employee of a large firm. Yet small businesses are concentrated in labor-intensive industries, and were therefore unable to reduce their biggest expense category.

---

[5] "The State of Small Business: A Report of the President," March 1982, p. 79.

Business Failures and Bankruptcies

Year	Bankruptcies	Business Failures
1982	65,657	25,343
1981	47,555	17,043
1980	43,374	11,719

Sources: Small Business Administration, Dun & Bradstreet.

High fixed costs, enormous monthly loan payments and reduced income exacerbated cash-flow problems for small-business owners. But they received little sympathy from their business creditors, many of whom were pressed small-business owners themselves. As late payments increased — "delinquent" receivables averaged 17 percent through the first three quarters of 1982[6] — creditors tightened up. "We have to take a much closer look at anything we send out for credit, and we do a lot more C.O.D. [cash-on-delivery] business than we've done in years," said Howard Yagoda of Turkeltaub & Schiffer Inc., a Queens, N.Y., carpet distributor.

This picture of recessionary distress is accurate for many small businesses. But some economists question the degree to which small businesses have been hurt worse than large businesses in this recession. Gray, discussing his economic analysis for the president's report, said, "We did go in with a bias that small businesses are generally hurt worst in a recession ... [but] it turns out that small business has not been hurt quite as bad as we thought relative to big business." Gray pointed out that two of the three worst-hit industries in the recession, manufacturing and mining, are dominated by large companies; only construction is a small-business province. There is a regional factor as well. Small businesses in the Midwest have been buffeted by the ripple effect from the decline in heavy industries, such as automobiles and steel. In New England, though, traditional industries that were decimated in the 1974 recession were replaced in many cases by service and high-technology firms that have weathered the current recession relatively well.

And despite the recession, businesses are being formed at a rapid rate. The SBA reported that about 560,000 new businesses were incorporated in 1982, down just 4 percent from the record year of 1981. Many of the new firms were in high-technology fields, such as computers, software and genetic engineering. "You read the newspapers and sort of wring your hands ... everything's supposedly come to a halt. But you'll always find good businesses that are able to expand and grow in just about any economic environment," said John Sower, director of the

[6] "NFIB Quarterly Report for Small Business," October 1982.

29

National Development Council.[7] Hard times notwithstanding, small-business owners are generally optimistic. In the NFIB's October survey, 51 percent of the respondents said they expected better business conditions within the next three-to-six months, while only 11 percent expected things to get worse.

Place of Small Business in U.S. Economy

The nation's interest in small business has deep historical roots. The entrepreneurial spirit — from the early shopkeepers to the pioneers who settled the West to the inventors who sparked the Industrial Revolution — has been a dominant force in American history. "If there's any thing in this body politic that is sacred, it is motherhood, apple pie and small business, and maybe not in that order," said Thomas Gray.

For economists, the interest in small business is a matter of numbers. According to a longtime standard that was certified by the 1980 White House Conference on Small Business, small businesses are defined as those with less than 500 employees.[8] By that standard, 98-99 percent of all businesses can be classified as small.[9]

Analysis of available data indicates that small business has lost some of its economic clout in recent decades, mainly because of the growing concentration of manufacturing and the expansion of chain retailing. According to an SBA breakdown of 1977 data provided by the Commerce Department's Bureau of Economic Analysis, the 10,000 "national" businesses had 415,000 subordinate establishments, created 62 percent of the Gross National Product (GNP) and employed 53 percent of the non-government work force. Most of these companies were in the manufacturing, mining, finance or transportation industries. Small businesses created 38 percent of the GNP, down from 43 percent in 1972, and 47 percent of non-government jobs, and were concentrated in construction, wholesale and retail trade, agriculture, fishing and forestry, and services.

Despite their declining share of the nation's wealth, small businesses are still seen by many as the engine that propels the

---

[7] The Washington-based National Development Council provides technical assistance and helps coordinate financing for state and local economic development projects, such as downtown revitalization and industrial parks.

[8] The White House Conference on Small Business, attended by about 2,000 small-business leaders, was held Jan. 13-17, 1980, in Washington, D.C.

[9] Unfortunately for researchers, complete data is available only on those firms that are publicly traded and must file quarterly reports with the Securities and Exchange Commission (SEC). The lack of data on smaller firms has led to confusion among economists and researchers. For instance, the Census Bureau, which conducts a business census every five years (the most recent was in 1982, with results to be released later this year), used the SEC file as its data base. The SBA, ordered by the Small Business Economic Policy Act of 1980 to construct a small business data base, has started with the Dun & Bradstreet Market Indicator File of 3.7 million small businesses.

Despite the recession, businesses are being formed at a rapid rate.

American economy into the future. Entrepreneurs have been the source of many innovations that are now part of daily life. Thomas Edison began his prolific career in a home laboratory. Orville and Wilbur Wright began their experiments in flight at their bicycle shop in Dayton, Ohio. Henry Ford's garage was so small that a wall had to be knocked down to get his first automobile into the street. The helicopter, the Polaroid camera and xerography are each the product of one fertile imagination. More recently, Steven P. Jobs and Stephen G. Wozniak, a pair of young college dropouts, tinkered in Jobs' garage and begat Apple Computer, the originator and dominant force of the personal computer industry. "The major strength of small business . . . is that in moving to exploit new demands, small businesses generally move first and fastest," said Thomas Gray.

Although many areas of research and development — medicine, for example — have been co-opted by large businesses and universities, small-business advocates are fond of quoting a 1976 National Science Foundation study that found small businesses to be two-to-three times as innovative per employee as large corporations. There are skeptics though. Economics writer Robert J. Samuelson pointed out that if a solo inventor hires people to produce and market his invention, his innovation-per-employee will inevitably decrease.[10]

There is even more controversy over the role of small business in job creation. Perhaps the most quoted statistics by small-business lobbyists are those from a 1979 study by Dr. David Birch of the Massachusetts Institute of Technology (MIT). Birch said that between 1969 and 1976, 86 percent of all new jobs were created by firms with under 500 employees, 80 percent

---

[10] Writing in *National Journal*, Nov. 20, 1982.

by firms with under 100 employees and 66 percent by businesses with under 20 workers. However, a more recent Brookings Institution study by Catherine Armington and Marjorie Odle, using the same data as Birch, found that only 39 percent of the new jobs were created by small businesses.[11] One reason for the disparity was that while Birch counted individual business establishments as small businesses even if they were franchises of large corporations, the Brookings researchers counted them only as parts of the parent firm. Their rationale was that while the local McDonald's owner may well be a small-business person, he or she operates in a far more controlled purchasing, marketing and credit environment than the independent businessman or businesswoman.

This debate is more than an esoteric exercise in statistics: it has policy implications as well. "It is critically important for the federal government to know where jobs come from," said Gray. "If you can focus your dollars where growth is coming from, you might well be able to get a net job gain much more quickly."

Problems and Opportunities

WHATEVER the resolution of the "job-creation" debate, it is clear that the small-business community is a provider of innovations and jobs, as well as the diversity so important to a pluralistic society. Small businesses also have a unique set of problems. Chief among them is capital formation. Small businesses tend to be undercapitalized, meaning they must obtain external funding to grow or, in tough times, to finance their inventories and stay above water.

Often, capital formation for a small business means a bank loan, and the exorbitant interest rates of recent years have been a serious detriment to small-business borrowers. Although the nominal prime interest rates — those charged to the most creditworthy, usually large businesses — have declined from a high of 21.5 percent in mid-December 1980 to 11 percent today, the "real" interest rates, measured by the difference between the inflation rate and the prime rate, have remained high. "The small-business men find it easier to borrow at 21, 22, 23 percent during runaway inflation when you can crank it into your product prices than to pay 13 or 14 percent when you're not selling and people aren't buying," said Jerome Gulan, vice president for government affairs of the National Small Business Association.

[11] "Small Business — How Many Jobs?" *The Brookings Review,* winter 1982.

Problems Facing Small Business

Four times a year, the National Federation of Independent Business asks small-business owners to name the most important problem facing them. The following are the results of the latest available surveys:

	October 1982	July 1982	April 1982
Interest Rates and Financing	25%	37%	37%
Poor Sales/Inadequate Demand	23	12	10
Taxes	13	13	14
Inflation	12	16	15
Govt. Regulations/Red Tape	6	4	4
Large Business Competition	6	6	6
Minimum Wage Costs/ Labor Costs	4	2	3
Quality of Labor	3	3	3
Other/No Answer	8	7	8

Even in the best of times, small businesses pay a premium on money. Because they are regarded as greater risks than large corporations, small businesses generally have to pay 2-5 percent above the prime rate. During tight money times, small businesses often have to sign variable rate agreements that allow interest rates to float up with increases in the prime. Those firms that are unable to obtain financing from banks have to turn to finance companies, which usually charge even higher interest rates. Some minority businesses not only have to pay higher rates, but frequently have to come up with more real collateral, instead of banking on projected sales — this despite a study by the Commerce Department's Minority Business Development Administration that found minority businesses to be no more risky than non-minority businesses.[12]

Many small-business owners believe the system is biased against them. But economists see the risk-based premium as the rational workings of the market. According to Thomas Gray: "It appears that small businesses are generally perceived as more risky and that's probably a correct perception. If that's true, then the financial community will find a way to incorporate that into interest rate decisions. Hard to argue against that." SBA has programs that provide direct or guaranteed loans, but they assist a very small percentage of small businesses and are being cut back by the Reagan administration (see p. 43).

Small-business owners are concerned about the effects of large federal deficits on interest rates. Many are convinced that

[12] William C. Scott, Antonio Furino, and Eugene Rodriguez, Jr., "Key Business Ratios of Minority-Owned Businesses," Center for Studies in Business, University of Texas, San Antonio, January 1981.

projected $200 billion deficits will absorb most of the available capital pool, resulting in the "crowding out" of capital-starved small businesses. According to Gray, "[Small-business owners] would prefer the federal deficit to come down because they see it as a proxy for pressure on interest rates and inflation."

SBA Administrator James C. Sanders suggested that debt financing should be avoided by small businesses if at all possible. "If he has an equity situation, then he doesn't have to meet monthly payments, which oftentimes submerge a young business," said Sanders. But significant funds are hard to raise from family and friends. Business acquaintances or strangers often demand a piece of the business in exchange for equity investment, something many entrepreneurs are reluctant to concede. Most small businesses are too small for public stock offerings or cannot afford the expensive SEC registration requirements.

The one bright spot for the capital-hungry entrepreneur is the booming venture capital industry *(see box, p. 39)*. Venture capital firms, which make equity investments in new businesses with big growth potential, virtually disappeared after capital gains taxes went up to 49 percent in 1969 but came roaring back with the reduction of the capital gains rate to 28 percent in 1978 and 20 percent in 1981. The industry's assets jumped from $5 billion to $6.6 billion between September 1981 and September 1982 alone. Still, this is a small pool of capital in a $3 trillion economy, and because of the risk involved, investments are made mainly in businesses that do not intend to remain small for long.

Tax Problems; Recent Relief Measures

Taxes are another problem for small-business owners, especially fixed payroll taxes such as Social Security. Since small businesses are concentrated in labor-intensive industries, Social Security taxes[13] are a relatively larger burden for them than for capital-intensive (mainly large) businesses. The Social Security system is currently in desperate financial straits.[14] Among the proposals to bail out the system made by a bipartisan presidential commission on Jan. 15, 1983, was acceleration of the payroll tax increases scheduled for later in the 1980s. Small business advocates argue that an increase will not only hurt them, but will hurt the economy, since an increased tax on labor dampens incentive to hire workers. "The more you increase the costs of hiring people, the more that discourages the creation of jobs," said Herbert Liebenson, president of the National Small Business Association.

---

[13] Currently 6.7 percent on the first $35,700 of a worker's salary from both employer and employee.
[14] See "Social Security Options," *E.R.R.*, 1982 Vol. II, pp. 929-948.

Mike McKevitt, a former Republican congressman from Colorado[15] and now chief lobbyist for the National Federation of Independent Business, was more emphatic, saying, "We don't want to hurt the old folks, but for God's sake, don't throw out the baby with the bath, because small business means jobs." In a survey of small-business owners by the Small Business Center of the U.S. Chamber of Commerce, only 2 percent of the respondents said Social Security taxes should be raised. Almost 75 percent said reduction in future benefit growth should be used instead to save the system.[16]

Though unable to provide small businesses with relief from Social Security taxes, the Reagan administration says many provisions of the Economic Recovery Tax Act (ERTA) of 1981 specifically benefited small business. The 25 percent reduction in individual income tax rates is singled out, since many small businesses are sole proprietorships, partnerships or small corporations that pay taxes at individual rather than corporate rates. The maximum size of corporations that can pay at individual tax rates, incorporated under Subchapter S of the Internal Revenue Code, was increased to 25 employees from 15. Corporate tax rates on the first $25,000 of profits dropped from 17 to 16 percent in 1982 and to 15 percent this year; on the next $25,000 of profits, there was a similar decrease from 20 to 19 percent in 1982 and then to 18 percent in 1983.

Of special interest to small businesses were changes in estate tax laws. Small business advocates complained that family members were often forced to sell off businesses because of high estate taxes. Under ERTA, the maximum property exemption from estate taxes will more than triple to $600,000 by 1987. The installment period for payment of estate taxes was lengthened from 10 to 15 years, and interest on the first $1 million of assets was limited to 4 percent. Reduced gift taxes will also allow small-business persons to pass on more of their holdings while they are still alive.

Several other provisions of ERTA benefited small business, including a 25 percent write-off for certain research and development activities and an increase in the ceiling on the investment tax credit for purchase of used equipment from $100,000 to $125,000 in 1982 to $150,000 in 1983. But small-business leaders were generally disappointed in the tax act. The main business tax break, the liberalization of depreciation schedules on plant and equipment, did little for small business. "They did complain with validity that most small companies are not capital intensive and there's nothing in the act that does anything

---

[15] McKevitt served one term from 1971 to 1973.
[16] *Washington Report*, Sept. 21, 1982. *Washington Report* is a publication of the U.S. Chamber of Commerce.

Women and Minorities in Business

Entrepreneurship, particularly in the retail and service trades, continues to provide growing opportunities to women and minorities, groups that until recently were rather thinly represented in business ranks. The Internal Revenue Service reported last year that women owned 22 percent of all sole proprietorships in 1980 — an increase of 7 percent from 1979. These establishments accounted for $40.1 billion in receipts and $6.2 billion in net income. About 43 percent of the women-owned sole proprietorships were in the service sector.

SBA Administrator James C. Sanders said last August that the increase in businesses owned by women reaffirmed his decision "to assign higher agency priority to the Office of Women's Business Enterprise," which provides technical and management assistance for female business owners. Many of the government-sponsored Small Business Institutes and Small Business Development Centers across the country provide special courses and counseling for women. Women in business can also turn to many women's groups for business information, including the Chicago-based National Association of Women Business Owners.

Economists believe that minority business ownership has increased also, but because the IRS does not break down business ownership by race, the latest figures that are available are the Business Census figures from 1977 (1982 figures will be available later this year). In 1977, there were 561,395 minority-owned businesses in the United States, up from 381,935 in 1972, an increase of 30.7 percent. Gross receipts jumped by 68.5 percent, from $16.5 million to $26.4 million.

However, business growth was uneven between minority groups. While the number of black-owned firms increased by 11.5 percent during the five-year period, businesses owned by persons of Spanish origin increased by 52.6 percent and those owned by Asian-Americans, American Indians and other minorities increased by 46.9 percent.

There are a number of governmental agencies with authority to assist minority small-business persons, including the Commerce Department's Minority Business Development Agency and the Small Business Administration's Office of Minority Small Business and Capital Ownership Development. SBA also helps finance minority venture capital firms through the Minority Enterprise Small Business Investment Company (MESBIC) program *(see box, p. 39)*. But members of the minority business community have been angered by Reagan administration moves to cut back SBA loans to minority businesses and to force the graduation of firms from the Section 8(a) government procurement set-aside program *(see p. 46)*. In an attempt to mend fences, President Reagan announced an executive order Dec. 15, 1982, that called for a 20 percent, or $15 billion, increase in the minority share of government contracts, and made $1.5 billion in credit assistance and $300 million in management assistance available to minority businesses.

to ease the cost of labor," said Ivan Elmer of the Small Business Center. In fact, Herbert Liebenson of the National Small Business Association claimed in a recent interview that the original Republican tax cut bill contained no benefits for small business and was changed to include $6 billion in benefits only after the Democrats proposed a $27 billion small business plan.

Regulatory Burden on Small Businesses

In his campaign to ease what he calls "burdensome government regulation," President Reagan has an ally in small business. Small-business owners have long complained that the price of complying with federal regulations dealing with such things as environmental protection, occupational health and safety, and equal employment opportunity is particularly onerous for them. Like many other overhead items, such as loan payments and payroll taxes, small businesses lack the capacity of large businesses to amortize the costs of complying with federal regulations over large production runs. "By-and-large, it costs the small operator many times as much to comply as it costs the large operator on a unit basis," said Ivan Elmer.

Most small businesses see large corporations as the real targets of federal regulations, Elmer said, and are trying to tell the government, "Look, guys, I don't think you were aiming at me, but you damn sure hit me." But there is evidence that regulators in the past picked on the little guys to a disproportionate extent. The Bureau of Labor Statistics reported in 1979 that the Occupational Safety and Health Administration (OSHA) performed about half of its inspections on firms with under 25 employees, despite the fact that firms with over 25 employees constituted 70 percent of the work force and 72 percent of all on-the-job fatalities.

A 1979 SBA study estimated that small businesses spend $12.7 billion a year just on government paperwork. Small-business owners are especially angered at overlap and duplication in many of the paperwork requirements. Joseph Voves, a Hawthorne, N.Y. businessman,[17] complained that the Business Census form he received recently was unnecessary, since the requested information concerning payroll and employment was already in the computers of the Social Security Administration. "Why not use the quarterly statements which every corporation files?" Voves asked.

The Reagan administration claims that the federal paperwork burden is being lightened by the Office of Management and Budget's efforts to get other federal agencies to stick to the

---

[17] Voves is founder and president of Metric & Multistandard Components, Inc., a distributor of metrically measured machine parts, such as screws, nuts and bolts.

mandates of the Paperwork Reduction Act of 1980, which required federal agencies to reduce paperwork burdens by 15
percent in 1982 and by 10 percent in 1983. Small-business
owners who feel abused by the regulatory system have some
other new weapons with which to fight back. The Regulatory
Flexibility Act and the Equal Access to Justice Act were passed
and signed in 1980 during the Carter administration but did not
take effect until 1981. The Regulatory Flexibility Act, com-
monly known as "RegFlex," requires federal agencies to con-
sider the effects of proposed rules and regulations on small
businesses, even to the extent of creating "tiered" regulations
with lighter requirements for small businesses. The SBA's Office of Advocacy, headed by Chief Counsel Frank Swain, is
charged with monitoring compliance with the law. "We have no
power to direct an agency to do anything, but we do have the
authority to shake our finger publicly at the agency and we've
not been reluctant to do that," Swain said.

Some agencies have voluntarily complied with the spirit of
RegFlex. OSHA, once one of small business' villains, has
exempted small businesses with good safety records from periodic inspections. Overall, though, compliance has been spotty.
"Some of the institutions that have traditionally tried to ignore
outside elements are continuing to ignore them," said Thomas
Gray. "Others are responding in a real good faith effort." Private sector observers are not yet convinced of the act's usefulness. According to Ivan Elmer, "There are teeth, but it's almost
like a set of false teeth. The question is whether they are in the
mouth ready to be used to bite with."

The Equal Access to Justice Act allows small-business owners
to recover more than their pride when courts find that they
have been wrongly accused of violating a federal regulation. In
the past, small businesses that wanted to challenge administrative penalties often found that legal fees were prohibitively
expensive. "A small-business man found it was cheaper to roll
over and pay a $5,000 fine even though he knew he was innocent
because it was going to cost him $50,000 to prove that," said
Jerry Gulan of the National Small Business Association. To
provide some balance, the Equal Access law requires federal
agencies to pay the legal fees of small-business owners who
successfully challenge regulatory or tax rulings. Since government attorneys lose about 25 percent of such cases,[18] the Equal
Access to Justice Act could result in substantial savings for
small businesses.

Small businesses may also benefit from the Export Trading

---

[18] According to Raymond S. Wittig, minority counsel for the House Small Business
Committee, quoted in *Nation's Business*, February 1982, p. 40.

Venture Capital

The "venture" or "risk" capital industry is one of the fastest growing segments of the investment business. The total capital committed to venture investments grew from $5 billion to $6.6 billion between September 1981 and September 1982, a jump of almost one-third in just one year. The reason for the rapid increase in popularity is clear: those venture capital firms that reached a previously planned date of termination between 1979 and 1981 enjoyed a median rate of return on investments of 25.5 percent and a mean rate of return of 27.6 percent.

A venture capital firm can be a completely private operation or can be licensed by the U.S. Small Business Administration as a Small Business Investment Company (SBIC) or a Minority Enterprise Small Business Investment Company (MESBIC). The advantage of federal licensing is that the venture capital firm can borrow up to $4 from the SBA at reasonable interest rates for every dollar of private investment. As of September 1982, $5 billion in capital was committed by private or corporate subsidiary venture capital firms and $1.6 billion was in SBICs.

A venture capital company takes its pool of funds and invests it in risky new businesses with innovative products or marketing ideas. The venture capitalists receive "equity," or a share in the business, and often an executive position or directorship with the new company, especially if it is the brainchild of an "ideas" person with little business or management experience. Many of the businesses fail, but others are enormous successes that give venture capitalists huge rates of return. According to Walter Stults, president of the National Association of Small Business Investment Companies, the rule of thumb is that for every 10 risk investments, two will be total losses, six will be "walking wounded" that require constant investor supervision, and two will be as successful as some of the best-known venture investments: Apple Computer, Tandem Computers, Intel (semiconducter) Corp. and Federal Express, among others.

The venture capital industry currently is a very small part of the economy. Small business advocates say it could grow substantially if limits on venture investment of pension funds are lifted. Under the "prudent man" rule of the Employee Retirement Income Security Act (ERISA) of 1974, pension-fund officers are held personally liable for investment losses, making investment in small and new businesses prohibitively risky. According to Herbert Liebenson, president of the National Small Business Association, the ERISA restrictions force many small businesses, in seeking safe investments on the New York Stock Exchange, to invest in large corporations.

Company Act of 1982, which removed a number of restrictions that had been seen as barriers to small business exporting. In other countries, export trading companies, which provide export management and marketing services for overseas traders, play a key role. For instance, the Mitsubishi and Matsui trading companies control over 51 percent of Japan's exports. But in the United States, laws that prevented banks from owning businesses blocked the formation of export trading companies. The 1982 law lifted the prohibition against bank ownership of trading companies.

Although the law will initially benefit larger businesses that already export, the export trading companies could also help small businesses work their way through the previously impenetrable maze of international regulations, market requirements and cultural differences. The law also provided exemptions from antitrust laws for small businesses that wanted to join in trading consortiums. The U.S. Commerce Department estimated that more than 25,000 small businesses, which had lacked the expertise or the economies of scale to get involved in trade, might become exporters because of the Export Trading Company Act.

Overall, the Reagan administration gets high marks from the small-business community for its regulatory relief efforts. In a survey of small businesses conducted by the Chamber of Commerce last August, 68 percent of the respondents said the administration was the branch of government most responsive to easing the regulatory burden. But the same poll indicated that the impact of those efforts had not yet been felt. Only 26 percent said the burden of regulation had declined in the previous two years, while 42 percent said it had remained the same and 32 percent said it had actually increased.

Effects of U.S. Procurement Policies

Small-business officials say that the federal government's purchasing policies do not provide small businesses with their rightful share. The federal government annually spends more than $110 billion on the procurement of goods and services. In fiscal year 1980, $25.4 billion of that went to small businesses, about 23 percent of the total and well below small business' 38 percent share of the gross national product, despite the fact that small businesses are entitled by law to all federal contracts under $10,000. The president's 1982 report on small business put much of the blame for this situation on the complexity of federal contract law. A 1979 Office of Federal Procurement Policy (OFPP) study found 485 federal offices operated under 877 sets of procurement regulations that totaled 64,600 pages in length, and that 21,900 new or revised procurement regulations were issued each year.

Not only is the process confusing, but the complex bidding processes mandated by the regulations put the cost of bidding for federal contracts out of range for many small businesses.

"No small business can afford to go through that massive amount of material in order to make a simple bid on a simple project," said Thomas Gray, who estimated that businesses spend almost as much money pursuing a federal contract as they do on the project itself.

A 1978 measure that amended the Small Business Act of 1958 and the 1958 Small Business Investment Act required solicitations of bids of over $1 million for construction contracts and $500,000 for other contracts to contain plans for subcontracting, in order to provide opportunities for small businesses. But the law has been of little apparent help to small business. According to the president's 1982 small business report, "The desired dramatic increase in small business participation has not been realized, partly because contracting officers have not been diligent in enforcing it and partly because SBA has been unable to monitor performance under this provision."

However, the Prompt Payments Act of 1982 should remedy one of the federal government's other bad habits: failure to pay its bills on time. The new law requires that the federal government pay suppliers within 45 days of delivery, or pay interest charges from day 31. In the past, late payments created severe cash flow problems for small businesses. A 1981 General Accounting Office study estimated the cost of late payments to the private sector at $150 million-$375 million a year.

Small-business advocates would like to see more programs that "set aside" federal contracts for small businesses. The term "set-aside" is usually linked with minority assistance programs, like the SBA Section 8(a) program *(see p. 44)*. But in July 1982, Congress overwhelmingly passed the Small Business Innovation Development Act which required all federal agencies with research and development budgets over $100 million to set up Small Business Innovation Research (SBIR) programs. These programs would, by 1987, guarantee 1.25 percent of agency R & D budgets to small businesses.[19] This set-aside law, intended to increase small business' 4 percent share of the federal government's $40 billion R & D budget, was hailed by small business associations. It passed despite the opposition of universities, the largest recipients of federal R & D dollars, who complained that money was being diverted from basic scientific research to product research, especially in the already capital-rich high-technology industries.

---

[19] The agencies currently involved include the departments of Defense, Health and Human Services, Energy, Interior, Transportation and Agriculture, the National Aeronautics and Space Administration, the National Science Foundation, the Environmental Protection Agency and the Nuclear Regulatory Commission. In addition, agencies with R & D budgets over $20 million will be required to set up SBIR goals.

Business-Government Issues

ACCORDING to the president's 1982 small business report, "Over the course of time, the business community in the United States has evolved into what some have called a *dual* system or even a *dual* economy, that is, an economy of two separate sectors composed of a small number of large corporations and a large number of small businesses." It was not always this way. America was founded as a nation of shopkeepers and small farmers. "Big business" was a creature of the Industrial Revolution; other trends in business concentration, such as chain retailing, awaited 20th century revolutions in communications and transportation. However, the duality in our economic system is not a recent occurence, but was recognized by the late 19th century. The Sherman Antitrust Act of 1890 and the Clayton Antitrust Act of 1914 were passed in great part to protect small-business owners from huge industrial empires that were seen as threatening to monopolize all commerce in the United States.

Despite the apparent interest in the viability of small business, no single federal entity was created to look after small-business interests until well into the 20th century. In 1942, the Smaller War Plants Corporation (SWPC) was formed "to mobilize the production capacity of all small business concerns." The SWPC had authority to make loans or guarantee bank loans to small businesses involved in the war effort. The SWPC was absorbed by the Reconstruction Finance Corporation (RFC) at the end of World War II. But the concept was revived in 1951, during the Korean War, with the establishment of the Small Defense Plants Administration, which made small-business loan recommendations to the RFC.

By 1953, strong pressure was being felt in Washington for the creation of a small business agency. A report that year by the Senate Banking and Currency Committee said, "While ... primary reliance should be placed upon individual initiative and private enterprise, the Congress cannot lose sight of the fact that in some areas, federal machinery is still required to enable small business to play its full part." In July 1953, a law was passed to create an experimental "Small Business Administration" with authority to provide small businesses with loans, management assistance and guidance in obtaining federal contracts. The SBA was granted its permanent authorization in October 1958.

The SBA, which has grown from 432 employees at its inception to 4,400 today, is probably best-known for its loan-making capacity. As of the end of fiscal year 1982 the SBA had made 449,769 business loans worth $34.23 billion. Most of these have been "guaranteed" loans, in which the SBA pledges to pay the lending institution, usually a local bank, 90 percent of the outstanding debt if a loan recipient defaults. A small percentage of SBA loans have been "direct," with the SBA acting as the lending institution for small businesses. The SBA is also in charge of federal disaster loans, of which 898,976, worth over $11.62 billion had been made through fiscal year 1982. Most of these loans went to owners whose businesses were disrupted by natural disasters — floods, earthquakes, tornadoes, blizzards — but there were exceptions. For instance, a $200 million disaster loan program was instituted last September to aid businesses along the Mexican border that were hurt by the devaluation of the Mexican peso.[20]

Loans and Other Services Provided by SBA

The SBA has several other financial assistance programs. Loans are made under Section 503 of the Small Business Investment Act of 1958 to local development corporations (LDCs) and state development corporations (SDCs), coalitions of government agencies, businesses and financial institutions with projects for economic development or renewal.[21] The SBA finances Small Business Investment Companies (SBICs) that provide venture capital to small businesses *(see box, p. 39)*. The agency also guarantees surety bonds — a financial commitment by contractors that they will finish a project — for those small businesses that are unable to obtain them through normal channels.

The SBA also provides management assistance to small businesses. Many small companies fail because entrepreneurs, while blessed with brilliant ideas or talents in their trades, lack knowledge in basic business skills, such as accounting, cash flow management, purchasing and marketing. To help overcome these disadvantages, the SBA provides small-business persons with management assistance through such programs as: Service Corps of Retired Executives (SCORE) and Active Corps of Executives (ACE), which rely on the voluntary counseling efforts of experienced businesspersons; Small Business Institutes (SBIs) on more than 500 university, college and community college campuses, with graduate business students and faculty

---

[20] Since Mexican currency was worth less, it took almost twice as many pesos to purchase American goods than before devaluation. Many American border businesses experienced a 40 to 60 percent dropoff in sales.

[21] On Oct. 22, 1982, the Reagan administration announced a Small Business Revitalization Program, which combined the resources of federal, state and local governments for use in economic development projects. Federal programs to be utilized include SBA Section 503 loans and the Department of Housing and Urban Development's Urban Development Action Grant (UDAG) and Community Development Block Grant (CDBG) programs. Twenty-one states are taking part in the project.

members providing advice; Small Business Development Centers (SBDCs), also usually university-based, which draw on the resources of both public and private sector for management assistance; business management courses, cosponsored with chambers of commerce, trade associations and academia; and numerous publications.

The SBA also continues to help small businesses find their way through the government procurement maze. A computerized data base, known as the Procurement Automated Source System (PASS), matches small businesses with relevant federal projects. The SBA also supervises small business "set-aside" programs. For 14 years, the SBA has assisted minority businesses through the set-aside program created under Section 8(a) of the Small Business Act. The agency acts as prime contractor for projects submitted by other federal agencies, then subcontracts them to eligible "socially and economically disadvantaged persons." The SBA is also in charge of the SBIR program created by the Small Business Innovation Development Act of 1982 *(see p. 41)*.

In 1976, Congress created an Office of Advocacy within the Small Business Administration. Small business interests had been critical of the SBA's inability to respond to congressional inquiries about the effects of proposed legislation on small businesses or to defend small-business interests when other agencies were prejudicial to them. The Office of Advocacy provides policy analysis and congressional testimony on proposed legislation, and acts as a small business ombudsman, with oversight of the provisions of the Regulatory Flexibility Act. "The Office of Advocacy was established to make sure there is an ability to assess and analyze the impact of federal policy on small-business interests, and try to articulate that impact when the debates come up," said Frank S. Swain, chief counsel of the advocacy unit. Last October, SBA added a new service called the "Answer Desk." SBA specialists provide answers to questions from current or prospective small-business owners on a toll-free "800" phone line. According to Swain, the "Answer Desk" has averaged about 250 calls per day.[22]

Continued Criticism of Agency's Programs

On the occasion of its 20th anniversary in 1973, SBA printed a short history which described the agency as "a model in its field and the *sine qua non* of a healthy and viable small business community." But in recent years, the Small Business Administration has been the subject of controversy. Chief among its

---

[22] The Answer Desk phone number is 800-368-5855 on the U.S. mainland, 653-7561 in the Washington, D.C. area. The service is not available in Alaska and Hawaii.

problems has been a reputation for waste and fraud. Billions of dollars allegedly have been lost because the SBA unwittingly made loans to a variety of mobsters and swindlers.[23] SBA Administrator James C. Sanders, a former San Diego businessman who was appointed in 1982, appears to be well-regarded in the small business community. But the agency still has a reputation as a patronage playground. "The fact that it is now a political dumping ground has prevented it from becoming the effective agency for small business which it should be," said Rep. Mitchell.[24]

The direct-loan program has also come under fire. In this program, the federal government acts as the lender of "last resort" for business owners who have been turned down by two local banks. The rationale is that many worthy business ideas never get off the ground because they are regarded as too risky by financial institutions. However, critics think the government has no right to intervene in such market decisions. "How can the SBA be expected to make a better credit judgment than the businessman's banker ... who knows his customer, the neighborhood and the competition much better than anyone in SBA?" asked Taylor C. Lattimore, a Miami-based SBA official, in 1981 testimony before the Senate Small Business Committee. The Reagan administration has tried to eliminate the program. But the program has strong congressional support. The fiscal year 1983 budget includes $215 million for direct loans, far more than the $41 million requested by the administration.

Some observers also have doubts about the necessity of the guaranteed-loan program. According to Ivan Elmer of the Chamber of Commerce's Small Business Center, SBA's loan-making efforts are so small that they are hardly worth having at all. SBA actually has already made substantial cuts in its lending programs. In fiscal year 1982, the total number of business loans — direct and guaranteed combined — declined 46.3 percent from 1981 levels. The dollar total of those loans fell by 44.5 percent. Loans to minority businesses also fell sharply, down 51.9 percent in number of loans and 47.9 percent in dollars.

There is also much debate over the SBA's handling of the Section 8(a) minority procurement program. By law, businesses whose employment or income grow beyond certain standards are supposed to be "graduated" from the 8(a) program. Of the more than 2,000 minority businesses that have entered the program, less than 200 have been graduated. Critics say these

---

[23] See "SBA Enters the Fraud-and-Waste Hall of Fame," *U.S. News & World Report*, July 27, 1981, and "SBA: A Ripe Target For Big Ripoffs," *U.S. News & World Report*, March 22, 1982.

[24] Quoted in "Entrepreneurial Economics," *Venture*, January 1983, p. 35.

businesses have been given an unfair special status, and are blocking other small businesses from taking advantage of the program. Last August, the Reagan administration tried to force the graduation of 23 firms, but delayed the action after protests from the minority community and the businesses involved, which say that much of their business in federal contracts would be lost if they left the program. The administration says it will implement the forced graduation on Feb. 14, a move Rep. Mitchell referred to as "a major mistake."

Despite its role as a small-business representative in Washington, the SBA has less than unanimous support from the small-business community. A 1981 survey by the Louisville Area Chamber of Commerce found that a vast majority of its members wanted the SBA eliminated. Many small-business owners, a basically conservative constituency, are affected not only by the waste and corruption accusations, but also by a strong disinclination against anything that smacks of "special interest." "There are very genuine, sincere recommendations that we should abolish the SBA, that it is sort of the antithesis of the philosophy of the constituency that it was put in place to serve," said Elmer. But the agency has its backers. "We have always been a strong supporter of a free and independent SBA," said Jerome Gulan of the National Small Business Association. Administrator James Sanders defends his agency as well: "Unless you have some agency that is devoted to [small business] it inevitably gets taken over by bigger interests."

Political Influence of Small Businesses

Although most of the discussion about government assistance to small business focuses on the federal Small Business Administration, there recently has been a great deal of small business assistance activity on the state level. Among the states, 27 have established state-level small business assistance offices; 29 cosponsor other kinds of small business assistance programs; 20 have created Governor's Advisory Councils or Task Forces on Small Business; nine have passed their own Regulatory Flexibility Acts; six have Equal Access to Justice laws; three have passed Paperwork Reduction acts; 28 have sponsored small business conferences; and 21 have Small Business Development Centers. In addition, eight state legislatures have small business committees.[25]

The growing number of small business programs and agencies in Washington and around the country can be seen as proof that government officials have recognized the important role of small

---

[25] See "Directory of State Small Business Assistance Offices and Activities, 1982 Edition," Office of the Chief Counsel for Advocacy, U.S. Small Business Administration.

business in economic stability and growth. But it is also evidence of the growing political power of the small-business community. "I think they've learned this is a pretty strong force," said Herbert Liebenson of the National Small Business Association. "General Motors doesn't have a vote; the corner grocery does."

The greater political presence of small business is in part attributable to greater cohesion between the various small business lobbying groups. Small business is not a monolithic entity, but is rather a loose agglomeration of millions of businesses with differing financial and demographic backgrounds and often differing political needs. Thus, small business suffered from political splintering that was exacerbated by the competition between the small-business interest groups, such as the National Federation of Independent Businesses, the National Small Business Association, and the hundreds of individual trade associations. In the past few years, though, observers have noted a change in the small-business community. "The major groups are cooperating fairly effectively in the last couple of years," said Thomas Gray.

Small-business owners are also getting more heavily involved in electoral politics. In 1980, small business activists took credit for a number of political victories, including the defeat of Sen. Gaylord Nelson, D-Wis., then chairman of the Senate Small Business Committee. In a poll taken in June 1982 by the Chamber of Commerce, 76 percent of the respondents said they intended to work for federal, state or local candidates, and 67 percent said they planned to make financial contributions to political candidates.

The political activity has resulted in more competition between the parties for the small business vote. Discussing the 1981 tax act, SBA Chief Counsel Frank Swain said, "Really for the first time, in that tax bill, the two sides of the aisle were openly vying for how good they could make the bill from a small business perspective." Although small business will not win all of its legislative battles, it is almost certain to be heard this year when it speaks up against Social Security payroll tax increases and huge federal deficits, and in favor of various tax benefits for small-business owners. "I think from now on the small business community will be recognized as a real political entity," said Rep. Mitchell.

Selected Bibliography

Books

Hancock, William A., *The Small Business Legal Adviser,* McGraw-Hill, 1982.

Lowry, Albert J., *How To Become Financially Successful Owning Your Own Business,* Simon & Schuster, 1981.

Mancuso, Joseph R., *Have You Got What It Takes?,* Spectrum, 1982.

Pratt, Stanley E., *How To Raise Venture Capital,* Scribner's, 1982.

Articles

Armington, Catherine and Marjorie Odle, "Small Business — How Many Jobs?," *The Brookings Review,* winter 1982.

Dizard, John W., "Do We Have Too Many Venture Capitalists?," *Fortune,* Oct. 4, 1982.

Kelly, Orr, "SBA Enters the Fraud-and-Waste Hall of Fame," *U.S. News & World Report,* July 27, 1981.

Levitt, Arthur Jr., "In Praise of Small Business," *The New York Times Magazine,* Dec. 6, 1981.

Pauly, David et al., "The Ills of Small Business," *Newsweek,* July 6, 1981.

Samuelson, Robert J., "A False Religion," *National Journal,* Nov. 20, 1982.

Taylor, Alexander L. III et al., "Hard Times on Main Street," *Time,* Oct. 26, 1981.

Thoryn, Michael, "A Fairer Shake for Small Business," *Nation's Business,* February 1982.

—— "SBA: Confronting Its Own Problems," *Nation's Business,* August 1982.

"Venture Capitalists Get Bolder," *Business Week,* Nov. 30, 1981.

Reports and Studies

Heller Small Business Institute, "After Two Years: Small Business Assesses the Reagan Administration," December 1982.

National Federation of Independent Business, "NFIB Quarterly Economic Report for Small Business," October 1982.

—— "NFIB Report on Small Business in America's Cities," November 1981.

Office of Advocacy, Small Business Administration, "Social Security: A Tax on Labor," Nov. 11, 1982.

Small Business Administration, "From Probation to World Renown," July 30, 1973.

"The State of Small Business: A Report of the President," March 1982.

The White House Conference on Small Business, "Conference Report," January 1980.

Cover illustration by Staff Artist Robert Redding.

Social Security Options

by

William Sweet

**Dec. 17
1982**

Editor's Note: Before leaving Washington for its 1983 Easter recess, Congress passed a bill to shore up the Social Security system. The measure was based primarily on recommendations made earlier in the year by the president's bipartisan National Commission on Social Security Reform.

The bill seeks to increase Social Security revenues and cut costs a total of $165 billion over the next seven years. It would speed up previously scheduled tax increases and postpone a cost-of-living increase due in mid-1983 until the following Jan. 1. Additionally, the Social Security tax would be increased on the self-employed.

Other provisions bring new federal employees under Social Security coverage beginning Jan. 1, 1984. And in the next century, the age for retirement at full benefits would gradually be raised from 65 to 67.

While these steps were expected to keep the Social Security system's retirement fund solvent at least for several years, the legislative package left unresolved the impending bankruptcy of Medicare's Hospital Insurance (HI) trust fund. That matter awaits later congressional action.

SOCIAL SECURITY OPTIONS

W HEN the 98th Congress convenes in January,[1] one of the first items on its agenda will be reform of the nation's troubled Social Security system. The largest of the system's three trust funds, Old Age and Survivors Insurance (OASI),[2] already is running at a deficit, and by sometime in 1984 the system as a whole is expected to go into the red. While nearly everyone agrees that something must be done to shore up the Social Security trust funds, there are sharp partisan differences on how to approach the problem and it is not clear how quickly they can be resolved.

In principle, Congress should be able to reach a compromise between revenue increases, which Democrats tend to favor, and benefit cuts, the Republican preference. But any kind of tax increase can be politically explosive, especially at a time of economic recession, and any reductions in benefits could antagonize Social Security beneficiaries — roughly one-seventh of the U.S. population.

In 1981 President Reagan recommended sweeping cuts in Social Security benefits, including elimination of the minimum monthly payment for low-income beneficiaries.[3] But the public and congressional outcry was so great that the administration beat a hasty retreat. Instead, the president announced that he was setting up a 15-member bipartisan commission to find a permanent solution to Social Security's financial woes. Chaired by Alan Greenspan, the head of the Council of Economic Advisers under President Ford, the commission includes five members appointed by the president, five appointed by Senate Majority Leader Howard H. Baker Jr., R-Tenn., and five by House Speaker Thomas P. O'Neill Jr., D-Mass.

The Greenspan commission is to report to the president by the end of December, but it appears unlikely that it will produce

---

[1] Congress will convene at noon on Jan. 3, but the Senate then plans to recess until Jan. 25. The House will work at organizing itself the week of Jan. 3 then adjourn until Jan. 25, the tentative date of President Reagan's State of the Union address.

[2] OASI pays benefits to retirees, their dependents and survivors. The other trust funds are Hospital Insurance (Medicare), which provides health care insurance for the elderly and for disabled Social Security beneficiaries, and Disability Insurance, which provides benefits for disabled workers. Nearly 36 million Americans receive Social Security checks each month. Total outlays from the three funds are projected at $229 billion for fiscal 1983.

[3] See Congressional Quarterly's 1981 CQ Almanac, pp. 117-121.

a single set of recommendations. At its Dec. 10 meeting the committee admitted that it was deadlocked and Chairman Greenspan postponed until Dec. 17 a vote on the various options the committee is considering to preserve the soundness of the system.

At a three-day meeting in November, committee members did agree on the scope of the problem. They concluded that the Social Security shortfall in the next seven years could be as high as $150 billion to $200 billion and that the system needed the equivalent of a 1.8 percent increase in payroll taxes to survive the next 75 years in sound condition. Commission members also appear to be in agreement that the cost-of-living formula needs to be modified in some way, that employees of the federal government and some non-profit organizations should be brought into the system to increase the revenue base and that some kind of "stabilizer" is needed to make the system less vulnerable to fluctuations in the economy.

Numerous Proposals for Reforming System

Anticipating congressional action on Social Security, many groups and individuals have issued proposals for a fundamental restructuring of the system. Critics on both the political right and left have charged that the government is relying on "Band-Aid" solutions. Without a radical reorganization of the whole system, they claim, people who have paid into the system for years may never get a fair return on their contributions.

What particularly irks conservative critics is the absence of any direct relationship between the amount one pays into Social Security and the amount one draws out in benefits. In contrast to private pension plans, in which benefits are proportional to the contributions individuals have made over the years, Social Security is a "pay as you go" system. Every individual who is a member of the system is entitled to certain benefits, on the basis of fixed criteria, regardless of how much the individual has contributed. Thus, in any given year, enough revenues must be obtained from working contributors to cover retiree benefits.

The Heritage Foundation, an ultra-conservative think tank in Washington, D.C., has called for greater reliance on privately offered retirement accounts and for separation of the "insurance" and "welfare" portions of Social Security. The welfare portion — such as spouses' payments — would be financed out of general revenues. The foundation's proposal is similar to a "family security plan" prepared by Peter J. Ferrara, who is currently a White House adviser.[4] Ferrara proposed that, start-

---

[4] Peter J. Ferrara, "Social Security Reform: The Family Plan," The Heritage Foundation, 1982.

Social Security and the Federal Budget

The National Commission on Social Security Reform voted Nov. 10 to recommend removing Social Security from the rest of the federal budget. While such a step would amount to no more than a technical change in bookkeeping procedures, it could have an important influence on the way the public perceives certain policy issues. However, the idea is opposed by Senate Budget Committee Chairman Pete V. Domenici, R-N.M., House Budget Committee Chairman James R. Jones, D-Okla., and the administration's budget director, David A. Stockman.

Social Security has been included in the federal budget only since 1969, when President Johnson "unified" the budget at the recommendation of a special commission. At that time, the Social Security trust funds were running at a surplus, and so the effect of combining them with the rest of the government's finances was to reduce the apparent size of the federal deficit.

The rationale for consolidation of the budget was that Social Security receipts and expenditures affected general economic activity, just as other government spending did. Critics charged, however, that the government's deeper motive for unifying the budget was to conceal the impact of Vietnam War expenditures.

The unexpected long-term effect of consolidating the budget has been to confuse thinking about trends in government activity. If pre- and post-1969 budgets are compared, without taking the addition of Social Security into account, increases in social expenditures relative to other federal outlays are overstated, and decreases in defense spending seem more significant than they really are.

---

ing in 1986, individuals be allowed to deduct 20 percent of their Social Security contributions for investments in private retirement accounts (IRAs). They could also have their employers contribute up to 20 percent of the employer share of the tax to IRAs. Ferrara believes that more investment in IRAs would help stimulate the economy, ultimately assuring individuals a higher return on their contributions than they would get from Social Security.

Another conservative group, The National Taxpayers Legal Fund, has been promoting a proposal that also calls for the separation of Social Security's welfare and insurance functions and for greater reliance on private retirement accounts.[5] Under the Legal Fund's plan, the Supplemental Security Income program, which provides benefits for the elderly poor and which is funded from general revenues, would take over responsibility for the welfare functions. Benefits from "future security individual retirement accounts" would be tax-exempt, as Social Security benefits are now.

---

[5] The National Taxpayers Legal Fund, "The Social Security Crisis: Mandate for Reform," Washington, 1982.

Liberals and leftists, in contrast to conservatives, have proposed bolstering Social Security finances with an infusion of general tax revenues. Ralph Nader's Congress Watch suggests taxing Social Security benefits received by the wealthy and funding Medicare out of general revenues. The Gray Panthers and the National Council of Senior Citizens, two lobbying groups for the elderly, also have called for some general revenue financing of Social Security. The American Association of Retired Persons has suggested that revenues could be raised by means of special excise taxes on such products as alcohol and tobacco or by delaying tax cuts scheduled for mid-1983. House Majority Leader Jim Wright, D-Texas, has suggested earmarking revenues from offshore oil leases to Social Security and providing people of retirement age with tax credits to encourage them to keep working.[6]

Lack of Support for Fundamental Changes

Many European countries rely heavily on general revenue financing for their old-age security systems. Austria, for example, funded nearly 35 percent of its old-age benefits out of general revenues in 1977, and the Federal Republic of Germany drew 25 percent from general tax receipts.[7] In the United States, however, the principle that Social Security should be self-financing is still almost sacrosanct. Among politicians and pollsters, it is widely believed that Americans would lose faith in a system that depended heavily on the vagaries of year-to-year appropriations.

Private and corporate pension plans have grown enormously since the Social Security system was established in 1935, but two out of three elderly persons still get half their cash from Social Security. Among elderly women, dependence on Social Security is especially acute. Some 60 percent of all unmarried women over age 65 rely on Social Security as their sole source of income.[8] Any talk of radically restructuring Social Security touches raw nerves, as Republicans found out in the 1982 elections.

The week before Election Day, the National Republican Congressional Committee found it advisable to withdraw a controversial fund-raising letter, in which contributors to the party were asked to choose between different options for reforming the Social Security system — among them a proposal to make the system voluntary. Speaking for the Democratic Party the Saturday before the election, Sen. Edward M. Kennedy,

[6] Wright's remarks were made on "Meet the Press," NBC-TV, Nov. 7, 1982.
[7] See U.S. Senate Special Committee on Aging, "Social Security in Europe: The Impact of an Aging Population," Washington, December 1981, pp. 13, 27.
[8] See "Women and Aging," *E.R.R.*, 1981 Vol. II, pp. 713-732.

'Opting Out' of Social Security

Some people believe that individuals should be allowed to "opt out" of the Social Security system and contribute some or all of their payroll taxes to private retirement accounts or group pension plans. Advocates of this approach believe that it would reduce the system's long-term liabilities and at the same time pay individuals higher returns on their contributions. Opponents say it would aggravate short-term financing problems by reducing the number of Social Security contributors. While the Greenspan commission has not given much consideration to the idea of "privatizing" Social Security, some foreign governments have embraced the concept.

Chile's military regime established a plan in May 1981 that allows individuals to withdraw completely from the state's old-age pension system. Individuals opting out are required to pay at least 10 percent of their income into private retirement funds, which must be managed by accredited firms. By the end of last year, about half the eligible people in Chile were reported to have withdrawn from the state system.

In 1978, a Labor Party government in England adopted a two-tier state pension plan, which the Conservatives endorsed as well. The first tier guarantees all individuals benefits up to fixed amounts, regardless of their income; all working people are required to contribute payroll taxes toward this fund. The second tier pays higher benefits that are dependent on earnings, but companies are allowed to withdraw from Tier II, provided they offer their workers private pension plans that promise benefits at least as good as the state system's. According to University of Dallas Professor John G. Goodman, an expert on the British system, companies representing about 45 percent of England's eligible workers have opted out of Tier II. The effect of introducing this reform, Goodman said, was to reduce the old-age system's unfunded liabilities by 30 percent.

In the United States, employees of state and local governments and non-profit organizations are allowed to withdraw from Social Security, with two years' notice, but until recently few chose to do so. As of June 1980, roughly 10 million state and local employees were covered by Social Security, and only 130,000 voluntarily terminated their enrollment. Between 1959 and 1981, the Social Security Administration received 881 termination notices from state and local groups. In 1982-84, around 800 will take effect, a big increase. State and local government employees have been "opting out in droves" during the past two years, Goodman said, and so have hospital employees.

D-Mass., charged that the administration was "waiting to spring a November surprise — a secret post-election plan to slash Social Security and tarnish the golden years of the elderly." President Reagan's efforts to defuse the issue with promises to "protect the solvency" of the system were apparently not completely effective. A *New York Times*/CBS survey of voters leaving polling places on Nov. 2 indicated that concern about Social Security was an important factor in Democratic House victories.

Even among business-oriented groups, proposals to slash Social Security benefits or make the system voluntary *(see box, p. 55)* do not necessarily meet with enthusiasm. A recent article in *Industry Week* pointed out that many companies would have to compensate for cuts in Social Security benefits because most "have chosen to integrate their pension plans with Social Security — that is, they rely on formulas that adjust company-paid benefits to reflect the amount a retiree receives from Uncle Sam." [9]

Probable Short-Term Funding Solutions

Since preservation of the Social Security system in roughly its current form seems likely, Congress will probably settle on a package of limited measures, designed partly to bolster confidence in the system, partly to ease the funding crunch. Confidence-building measures could include giving the Social Security Administration greater autonomy, perhaps by separating it from the Department of Health and Human Services, and/or the addition of two members to the Social Security Board of Trustees to represent the general public — a step advocated by Sen. Daniel Patrick Moynihan, D-N.Y.[10] Suggestions for strengthening the system's finances include changing procedures used to invest trust funds' reserves and elimination of the so-called "windfall" benefits received by those who have worked in both non-covered employment and in jobs covered by Social Security. This last measure would affect federal employees who took private-sector jobs after leaving government service and are able to "double-dip" upon retirement.

There appears to be growing support for the idea of extending the system to include employees of federal and perhaps state governments, as well as people working for some non-profit organizations. Immediate inclusion of all federal and state employees could generate up to $50 billion in the next five years. It is much more likely, however, that Congress would vote to include only new government employees, perhaps those with less than five years of service. This would generate only about $13.5 billion in additional revenues.[11]

---

[9] Marilyn Much, "Social Security: Who Pays for the Cure?" *Industry Week*, Nov. 15, 1982, p. 62.
[10] The board currently has four members: the secretaries of labor, health and human services and the Treasury, and the commissioner of Social Security.
[11] Unions representing government employees oppose their incorporation into Social Security, since their current plans generally provide superior benefits. In 1977, Congress rejected a proposal to extend coverage to all federal workers, though they are required to contribute to Social Security's Medicare Fund.

Easily the biggest increase in revenues would be obtained by advancing to 1984 the payroll tax increases scheduled to come into effect between 1985 and 1990. Acceleration of the tax hikes could yield close to $160 billion over five years. Former Social Security Administrator Robert M. Ball, one of the most influential members of the Greenspan commission, has suggested coupling a speedup of payroll tax hikes with optional tax breaks for Social Security contributions. Those taking advantage of the breaks would have to pay taxes on benefits after retirement, which is the way IRAs and Keogh plans work.[12]

Modifying the way benefits are indexed to inflation also could have a relatively big impact on Social Security finances. One simple measure would be to postpone the 1983 cost-of-living adjustment from July to October, which — because benefits compound on whatever new base is established — could yield as much as $35 billion over six years. Many economists advocate linkage of benefits to wages rather than the cost-of-living index, since that would strengthen the tie between contributions and returns. Another possibility would be to construct a special cost-of-living index for the elderly, since it is generally assumed that the regular cost-of-living index overstates the increases in prices that affect old people. Housing costs are an important component in the cost-of-living index, for example, but most elderly homeowners have paid off their mortgages.

Cutting benefits for the elderly is not popular in any political quarter, but it is usually recognized that some groups of retired people may be getting more than they really need from Social Security. House Speaker O'Neill has indicated that he might support partial taxation of Social Security benefits to people over some income level. The exemption of investment income from the amount retirees can earn, without losing benefits, could come under fire as well.[13]

Long-Term Funding Problems

THE Social Security system's basic difficulties can be traced to demographic and legislative trends that have conspired to place an ever greater burden of supporting the elderly on current workers. Since 1935, when the system was established, Congress has steadily increased the number of people eligible

[12] Keogh plans allow self-employed persons to set aside up to 15 percent of their earnings, to a limit of $7,500, in retirement accounts.
[13] In 1983, pensioners aged 65 to 69 can earn up to $6,600 without cutting into their Social Security benefits.

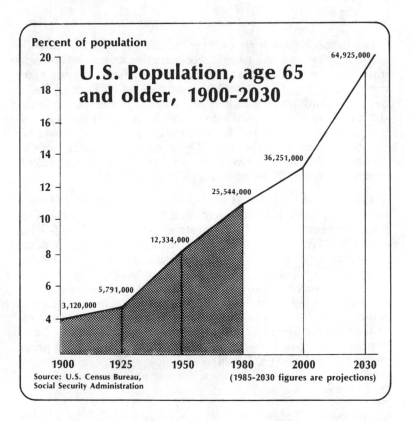

Percent of population

U.S. Population, age 65 and older, 1900-2030

64,925,000

36,251,000

25,544,000

12,334,000

5,791,000

3,120,000

1900 1925 1950 1980 2000 2030

Source: U.S. Census Bureau,
Social Security Administration

(1985-2030 figures are projections)

for benefits. Survivors and dependents of insured workers became eligible in 1939; self-employed persons other than farmers and professionals were brought into the system in 1950; farmers and professionals, including members of the clergy, were included in 1954. In 1956, only 20 percent of the people over age 65 received Social Security benefits, but today over 90 percent do. Average monthly benefits increased between 1950 and 1980 by a factor of about 2.5, after correcting for inflation.[14] At the same time, the proportion of the population over 65 has increased *(see graph, above)* and Americans have taken to retiring somewhat earlier. Average life expectancy has gone from 62 in 1935 to about 74 today. Since 1960, the labor force participation rate among workers aged 55-64 has dropped from 85 percent to less than 70 percent.[15] In 1961, men as well as women became eligible to receive 80 percent of their monthly Social Security benefits if they retired at 62 rather than 65. Critics say that this provision encourages a lower labor force participation rate.

As a result of the aging of the U.S. population and the trend toward earlier retirement, the ratio of Social Security contribu-

---

[14] The average monthly benefit in 1980 was about $300.
[15] See Tom Bethell, "Social Security: Permit for Idleness," *The Journal of The Institute for Socioeconomic Studies*, autumn, 1981, p. 47.

tors to beneficiaries has steadily deteriorated. In 1940 there was an average of 8.5 people aged 20-64 for every person 65 or older; in 1980 there were just over five people under 64 for every person older.[16] In 1950, an average of 16 workers paid Social Security taxes for every retiree supported by the system, but now the ratio is about 3-to-1, and by the year 2020 it could drop to 2-to-1.[17]

During the 1950s and 1960s, high rates of economic growth and a widening base of payroll contributions enabled Congress to increase Social Security benefits. As late as 1972, the Social Security Advisory Council informed Congress, on the basis of optimistic economic projections, that the system would accumulate reserves of up to $1 trillion in the following 50 years. In response, Congress enacted hefty benefit hikes, cut future tax rates and linked benefit levels to the consumer price index.

In 1973, however, soaring oil prices sent the economy into a protracted slump, and by the mid-1970s, Social Security revenues were falling far below anticipated levels. The system's reserves, instead of increasing to $1 trillion, fell to a small fraction of annual outlays *(see box, p. 61)*. In 1977, Congress sought to alleviate the crunch by raising Social Security tax rates, increasing the maximum income level taxed and modifying the formula for cost-of-living adjustments.

By the end of the 1970s, however, a combination of inflation and recession had put another squeeze on the system. Steps taken in 1981 to tighten benefits proved insufficient to get the books back into balance and during the past two years the old age fund has had to borrow from the health and disability funds to stay afloat.[18]

Rising Economic and Demographic Burdens

Since efforts by Congress to rectify Social Security's finances have failed repeatedly in recent years, many experts have argued that Congress needs to confront the "fundamental" problems confronting the system and not just "tinker around the edges." Writing in a recent issue of *The New York Review of Books,* Peter G. Peterson, a former secretary of commerce, asserted that Social Security's "financial problems are not minor and temporary, as most politicians, at least in election years, feel compelled to insist.... To put the matter bluntly, Social

---

[16] See "How to Save Social Security," *Business Week,* Nov. 29, 1982, p. 81.
[17] See *U.S. News & World Report,* Nov. 8, 1982, p. 44.
[18] While the Medicare health fund is currently flush, it too could be in trouble by the end of the 1980s unless something is done to curb rising hospital costs. The disability fund's costs have been cut partly by means of an accelerated review of the rolls, which Congress mandated in 1980. Groups representing the disabled have charged that deserving individuals are losing benefits. See "Mental Health Care Reappraisal," *E.R.R.,* 1982 Vol. II, pp. 609-632.

Security is heading for a crash . The Social Security system has become a high-risk gamble on economic progress and population growth." [19]

Drawing on work done in the early 1970s by Martin Feldstein, who is currently chairman of the president's Council of Economic Advisers, and A. Haeworth Robertson,[20] chief actuary of the Social Security Administration from 1935 to 1978, Peterson argued that the growing burden of Social Security taxation is retarding the country's rate of investment and economic growth. Comparing the United States to Japan, where rates of investment in new plant and equipment, public infrastructure and civilian research and development have been much higher, Peterson attributed the difference partly to the fact that "pensions in Japan — both public and private — are meager, forcing workers to save for their retirement."

Not all economists agree with this line of reasoning. In a book published last November, Henry Aaron, a senior fellow at the Brookings Institution in Washington, D.C., asserted that the evidence is inconclusive as to whether Social Security has had significant detrimental effects on the U.S. savings rate and labor supply.[21] On the other hand, Aaron cited strong evidence that Social Security has greatly improved the economic status of the aged. Aaron found that Social Security provided 39 percent of the total money income of the elderly in 1978, and 76 percent of the income of the elderly poor.

Challenge Posed by Baby-Boom Generation

According to most reputable analyses, if the problems currently afflicting the Social Security system can be solved for the rest of the decade, the situation will ease somewhat for the following 20 years or so, as the relatively small generations of people born during the Depression and World War II reach retirement age. In the second decade of the 21st century, however, when members of the baby-boom generation start reaching age 65, the system could encounter a crisis even more serious than the current crunch. At that point, if current economic and demographic trends continue unabated, everybody agrees that Social Security will be facing truly fundamental problems.

How serious is the long-term danger? In an article published last fall by the Federal Reserve Bank of New York, the authors said the "basic problem is that ... average retirees both now and in the future can expect to receive benefits that, by any

[19] Peter G. Peterson, "Social Security: The Coming Crash," *The New York Review of Books*, Dec. 2, 1982, p. 34.
[20] See A. Haeworth Robertson, *The Coming Revolution in Social Security* (1981).
[21] Henry J. Aaron, *Economic Effects of Social Security* (1982).

Trust Fund Assets as a Percentage of Annual Outlays, 1972-1982

Year*	Old Age and Survivors Insurance (OASI)	Disability Insurance (DI)	Hospital Insurance (HI)	OASI, DI, and HI Combined
1972	88%	140%	47%	87%
1973	75	125	40	76
1974	68	110	69	73
1975	63	92	79	69
1976	54	71	77	60
1977	47	48	66	50
1978	39	26	57	40
1979	30	30	54	34
1980	23	35	52	29
1981	18	21	45	23
1982**	15	16	52	22

* Beginning of the year.
** Ratios for 1982 based on outlays projected by the Congressional Budget Office.

SOURCE: David Koitz, "A Summary of the 1982 Trustees' Report and Supplementary Historical Information," Congressional Research Service, Report No. 82-75 EPW, April 1982.

measure, are far in excess of lifetime contributions. For example, the average 65-year-old retiree in 1982 (with a non-working spouse) recovers his lifetime contributions within nine months after retiring.... The difficulties of Social Security are almost entirely the result of the fact that a self-financed system cannot continue to pay out subsidies forever." [22]

The implication is that each generation cannot go on subsidizing the retirement of the previous generation forever. But of course that depends on how big and how rich each successive generation is, and on how big the subsidies are. The authors of the Federal Reserve Bank article concede, after introducing certain refinements into their calculations, that the situation is not quite as dire as it looks at first glance. If the employer's contributions are taken into account, and if contributions are assigned compound interest comparable to what they would earn in a private retirement fund, the average 1982 retiree would need well over five years to recover in benefits the full value of contributions he made to the system.[23] Still, taking all refinements into account, the system provides the retiree with benefits that are almost three times the value of his (or her) contributions.

[22] James R. Capra and others, "Social Security: An Analysis of Its Problems," *Federal Reserve Bank of New York Quarterly Review*, autumn 1982, pp. 1-2.
[23] The rationale for including the employer's contributions is that they can be considered a part of the employee's wages, an argument accepted by many but not all economists.

What makes the situation especially alarming is that current workers are having to subsidize current retirees at rather high rates *and* at the same time build up reserves for their own retirement. This is because the dependency ratio is expected to further deteriorate when the baby-boom generation retires. According to a frequently cited estimate by the Social Security Administration, the system needs an accumulated reserve of about $1.5 trillion to cover benefits for the baby-boom generation.

Whether the burden proves bearable or not will depend on a number of long-range factors that cannot be predicted with any great certainty: the evolution of political attitudes, economic growth rates and demographic trends, among others. Demographic trends, in particular, are remarkably volatile, and many key developments in recent decades — the baby boom, for example — were not predicted by professional demographers. If fertility rates rise more sharply than expected in the next two decades, then the burden of supporting the baby-boom generation in retirement could be smaller than currently anticipated. Of course fertility rates could also turn out to be even lower than expected, and in that case the problems facing the system after the year 2010 will be even more fundamental than the pessimists now predict.

In any event, as one expert pointed out, as long as Social Security is "financed by intergenerational transfers instead of by the contributions of the recipients themselves, the system will be vulnerable to demographic shifts that legislation cannot fully anticipate." [24] One wild card is the role illegal immigrants will play in the coming decades. Since immigrants tend to be younger than the population as a whole, many of them could still be in the work force when the baby-boom generation retires. Moreover, many illegal immigrants may never claim the benefits to which they are entitled, either because they are afraid to disclose their identities to authorities or because they have left the country.

Reconciling Short- and Long-term Answers

AFL-CIO President Lane Kirkland has warned against characterizing the Social Security crunch as an intergenerational dispute. Young people benefit from survivor and disability payments, he pointed out, and they live more happily in the knowledge that their parents will be provided for. Wilbur J. Cohen, a founding father of Social Security and a former secretary of health, education and welfare, has said — in much the same

---

[24] Peter A. Morrison, "Demographic Certainties and Uncertainties in the Future of Social Security," The Rand Corporation, July 1981, p. v.

Social Security Tax Schedule

Years	Maximum taxable earnings	Combined payroll tax rate[a]	Maximum tax*
1937-49	$ 3,000	1.0 %	$ 30.00
1950	3,000	1.5	45.00
1951-53	3,600	1.5	54.00
1954	3,600	2.0	72.00
1955-56	4,200	2.9	84.00
1957-58	4,200	2.25	94.50
1959	4,800	2.5	120.00
1960-61	4,800	3.0	144.00
1962	4,800	3.125	150.00
1963-65	4,800	3.625	174.00
1966	6,600	4.2	277.20
1967	6,600	4.4	290.40
1968	7,800	4.4	343.20
1969	7,800	4.8	374.40
1970	7,800	4.8	374.40
1971	7,800	5.2	405.60
1972	9,000	5.2	468.00
1973	10,800	5.85	631.80
1974	13,200	5.85	772.20
1975	14,100	5.85	824.85
1976	15,300	5.85	895.05
1977	16,500	5.85	965.25
1978	17,700	6.05	1,070.85
1979	22,900	6.13	1,403.77
1980	25,900	6.13	1,587.67
1981	29,700	6.65	1,975.05
1982	31,800	6.70	2,130.60
1983	33,900[b]	6.70	2,271.30[c]
1984	36,000[b]	6.70	2,412.00[c]
1985	38,100[b]	7.05	2,686.05[c]
1986	40,200[b]	7.15	2,874.30[c]
1987	42,600[b]	7.15	3,045.90[c]

a. Employee and employer, each. Combined tax rate includes retirement, survivors, disability and hospital insurance programs.

b. Estimates based on an automatic adjustment mechanism that increases the wage base as incomes increase.

c. Dependent on maximum taxable earnings (see note b).

SOURCE: Social Security Administration

vein — that short- and long-term problems should not be lumped together. "It doesn't seem to me that we have to worry so much about the crunch of 2015 right this year or this month," he said. "We've got to solve the problem of 1984 first." [25]

---

[25] Quoted in *National Journal*, Nov. 20, 1982, p. 1995.

Most Social Security experts would agree that it is not necessary to get obsessed, as yet, with problems that will not be cropping up for another 25 years. But at the same time, it obviously is important to avoid near-term solutions that will aggravate long-term problems. Susan Lee, an editorial writer for *The Wall Street Journal,* pointed out in a recent article that incorporation of government workers into Social Security would yield added revenues in the next few years but add to the system's unfunded liabilities eventually. Citing estimates by the Congressional Budget Office, Lee said that the Civil Service Retirement System's unfunded liabilities "will rocket" in four years "almost 70 percent to $840 billion." [26]

Linking inflation adjustments to wages rather than the cost-of-living index, another popular idea, could also backfire. In recent years, wage hikes have been running behind price increases, a normal pattern in recessionary times when unions are trying to protect jobs. But in times of economic expansion, when employers are eager to draw workers into the labor force, wages often run ahead of prices. If the economic picture were to improve in the coming years, linkage of Social Security benefits to wages rather than prices could add to the system's costs. [27]

Acceleration of Social Security tax increases scheduled for the late 1980s or additional tax hikes would ease current financial problems but could also cause a political backlash — not just among Republican opponents of high taxation but among working-class Democratic voters as well. In contrast to the federal income tax, which is a graduated or progressive tax that rises with income levels, the Social Security tax is regressive. As a member of *The Washington Post's* editorial staff pointed out in a recent column, "it's a flat tax on earnings up to $32,400 a year, with no exemption and no deductions." [28]

In light of such factors, it may be best to design Social Security reforms for the short- and long-term that allow for more or less automatic adjustment to unexpected changes. This was the conclusion reached by Sylvester J. Schieber, research director of the Employee Benefit Research Institute, in a study released Nov. 8. "The uncertainty in the extent of changes in the economy, productivity, birthrates, life expectancy, and a host of other factors suggests that Congress should adopt a Social Security policy that allows for some margin of error," he wrote. [29]

---

[26] Writing in *The Wall Street Journal,* Dec. 2, 1982.
[27] This is what happened in West Germany during the 1970s, when inflation was low and real wage increases big. See Bethell, *op. cit.,* p. 51.
[28] J. W. Anderson, writing in *The Washington Post,* Sept. 14, 1982.
[29] Sylvester J. Schieber, "Social Security: Perspectives on Preserving the System," executive summary, Employee Benefit Research Institute (1982), p. 18.

Future Political Outlook

CONGRESS could act on Social Security during the current lame-duck session, but it is much more likely that members will wait until early next year to tackle the issue. Sen. William L. Armstrong, R-Colo., a member of the Greenspan commission and chairman of the Senate Social Security Subcommittee, said in an interview Nov. 16 that "if we could put together a package sometime in the next four or five weeks . . . , it would be on the docket for early next year and hopefully [could be passed] very early before the next campaign cycle starts and it again gets to be a problem." [30] Rep. Dan Rostenkowski, D-Ill., chairman of the House Ways and Means Committee, which has jurisdiction over the issue, has scheduled Social Security hearings for Feb. 1. He hopes to bring legislation to the floor in the spring.

In a letter to congressional colleagues in mid-November, Rostenkowski called for legislation that would balance the interests of current Social Security beneficiaries against those of taxpayers. Rostenkowski warned against sharp tax increases or reliance on general revenues, but he also said Congress "must be willing to at least discuss new sources of revenue . . . including excise taxes and taxing cash benefits." Among political analysts in Washington, it is believed that Rostenkowski stands a good chance of hammering out a bipartisan bill, provided House Speaker O'Neill and President Reagan become more actively involved in forging a compromise, and provided he retains the backing of Rep. Claude Pepper, D-Fla.

Pepper, the oldest member of Congress and one of the most popular, has given up his chairmanship of the House Committee on Aging to take over the Rules Committee, which puts him in a strategic position to influence Social Security legislation. In a column distributed by Newspaper Enterprise Association on Nov. 10, Pepper cited survey data indicating that it will not be easy to sell new members of Congress on remedies to the Social Security problem. Reduction of inflation adjustments was opposed by 89 percent of the newly elected members of Congress, according to a *New York Times*/CBS survey. Increased Social Security taxes were opposed by 78 percent, and 67 percent were against increasing the age at which benefits can be drawn.

Deliberations of the Greenspan Commission

Immediately after the Nov. 2 elections, Sen. Robert Dole, R-Kan., said "the Democratic leadership now has an obligation to

---

[30] Interview on ABC's "Good Morning America," Nov. 16, 1982.

Commission Members
Alan Greenspan, Chairman

Rep. Bill Archer, R-Texas
Sen. William L. Armstrong, R-Colo.
Robert M. Ball
Robert A. Beck
Rep. Barber B. Conable Jr., R-N.Y.
Sen. Robert Dole, R-Kan.
Mary Falvey Fuller
Sen. John Heinz, R-Pa.
Ex-Rep. Martha Keys, D-Kan.
Lane Kirkland
Sen. Daniel Patrick Moynihan, D-N.Y.
Rep. Claude Pepper, D-Fla.
Alexander B. Trowbridge
Ex-Rep. Joe Waggonner, D-La.

come forward with concrete proposals" on Social Security because of its enlarged majority in the House. Days after Dole
issued that challenge, the Greenspan commission held one of its
final meetings and considered a plan drafted by key Democratic
members. The compromise package was reported to include the
following provisions: Acceleration of all or some of the payroll
tax increases scheduled for 1985, 1986 and 1990; extension of
the system to embrace all federal employees with less than five
years of service and employees of non-profit organizations;
deferral of the 1983 cost-of-living increases from July to October; an additional tax increase after the year 2020, if needed;
and, that same year, a reduction of benefits relative to wages, if
necessary.

The Democratic proposals were largely the work of Robert
Ball, a former Social Security commissioner and an O'Neill-
appointee to the Greenspan commission. In addition to the
measures contained in the Democratic plan, Ball also has

spoken in favor of raising the Social Security tax on self-employed people. Ball would raise the tax on self-employed people 100 percent but allow them to deduct half for federal income tax purposes. Self-employed people currently pay half the combined amount employees and employers contribute.

As of Dec. 15, the commission's Republicans had not responded with a formal proposal of their own, but one Republican member, Robert A. Beck, chairman of Prudential Insurance Co., did draft a list of ideas that Republicans generally support.[31] Beck advocated linkage of cost-of-living adjustments to the wage index, minus 1.5 percentage points each year. Greenspan and the commission's staff director, Robert J. Myers, have endorsed the same idea. Beck also would like to shift the retirement age at which people become eligible to receive full benefits from 65 to 68, starting in 1990.

House Speaker O'Neill and President Reagan have kept low profiles so far and have not publicly commented on the Greenspan commission's deliberations. But among members of the commission, especially the Republican appointees, there is increasingly strong sentiment that the top political leadership has to enter the fray if a timely compromise is to be reached. "Negotiations between the president and congressional leadership are urgently needed if a bipartisan agreement is ever to be reached," Sen. John Heinz, R-Pa., wrote in a column published in *The Washington Post* Dec. 10. "Without such an agreement in advance, we risk a congressional deadlock on Social Security for the duration of the new Congress."

---

[31] For a detailed account of Beck's views, see "Social Security: Horn of Plenty or Can of Worms?" *Journal of American Insurance,* summer 1982.

Selected Bibliography

Books

Aaron, Henry J., *Economic Effects of Social Security,* Brookings, 1982.
Crystal, Stephen, *America's Old-Age Crisis: Public Policy and the Two Worlds of Aging,* Basic Books, 1982.
Robertson, A. Haeworth, *The Coming Revolution in Social Security,* Security Press, 1981.
Russell, Louise B., *The Baby Boom Generation and the Economy,* Brookings, 1982.
Social Security Administration, *Social Security Handbook,* seventh edition, 1982.

Articles

Bethell, Tom, "Social Security: Permit for Idleness," *The Journal of The Institute for Socioeconomic Studies,* autumn, 1981.
Capozzi, Robèrt, "Social Security: Why It's Going Bankrupt," *Inquiry,* October 1982.
Capra, James R. and others, "Social Security: An Analysis of its Problems," *Federal Reserve Bank of New York Quarterly Review,* autumn 1982.
Ehrbar, A. F., "Social Security: Heading for the Wrong Solution," *Fortune,* Dec. 13, 1982.
Fessler, Pam, "Social Security Returns From Political Limbo," *Congressional Quarterly Weekly Report,* Oct. 9, 1982.
Much, Marilyn, "Social Security: Who Pays for the Cure?" *Industry Week,* Nov. 15, 1982.
Peterson, Peter G., "Social Security: The Coming Crisis," *The New York Review of Books,* Dec. 2, 1982.
Social Security Bulletin, selected issues.
"Social Security: Horn of Plenty or Can of Worms?" *Journal of American Insurance,* summer 1982.

Reports and Studies

Congressional Budget Office, "Financing Social Security," Washington, November 1982.
Editorial Research Reports: "Social Security Reassessment," 1979 Vol. I, p. 461; "Social Security Financing," 1972 Vol. II, p. 707; "Plight of the Aged," 1971 Vol. II, p. 863.
Ferrara, Peter J., "Social Security Reform: The Family Plan," The Heritage Foundation, Washington, 1982.
Morrison, Peter A., "Demographic Certainties and Uncertainties in the Future of Social Security," The Rand Corporation, Santa Monica, Calif., July 1981.
National Taxpayers Legal Fund, "The Social Security Crisis," Washington, 1982.
Senate Special Committee on Aging, "Social Security in Europe: The Impact of an Aging Population," Washington, December 1981.
Schieber, Sylvester J., "Social Security: Perspectives on Preserving the System," Employee Benefit Research Institute, Washington, 1982.

FARM POLICY'S NEW COURSE

by

Roger Thompson

**Mar. 25
1983**

FARM POLICY'S NEW COURSE

THREE YEARS AGO, President Carter's secretary of agriculture, Bob Bergland, announced the federal government saw no need to pay farmers to take a single acre of crop land out of production. What could not be sold at home could be shipped abroad to satisfy a seemingly insatiable world market that already was claiming one-third of this country's grain production.

In the topsy-turvy arena of global food needs and U.S. farm policy, such optimism now seems like ancient history. As farmers prepare for spring planting this year, the message from Washington is dramatically different. Bergland's successor, John R. Block, is offering farmers new and old incentives, including paying them with surplus crops, to leave up to 50 percent of their wheat, feed grain, rice and cotton lands idle. Bumper crops in 1981 and 1982, falling demand, rising export competition and the dollar's strength abroad have left farmers and the government stocked with price-depressing surpluses.

Market prices for wheat, corn and other important grains have shrunk by one-third in the past two years. Cotton prices dropped 25 percent. Farm income has nose-dived along with prices, from a historic high of $32.7 billion in 1979 to an estimated $19 billion last year. That is less than the interest payments on outstanding farm debt of $215 billion — a figure that has nearly doubled since 1977 and quadrupled since 1972, according to the Department of Agriculture. Adjusted for inflation, farmers' income last year was the lowest since 1933.

Adding to the farmers' plight is a reversal in the steadily upward rise in land values. The price of prime farm land is tumbling across the Midwest. As land values fall, so does the equity farmers need in order to borrow money for machinery, seeds, fertilizer and chemicals. Hardest hit are the young farmers who borrowed heavily at high interest rates to get started during the 1970s farming boom. The Department of Agriculture estimates that about 5 percent of the nation's farmers — about 120,000 farms — are in serious financial trouble.[1]

A farmer who finds his line of credit at the local bank abruptly cut short may turn to the Farmers Home Administra

---

[1] The department estimates that at least 50 percent of the nation's farmers are doing well, 25 percent are getting by and 20 percent are hurting — leaving 5 percent on the edge of bankruptcy. In general, producers of meat animals are faring better than grain farmers.

tion, the federally supported lender of last resort for about 12 percent of all farm operations. Even with below-market interest rates, more than a quarter of the agency's 271,000 loans last year were overdue, up from just 12 percent in 1979. While the number of farmers going out of business is up, it is still far below the Depression levels of the 1930s.[2]

Federal Efforts to Reduce Grain Crops

Fewer farmers succumb to hard times today because price support and production control programs begun in the Depression era hold out a financial safety net. Government commodity loan programs guarantee farmers a minimum price for their crops while attempting to keep production in balance with demand *(see box, opposite)*. Production controls, however, have a poor track record. The latest notable failure was Block's appeal to farmers to reduce 1982 wheat plantings 15 percent and other crops by 10 percent to avert back-to-back bumper crops and their disastrous effect on farm prices. Less than one-third of the farmers cut production.

The remainder took their chances with the market, and lost. The 1982 crop produced a record harvest of 2.8 billion bushels of wheat, 8.4 billion bushels of corn, 2.3 billion bushels of soybeans, and 1.9 billion bushels of oats, barley and sorghum. Even before the first bushel was harvested, one-half of the abundant 1981 wheat crop and one-quarter of the corn crop remained in storage.

As market prices sank in response to the glut, government loan and price supports soared to a record net level of $11.9 billion in fiscal year 1982 — $7 billion in commodity loans, $2.6 billion for purchases primarily of dairy products, $1.5 billion largely for "deficiency" and disaster payments, and $700 million mostly for grain storage. The Agriculture Department projects that the farm programs will cost $18.2 billion this year, when the impact of last year's bumper crop is felt. Program outlays lag a year behind the harvest.

Many farmers trace their current difficulties to the Carter administration's embargo on grain sales to the Soviet Union, announced Jan. 4, 1980, in retaliation for the Soviet invasion of Afghanistan. By the time the embargo was lifted by President Reagan in April 1981, the U.S. share of Soviet grain imports had dropped from 70 percent to 27 percent. However, American

---

[2] For example, there were 76,000 farm foreclosures in 1935 alone. In contrast, only 3 percent of FmHA's borrowers — 7,997 farmers — went out of business last year: 844 from foreclosures and 1,245 through bankruptcies. The remainder liquidated their holdings to pay off debts, many apparently in the face of imminent failures. For background, see *The Wall Street Journal*, Oct. 18, 1982.

Farm Commodity Programs

The Department of Agriculture is directed by Congress to support farm income through loans, target prices, subsidies, grain reserves and production limits. Minimum prices are guaranteed for wheat, corn, barley, oats, rice, cotton and dairy products.

Loans obtained from the Commodity Credit Corporation (CCC) are the chief market price-support mechanism. A farmer agrees to put a specified amount of his commodity in a government-approved storage facility in exchange for a loan, generally set well below the market level. At the end of the loan period, the farmer may repay the loan with interest and retain the commodity, or forfeit the commodity as payment for the loan. CCC loans are available for wheat, corn, sorghum, barley, oats, rice, cotton, rye, soybeans, peanuts, sugar, honey and tobacco.

Target prices are set higher than loan rates and are intended as income supplements. Target price levels are calculated to reflect the national average cost of producing a crop. If the market price fails to reach the target price, farmers are entitled to collect a "deficiency payment." It represents the difference between the target price and the market price, or between the target price and the loan rate, whichever is smaller.

Subsidies are used to support dairy prices only. The government buys what dairy farmers cannot sell at a current rate of $13.10 for each one hundred pounds of milk, cheese and butter. There is no limit to the amount dairy farmers may sell to the government.

The *grain reserve* was introduced during the Carter administration as a way of storing food to offset crop failures in the United States or abroad. Farmers may have their grain stored for three years in exchange for a per bushel loan rate slightly higher than CCC commodity loans. In addition, the government pays the farmer an annual storage fee of 25.6 cents a bushel. If prices rise, farmers may take their grain out of reserve storage in less than three years by repaying the loan but with no loan penalty.

Production limits may be announced at the discretion of the secretary of agriculture. While compliance is voluntary, only those farmers who sign up are eligible for commodity loans or supports. In addition, the secretary of agriculture may offer farmers cash to take land out of production.

grain found other foreign markets.[3] Export sales continued upward in 1980 despite the embargo, peaking at $43.3 billion in 1981 and dipping last year to $36.6 billion *(see table, p. 75)*. Total exports this year are not expected to surpass $36 billion.

Most analysts contend that two years of worldwide recession

[3] The U.S. share of the Soviet market rebounded to 35 percent, representing 13.9 million metric tons, in fiscal year 1982, just shy of the record 15 million metric tons shipped in 1979. A metric ton is 2,200 pounds.

and a strengthened dollar, which makes U.S. grain more expensive abroad, account for the slip in farm exports. Others point to an additional factor — export subsidies offered by the European Common Market countries and a handful of others enabling their farmers to undercut American food prices in world markets.[4]

Threat of Farm Trade War With Europe

American agriculture decries Common Market food export subsidies — amounting to an estimated $6 billion last year — as unfair and is pressing Congress to retaliate with U.S. subsidies. A number of subsidy bills are before Congress, giving rise to speculation that a trade war could break out unless both sides arrive at a negotiated settlement.

Common Market representatives defended their export subsidy practices at a meeting in Geneva last November of the 88 nations subscribing to the General Agreement on Tariffs and Trade (GATT), an international trade organization that oversees tariffs, subsidies and other aspects of trade among its members, including the United States.[5] The Common Market contends its food export subsidies do not violate a GATT agreement — an agreement which permits such subsidies if they do not result in the takeover of traditional markets of other GATT nations. The United States claimed that Common Market wheat exporters violated that agreement. But a special GATT judicial panel announced in late February it could find no evidence to support the U.S. charge.

President Reagan preaches the gospel of free trade for all exports, but the administration has been giving out mixed signals on trade issues. Last October the administration began to underwrite farm export sales with a $500 million "blended credit" program. It offers foreign food buyers loans with interest rates two percentage points below market rates. The lower rates are achieved by combining interest-free loans by the Agriculture Department's Commodity Credit Corporation with federally guaranteed commercial loans. In January, Reagan announced the program would receive $1.25 billion more lending funds.

The same month the administration negotiated the sale of one million tons of subsidized flour to Egypt, long considered one of France's markets for farm goods. The government will give U.S. millers enough surplus wheat to reduce the net per ton price to the Egyptians by $100, bringing it below the prevailing

---

[4] The 10 full members of the Common Market are Belgium, Britain, Denmark, France, Greece, West Germany, Ireland, Italy, Luxembourg, and the Netherlands.

[5] For background on the GATT meeting, see "Global Recession and U.S. Trade," *E.R.R.*, 1983 Vol. I, p. 178. See also Thomas R. Graham, "Global Trade: War and Peace," *Foreign Policy*, spring 1983, pp. 129-130.

Agricultural Exports

	U.S. Farm Exports (in billions)	Percent of all U.S. Exports	Percent of World Farm Exports
1970*	$ 7.3	17	14.3
1975	21.9	21	18.1
1980	41.3	19	18.4
1981	43.3	18.9	19.5
1982	36.6	17.7	N.A.

* calendar years

Source: U.S. Agriculture Department, Trade and Economics Division

U.S. price of $255 a ton. The net cost to the government is expected to be about $130 million. The sale was viewed by an unidentified Common Market official as "a brutal takeover of one of our major markets." In response, Agriculture Secretary Block said the deal showed, "We mean business when we talk about competing for export markets." [6]

U.S. and Common Market trade negotiators set the end of March as the deadline to reach agreement, but prospects remain dim. Private talks in Brussels broke off late in February when the two sides agreed that the issue was so politically charged it should be handled at the Cabinet level.

The Common Market argues it is no more guilty of unfair farm export subsidies than the United States is. The main difference, said Ella Kruchoff, a spokeswoman for the European Community office in Washington, D.C., is "the U.S. government has a less transparent system of subsidies" than the Common Market. "Most congressmen are ignorant of the facts," she added. She pointed out that the Common Market is the American farmers' biggest export market. It bought $9 billion in agricultural products in 1981, primarily soybeans and feed grains, while the United States bought only $2 billion in European farm products that year.

With no negotiated settlement in sight, the Senate Agriculture Committee has approved an export subsidy bill requiring the secretary of agriculture to sell at least 150,000 metric tons of federally owned surplus dairy products abroad annually for the next three years at prices substantially below U.S. market prices. The bill, which has not come to the Senate floor for a vote, also authorizes an export payment-in-kind (PIK) program in which federally owned commodities would be given to buyers as bonuses, thereby lowering the overall purchase price. In

[6] Both quoted in *The New York Times*, Jan. 21, 1983.

75

addition, federal funds would be used to subsidize exports of eggs, raisins and canned fruit.[7]

New PIK Program for Temporary Relief

The domestic version of PIK is the government's primary assault on price-depressing surpluses. It is an about-face in the administration's farm policy. President Reagan came into office favoring less, not more, government regulation of farming. He sought unsuccessfully to eliminate from the 1981 farm bill the Agriculture Department's discretionary authority to control farm production.

Just two years later, Reagan stood before the American Farm Bureau Federation convention in Dallas on Jan. 11 and portrayed PIK, a novel production control program, as the farmer's road to salvation — though admittedly a temporary expedient. The program enables wheat, corn, sorghum, rice and upland cotton farmers to take up to 50 percent of their crop land out of production.

To participate in the program, farmers were required to sign up for a previously announced acreage diversion ("set-aside") program in which they agreed not to plant 20 percent of their land. They had to do that to become eligible for federal commodity loans, better known as price supports, and direct cash payments.[8] Under PIK, farmers may leave idle an additional 10 to 30 percent of their crop land. In return, wheat farmers will receive an amount of wheat equal to 95 percent of their average per acre production. This will come from surplus U.S. stocks or the farmer's own prior crops which were placed in government hands as collateral for loans he obtained. Farmers may store or sell the PIK crops.

Corn, sorghum, rice and cotton farmers will receive an amount equal to 80 percent of the per acre production of those crops. Wheat farmers are offered the higher incentive — 95 percent — because the winter crop in states south of the Dakotas already is in the ground. Agriculture officials figured it would take a greater crop guarantee to entice winter wheat farmers to sign up since most of their investment is already committed.

"This plan is aimed at bringing supply more in line with demand, and strengthening farm income in the future," Reagan

---

[7] Contrary to President Reagan's wishes, the bill contains a provision exempting export-PIK and blended-credit commodities from the federal cargo preference law. The law requires roughly half of the goods exported under federal programs to be carried on U.S.-flag ships. Farm interests dislike the requirement because U.S. shipping is more expensive, raising the cost of the food.

[8] For example, wheat farmers receive cash for 5 percent of the land they take out of production. Payment is based on average per acre yield, at $2.70 a bushel. Corn farmers receive cash on 10 percent of their diverted acreage, figured at a rate of $1.50 a bushel.

said in Dallas. "It makes our problem the solution." Block had estimated that PIK would take 23 million acres out of production but the actual amount, announced March 22, far exceeded expectations. Farmers pledged to put 69.1 million acres under PIK and 13.1 million acres under the acreage diversion program.[9] Together the 82.2 million acres to be left unplanted represents 36 percent of the farm land eligible for the two programs.

PIK's benefits to the government and farmers remain a matter of intense speculation. The Department of Agriculture projects savings of $3.7 billion in farm program outlays through fiscal year 1984. As for farm prices, the department predicts a slight rise this year under the program. Early indications of heavy farmer participation in PIK sent prices soaring on the Chicago futures market in mid-March. Reaction to the PIK program among farmers and farm organizations has been generally favorable.

While farmers stand to benefit from PIK, it poses frightening prospects to agriculture-related businesses. Farmers won't just cut back on planting. They are expected to reduce purchases of seed, fertilizer, farm equipment and storage bins. University of Missouri economist Abner Womack calculates the nationwide impact on farm supply manufacturers and dealers this year will add up to a loss of $4 billion. Small operators who lack the resources to weather a sharp drop in business, even for a year, will be hard hit.[10]

Food Giveaways for U.S., World Hunger

The administration argues that only drastic measures, such as PIK and increased exports, can reduce the American stockpile of surplus commodities. Domestic giveaway programs also can help, but by law they are limited to dairy products: cheese, butter and dried milk. These are "table ready" while grains must be milled before use. The cost of milling is what keeps the government from adding grain to its domestic giveaway programs, Secretary Block told the congressional Joint Economic Committee on Jan. 31.

Even without expensive processing, the cheese and butter giveaway program that was begun last year to aid the poor cost

---

[9] Some 22.5 million of the 69.1 million acres represent entire farms. This was done on the basis of bids submitted by farmers for the amount of crops they would receive in return.

[10] Farm equipment manufacturers are resigned to another year of sluggish sales that already have threatened the life of two ailing giants, International Harvester Co. and Massey-Ferguson Ltd. Harvester posted a $1.6 billion loss for fiscal year 1982; Massey-Ferguson refinanced its debt in March to avoid the immediate danger of bankruptcy. John Deere & Co., the largest producer of farm equipment, reported a loss of $28.5 million for the quarter ending Jan. 31, its first quarterly loss since 1968.

the government $287 million through Dec. 31. The Agriculture
Department's Food and Nutrition Service, which provides funds
and food for school breakfast and lunch programs and non-
profit groups, donated 166 million pounds of cheese and 18.9
million pounds of butter to the poor. Eleven million pounds of
dried milk were distributed in an experimental program. This
year, the nutrition service has been authorized to give away 500
million pounds of cheese and 125 million pounds of butter at a
cost projected to reach $975 million. These donations, however,
will hardly dent the growing stockpile of surplus dairy products.
By Sept. 30, the government expects to own 1.1 billion pounds
of cheese and 675 million pounds of butter.

The Senate Agriculture Committee, in response to pleas from
public interest and humanitarian groups known as the "hunger
lobby," on March 3 approved a bill to lift restrictions on domestic surplus commodity giveaways and authorize $200 million
through September 1984 for the cost of processing and
distributing surplus food.

Cost also limits food donations to feed the poor overseas,
Block told the Joint Economic Committee. The administration
spent $480 million on international food charity in 1982 and
expects to spend $650 million this year and next. CARE (Co-
operative for American Relief Everywhere) and other international aid agencies are lobbying Congress to make surplus
stocks available. Currently, CARE receives government grants
to purchase the commodities it distributes overseas. In addition,
the agency hopes to obtain surplus food to give away, sell or
barter. Richard Loudis, a CARE spokesman, is not impressed
with official excuses for limiting the distribution of food surpluses: "It is the principal irony of our times that when America
is drowning in overproduction, millions of people are
starving." [11]

Government's Role in Agriculture

THE INDEPENDENT family farm has long held a special
place in American political thought. Thomas Jefferson expressed it this way in *Notes on the State of Virginia:* "Those
who labor in the earth are the chosen people of God, if ever he
had a chosen people, whose breasts he has made his peculiar
deposit for substantial and genuine virtue." Similar thoughts
continued to find expression throughout the following 200 years.

---

[11] Quoted in *The Wall Street Journal*, Feb. 18, 1983.

The post-Revolutionary ordinances of 1785 and 1787 provided for the sale of public land for farming, opening up the upper Midwest — the Northwest Territory — to settlement.

President Lincoln rededicated the nation to a belief in the family farm when he signed the Homestead Act of 1862, starting the process that gradually transferred 147 million acres of frontier land to 1.6 million families. Each settler was allowed 160 acres of public land by paying a small filing fee and living on and working the land for at least five years. Once the government opened the West to the farm family, it induced railroads to follow by giving them vast tracts of land. It also encouraged, under the Morrill Act of 1862, the states to establish land-grant colleges to teach agriculture and mechanical arts.[12] They became the centers of agricultural research.

As late as 1910, one third of the people lived on small family farms. By 1980, 2.4 million farms remained, averaging 430 acres — nearly triple the size of 50 years earlier. Still, 95 percent of the farms today can be called family farms.

Farms perished but farm production rose. Improvements in machinery, fertilizers, pesticides and plant varieties increased per acre yields and reduced labor needs. Seventy years ago, it took 106 hours of labor and seven acres to produce 100 bushels of wheat. Today it takes only nine hours of labor and three acres. Similar advancements have been made with other crops. Production efficiency gradually has narrowed the gap between farm and non-farm income. In the 1930s, farmers earned one-third to one-half the amount that non-farm workers did. In the 1960s, they were earning three-quarters as much. By 1979, the best year ever for American farmers, their income was on a par with urban workers. Since then, farmers have lost ground.

Surviving Tradition of Depression-Era Aid

From the Agriculture Department's inception in 1862 until 1933, it functioned primarily as a booster of research and education through the land grant colleges. The government let farmers and the free market system make production and pricing

---

[12] See "Access to Federal Lands," *E.R.R.*, 1981 Vol. II, pp. 693-712, and "Protection of the Countryside," *E.R.R.*, 1971 Vol. II, pp. 550-552.
[13] Figures cited by Don Paarlberg in *Farm and Food Policy: Issues of the 1980s*, p. 20. Paarlberg is professor emeritus of agricultural economics at Purdue University, Lafayette, Ind., and has served in numerous sub-Cabinet positions in the Agriculture Department.

decisions. That changed in the Depression. Between 1929 and 1932 farm prices dropped 56 percent; net agricultural income fell from $6.3 billion to $1.9 billion. Farmers were desperate for help, and the New Deal came forth with a program to prop up prices and control production. Franklin D. Roosevelt, echoing Jefferson, said: "The American farmer living on his own land remains our ideal of self-reliance and spiritual balance." [14]

The new farm program, detailed in the Agricultural Adjustment Act signed into law May 12, 1933, aimed to control the supply of six basic crops: wheat, corn, cotton, rice, peanuts and tobacco. The concept of "parity" was introduced in farm policy as a means of setting the first price support levels, and it has been at the center of farm policy debate ever since. It is the relationship between the price of farm commodities and the cost of goods that the farmer buys. The base years initially used were 1910-14, a period of farm prosperity. One farmer explained the concept this way. If a bushel of wheat in 1910 sold for enough to buy a pair of overalls, then wheat prices should have risen enough to make the same purchase today. That is what farmers call 100 percent of parity.

Parts of the 1933 farm bill were struck down by the Supreme Court. But another law, in 1938, expanded the farm program, extending loans to farmers to store surpluses and release them during lean years. By the time the United States entered World War II in 1941, the government had made $5.3 billion in direct payments under the new program.

New Deal farm programs remained virtually intact long after the Depression ended. But they failed to keep surpluses in check. In 1953, for example, the government acquired 486 million bushels of wheat, 41 percent of the year's bumper crop. A year later Congress launched a new program to help absorb food surpluses. It passed Public Law 480 authorizing donations or low-interest loan sales to needy countries. By 1980, the government had put more than $30 billion into the program, $11.4 billion in donations and $19 billion in loans for food purchases.

But exporting food to the needy did not eliminate surpluses. The growing stores of commodities and food needs of poor Americans spotlighted by the Kennedy administration brought forth an experimental food stamp program for low-income families in 1961. People could use the stamps in stores to purchase certain kinds of food. The food stamp program became permanent in 1964 and remained relatively non-controversial until four years later with the publication of *Hunger, USA*.[15] The

---

[14] Quoted by Sandra S. Batie and Robert G. Healy in *The Future of American Agriculture as a Strategic Resource* (1980), p. 118.
[15] The report was compiled by an advocacy group called the Citizens' Board of Inquiry into Hunger and Malnutrition.

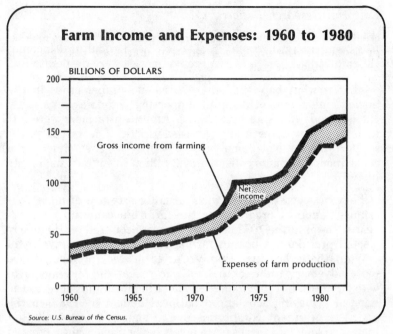

Farm Income and Expenses: 1960 to 1980

BILLIONS OF DOLLARS

Gross income from farming

Net income

Expenses of farm production

Source: U.S. Bureau of the Census.

report stated that one-half of all households in the United States had poor diets and only one-fifth of those, about five million, were reached by food programs.

The political fallout from the report triggered rapid growth in food assistance programs, primarily food stamps. Those lobbying on behalf of the poor received a sympathetic hearing, and considerable publicity, as they appeared before the Senate Select Committee on Nutrition and Human Needs, under the chairmanship of George McGovern of South Dakota. Food stamp assistance rose from $250 million in 1969 to $11 billion last year. The program, however, has had negligible impact on depleting government-stored surpluses.

Cutting Surpluses Through Foreign Sales

It wasn't charity at home or abroad that finally rescued farmers from chronic surpluses a decade ago. It was the Soviet Union, which in 1972 negotiated the first of several massive grain purchases with the United States and set farm prices soaring.[16] The deal ushered in a new era for American farmers.

Against this backdrop, Congress in 1973 passed an omnibus four-year farm bill that put an end to direct payments for taking acreage out of production and to guaranteed price supports. The mood at the time was that farmers needed less government assistance. However, the "target price" system was

---

[16] See "World Grain Trade," *E.R.R.*, 1973 Vol. II, pp. 709-732.

created as a concession to those who argued that farmers needed protection in the unlikely event that market prices again fell below production costs.

That is what happened in 1976 when bumper crops in the Soviet Union and other grain-importing countries drastically cut demands for American grains. American farmers were left with huge surpluses and depressed prices. The target price-support mechanism came into play for the first time. As a consequence, farmers collected $1.2 billion in support payments in 1977.[17]

They besieged Congress with pleas for a return of more government support programs as the farm bill came up for four-year renewal in the 1977 session. Farmers counted on the newly elected president, a peanut farmer from Georgia, to give them a sympathetic hearing. Jimmy Carter proved, however, to be more adversary than compatriot. He repeatedly threatened to veto any farm bill that exceeded spending levels he set — in the hope of achieving a balanced national budget by 1981. In the end, the president compromised and signed a farm bill that increased loan and target price levels beyond his wishes, created a farmer-held grain reserve and extended the secretary of agriculture's authority to mandate an acreage set-aside programs.

Farmers complained that the bill did not do enough, and the following winter the new, militant American Agriculture Movement staged public demonstrations, including a "tractorcade" into Washington, blocking city traffic with tractor parades. Carter's trouble with the farmers deepened when he reneged on a campaign promise never to use food as a diplomatic weapon and clamped an embargo on most grain shipments to the Soviet Union. Farm prices tumbled and stayed low for months.

Administration's Inability to Curb Supports

Farmers were dismayed and angry, and carried their grudge against the president to the ballot box in November 1980. Ronald Reagan, a man who told a farm audience he wasn't familiar with parity, carried the farm vote. Fulfilling his own campaign promise, he lifted the embargo scarcely more than three months after taking office, on April 24, 1981. By that time it was clear the Soviet Union had been able to satisfy most of its grain needs through other suppliers.

Some analysts contend that the embargo had a beneficial effect. U.S. exports now are more widely dispersed and there-

[17] For background, see "Farm Policy and Food Needs," *E.R.R.*, 1977 Vol. II, pp. 805-824. Also see Congressional Quarterly's *Congress and the Nation*, Vols. III, IV, V, and *CQ Almanac 1981*.

fore less susceptible to the on-again, off-again demands of the Soviet market.[18] Since the embargo was lifted, the Soviets purchased about 14 million metric tons in fiscal year 1981-82 and six million metric tons so far this year. At the time, Carter embargoed 17 million tons of wheat and feed grains that represented a single year's exports.

Whatever good will Reagan earned in the Farm Belt by ending the embargo, it was quickly expended in the administration's new farm bill. The farm programs were up for another four-year extension, beginning in September 1981. Secretary Block shocked the farm community with his major proposals: an end to production controls and the target prices, broad discretionary power to set commodity loan rates rather than fixing them in law, and drastic cuts in dairy subsidies. In short, the administration wanted Congress to begin weaning farmers of government income supports and production controls. To underscore its commitment to limit farm spend-

John R. Block

ing, the administration persuaded Congress to place a ceiling on spending.

The spending level for the four-year farm bill, roughly $11 billion, had the desired effect of causing a breakdown of the usually harmonious relationships among farm commodity groups. Instead of joining forces for mutual benefit, the traditional method of shaping farm legislation, lobbyists for grain, dairy, tobacco, sugar, peanut and other commodities were openly fighting one another for their share of diminished agriculture expenditures.

The final bill cleared Congress Dec. 16, 1981, by a two-vote margin in the House, reflecting the lingering resentment stirred by months of debate. The bill preserved and authorized gradual increases in loan and target price rates, although at lower levels than farmers wanted. It froze the dairy price support of $13.10 for every hundred pounds of unsold products rather than allowing it to rise as previously authorized to $14 on April 1, 1981. Ironically, an administration that tried to curb farm support spending settled for a farm bill that has allowed a stream of payments to expand into a torrent.

---

[18] This view is put forward by Robert L. Paarlberg in "Food as an Instrument of Foreign Policy," pp. 25-39 in *Food Policy and Farm Programs* (1982), Don F. Hadwiger and Ross B. Talbot, eds.

With each new farm bill debate, members of Congress have a renewed opportunity to frame their actions in terms of preservation of the family farm. Yet many farm policy analysts argue that federal farm programs have had the opposite effect.

When Bob Bergland was secretary of agriculture (1977-80), he launched a series of nationwide hearings on survival of the family farm — in the aftermath of the American Agriculture Movement's "tractorcade" to Washington. The results of those hearings and Agriculture Department studies were published in 1980 in a report entitled "A Time to Choose: Summary Report on the Structure of Agriculture." It suggested that federal farm policies had hastened the demise of small farms while encouraging larger operations.

This does not mean that farm ownership is concentrated in the hands of giant corporations. In fact, the study found that only 12 percent of all U.S. crop land was farmed by corporations. And nearly nine of every 10 of those corporations were family held. Clearly, families still are the primary force behind American agriculture, but there are fewer of them than ever, working larger farms than ever.

Farm economists point out that federally supported research has generated the new technology and plant hybrids that push farmers inexorably toward larger and larger operations. And commodity programs offer rewards by the bushel, thereby channeling more to those who are the largest. In 1980, roughly one-quarter of the farms, those with sales of over $40,000 a year, took in two-thirds of all government farm program payments.

Beyond Today's Farm Problems

AFTER PIK, then what? Secretary Block acknowledges it is a temporary program that applies only to 1983 crops unless he extends it for a second year. The American Farm Bureau Federation contends that present farm programs are a failure and need revision. Washington office spokesman Mike Durando said in an interview, "We see continued incentives to overproduce." The current grain glut and depressed prices have underscored for farmers the need to declare their independence from ineffective government programs, said Orlen Grunewald, an agricultural marketing economist at Kansas State University. "The agriculture policies we have today were put in place in the 1930s. Most farmers have come to realize that it needs to be changed," Grunewald said in an interview.

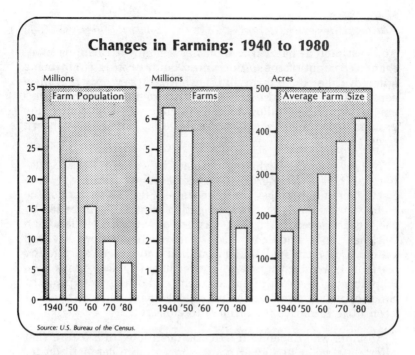

Changes in Farming: 1940 to 1980

Farm Population (Millions)
- 1940: ~30
- '50: ~23
- '60: ~16
- '70: ~10
- '80: ~6

Farms (Millions)
- 1940: ~6.3
- '50: ~5.6
- '60: ~4
- '70: ~3
- '80: ~2.5

Average Farm Size (Acres)
- 1940: ~150
- '50: ~210
- '60: ~300
- '70: ~375
- '80: ~430

Source: U.S. Bureau of the Census.

Discontent with federal farm programs is so widespread in the Midwest that Kansas Gov. John Carlin has started a search for ideas to draft a new farm policy. Carlin, a Democrat, appointed a blue-ribbon panel last September to study farm needs and come up with recommendations in time for presentation to the Midwest Governors' Conference next fall.

Western Soil Erosion and Water Scarcity

The commodity program is not the only farm problem that awaits solution. Soil erosion and water scarcity have worsened during a decade of all-out farm production. Some farm economists worry that the nation is depleting its soil and water resources to achieve short-term export gains. Since President Roosevelt signed the Soil Conservation Act in 1935, the federal government has channeled $25 billion into conservation programs through the Soil Conservation Service. Erosion was thought to be under control until millions of acres of marginal land were returned to production in the 1970s. Cultivated land rose from a post-World War II low of 333 million acres in 1969 to 391 million acres in 1981. A hidden price paid for this expansion was a sharp increase in topsoil erosion.

A General Accounting Office survey in 1977, "To Protect Tomorrow's Food Supply, Soil Conservation Needs Priority Attention," reported that random visits to 283 farms in eight states revealed 84 percent were suffering from unacceptably high rates of soil erosion. An Agriculture Department study in 1980, "Appraisal 1980: Soil and Water Resources Conservation

Act," estimated that soil erosion was a major problem on more than 20 percent of the nation's crop land. Erosion is not being ignored. The 1981 farm bill authorized a number of new conservation measures. And the PIK program requires farmers to plant their fallow crop land in an erosion-controlling ground cover such as clover or alfalfa. But great concern remains.

Water depletion is the big problem in western Texas, Oklahoma, Kansas, Nebraska, the Dakotas and westward to the Pacific mountain ranges. In those states, 80 to 90 percent of the water is used for agriculture. Irrigation, much of it provided by the federal government since passage of the 1902 Reclamation Act, has made arid land bloom with a steady flow of cheap water. It is estimated that 50 million acres receive irrigation water in 17 Western states. The government typically pays 80 to 90 percent of the cost of dams, canals and other water projects. Since operating subsidies help keep water prices low, there has been little incentive for farmers to conserve.[19]

Farmers who depend on irrigation can look to a future that offers less water at higher costs, and to more competition for available supplies. Based on present levels of use, almost every region west of the Mississippi has insufficient water from all sources for future agricultural production, according to the "Second National Water Assessment" published in 1978 by the U.S. Water Resources Council. The biggest issue is competition from municipal and industrial users. While agriculture's demand for water is projected to rise only 6 percent by the year 2000, other uses are expected to increase by 81 percent.[20]

World Challenge of Feeding Billions More

The depletion of natural resources affects not just the American farmer. Worldwide degradation of land, forests, lakes, rivers and oceans caused by rapid population growth portend a decline in living standards for millions of people, argues Lester R. Brown, president of Worldwatch Institute, an environmental-minded policy research organization in Washington, D.C. Brown makes what might be called the ultimate Malthusian argument: the Earth's biological systems eventually will break down under constant abuse by too many people.[21]

The wild card that Brown has not taken into consideration is

---

[19] See "Western Water: Coming Crisis," *E.R.R.*, 1977 Vol. I, pp. 21-40.
[20] Figures cited by Tom Fulton and Peter Braestrup in "The New Issues: Land, Water, Energy," *The Wilson Quarterly*, summer 1981, p. 127.
[21] Brown sets forth this argument in his book *Building a Sustainable Society* (1981). In 1798 Thomas Malthus advanced his famous thesis that the world population was increasing faster than the means of subsistence. Only war, famine, disease or some form of "moral restraint" could bring the population into equilibrium with the food supply, and then only at a bare subsistence level.

the possibility of a second "Green Revolution" by creation of new kinds of plants through genetic engineering. The first Green Revolution blossomed in the 1960s, resulting from years of concentrated effort in traditional plant breeding. New strains of corn, wheat and rice developed through cross-pollination produced stunning increases in yields when combined with chemical fertilizers. Newly developed pesticides and herbicides helped protect the hybrid crops from pests and weeds.[22]

The Green Revolution spread quickly where farmers could afford the agricultural chemicals and the soil was favorable. Many developing countries, however, had a difficult time affording the petroleum-based chemicals as costs soared along with world oil prices. Without fertilizer, the new grain varieties produced yields only slightly above the traditional varieties.[23]

Some argue that the first Green Revolution merely delayed a collision between population and food supply. Despite its successes, food production in developing countries increased little in the past decade and actually declined in Africa. Genetic engineering holds the potential of picking up where traditional plant breeding left off. Scientists hope to create custom-made plants that thrive in poor soil without fertilizer. Although research is proceeding at a fast pace, scientists predict it will be 10 to 20 years before genetic tinkering lives up to its advance billing.[24]

Meanwhile, as many as 100 million people are considered "desperately hungry," according to Harvard researcher Nick Eberstadt.[25] The world produces enough to feed everyone, but it is not evenly distributed — primarily because of economic and political considerations. Aside from distribution, Eberstadt writes, poor countries seem intent on taking the great leap into the industrial age while neglecting agriculture. As a result, India's cheap labor enables it to produce a ton of steel one-third cheaper than at a Bethlehem Steel, while the cost of growing a ton of wheat is 40 percent more in India than in Kansas. Eberstadt's thoughts provide yet another reminder that American farm policy, like the American economy generally, affects and is affected by the global market place.

[22] See "Green Revolution," *E.R.R.*, 1970 Vol. I., pp. 219-238.
[23] For a discussion of the limits of the new plant varieties, see Nyle C. Brady, "Chemistry and World Food Supplies," in *Science*, Nov. 26, 1982, pp. 847-853.
[24] For background on genetic engineering, see "Advances in Agricultural Research," *E.R.R.*, 1981 Vol. I, pp. 369-388. Also see Peter Steinhart, "The Second Green Revolution," in *The New York Times Magazine*, Oct. 25, 1981.
[25] Nick Eberstadt, "America and World Hunger," in *The Wilson Quarterly*, summer 1981, pp. 138-149. Eberstadt was a Visiting Fellow at the Harvard University Center for Population Studies in 1981 and is a doctoral candidate in political economy at Harvard's Kennedy School of Government.

Selected Bibliography

Books

Batie, Sandra S. and Healy, Robert C., eds., *The Future of American Agriculture as a Strategic Resource,* The Conservation Foundation, 1980.

Brown, Lester R., *Building a Sustainable Society,* W. W. Norton & Co., 1981.

Hadwiger, Don F. and Browne, William P.,eds., *The New Politics of Food,* Lexington Books, 1978.

Hadwiger, Don F. and Talbot, Ross B., eds., *Food Policy and Farm Programs,* Capital City Press, 1982.

Paarlberg, Don, *Farm and Food Issues of the 1980s,* University of Nebraska Press, 1980.

Articles

"Agriculture in America," articles in *The Wilson Quarterly,* summer 1981.

Agricultural Outlook (published by U.S. Agriculture Department's Division of Economic Indicators and Statistics), selected issues.

Batie, Sandra S. and Healy, Robert C., "The Future of American Agriculture," *Scientific American,* February 1983.

Brady, C. Nyle, "Chemistry and World Food Supplies," *Science,* Nov. 26, 1982.

Cox, Meg, "Farm Crisis Falls Short of Depression Agony But There Are Parallels," *The Wall Street Journal,* Oct. 18, 1982.

Farm Bureau News (published by the American Farm Bureau Federation, Washington, D.C.), selected issues.

Farm Journal (Philadelphia, Pa.), selected issues.

"Population and Environment," a series in *People* (published by International Planned Parenthood Federation), Vol. 10, No. 1, 1983.

Robbins, William, "Some Farmers Thriving as Others Go Under," *The New York Times,* Feb. 19, 1983.

"Why the Recovery May Skip the Farm Belt," *Business Week,* March 21, 1983.

Reports and Studies

Eckholm, Erik and Brown, Lester R., "Spreading Deserts — The Hand of Man," Worldwatch Institute, (1776 Massachusetts Ave., N.W., Washington, D.C. 20036), August 1977.

Editorial Research Reports: "Farm Policy and Food Needs," 1977, Vol. II, p. 807.

MacNeil-Lehrer Report, PBS-TV, "Grain Paybacks," Jan. 11, 1983, transcript No. 1902 (Box 345, New York, N.Y. 10101).

U.S. Bureau of the Census, *Statistical Abstract of the United States 1982.*

U.S. Department of Agriculture, "A Time to Choose: Summary Report on the Structure of Agriculture," 1981.

—— "Final Regulatory Impact Analysis" for payment-in-kind program, Jan. 11, 1983.

RISING COST OF HEALTH CARE

by

**Mary H. Cooper
and Sandra Stencel**

Apr. 8
1983

RISING COST OF HEALTH CARE

F OR Americans hard pressed by double-digit unemployment and high interest rates, one of the few encouraging developments during the current recession has been a fall in the rate of inflation. In 1982, the Consumer Price Index (CPI) rose by a relatively low 3.9 percent, five points below the 1981 figure.[1] But one component of the index continued to climb at a faster rate than other consumer prices. The amount Americans spent on health care in 1982 rose 11 percent over the previous year to a record $321.4 billion; hospital costs alone rose 12.6 percent last year. And while consumer prices actually fell by 0.2 percent in February 1983, medical costs went up 0.8 percent. The portion of the nation's gross national product (GNP) spent on health care has risen from 6 percent in 1965 to 10 percent today.

The federal government's contribution to the nation's health care bill also continues to climb, as rising hospital and physicians' charges are reflected in the cost of Medicare, Medicaid and other public health programs. Combined outlays for Medicare, the federal health care program for the elderly, and Medicaid, the state-federal program for the poor and disabled, are projected to reach $75 billion in fiscal 1983, accounting for 9.5 percent of the federal budget.

President Reagan has described the rate of increase in health care costs as "excessive," undermining "people's ability to purchase needed health care." [2] To help bring health costs under control, the administration has proposed a series of reform measures reflecting the president's often stated goal of reducing government influence and restoring public services to the private sector. One of these measures — a plan to set up a new system for reimbursing hospitals for treating Medicare patients — was approved by Congress March 25 as part of the Social Security rescue bill (see p. 94).[3]

Among the other cost-containment proposals Reagan sent Congress was one to set up a voucher system expanding "oppor-

---

[1] Published monthly by the Department of Labor's Bureau of Labor Statistics, the CPI follows a "market basket" of goods and services and determines the rate of price variation for each over the previous month.
[2] Message on his proposed budget for fiscal 1984, delivered to Congress Jan. 31, 1983.
[3] For background on the Social Security system's financial problems, see "Social Security Options," E.R.R., 1982 Vol. II, pp. 929-948.

tunities for Medicare beneficiaries to use their benefits to enroll in private health plans as an alternative to traditional Medicare coverage." Reagan also asked Congress to begin taxing employer-sponsored health insurance benefits *(see p. 96)* and to require Medicare beneficiaries to pay more out of their own pockets for short-term hospital stays. This plan would be coupled with "catastrophic" coverage for long illnesses *(see p. 97)*. Reagan also proposed that Medicaid beneficiaries be required to pay nominal fees of $1 to $2 for each visit to a doctor or hospital. Under current law, states may impose such "cost-sharing" requirements, but are not required to do so.[4]

While the administration's health care reform package was presented as a cost-control initiative, the projected savings would be relatively small, at least in the short term. The Department of Health and Human Services estimated that the package would save $4.2 billion in fiscal 1984. But even if all the proposals are enacted, federal outlays for health would increase nearly 10 percent in fiscal 1984, to $90.6 billion, from the 1983 level of $82.4 billion, according to the budget.

The Factors Behind Health Care Inflation

The reasons for mounting health care costs are varied and complex. They include such things as the growing size and age of the elderly population, higher salaries for nurses and other hospital workers, and the increase in the number of malpractice suits, which many believe has caused doctors to overtreat their patients in an effort to protect themselves from possible legal action.

Consumer expectations were regarded as a primary cause of the problem in a recent survey of health experts conducted by Yankelovich, Skelly and White, Inc., for *Prevention* magazine.[5] One reason for consumers' "nearly limitless expectations of the system," the report said, was the fact that the cost of medical treatment has to a great extent been shifted to third parties. Patients pay only 29 percent of the nation's health care bill out of their own pockets, not enough, critics say, to make them cost-conscious. Public funds, including Medicare and Medicaid, pay 42 percent of the nation's medical costs, while private insurance companies cover 27 percent *(see box, p. 95)*. Both private and public insurance plans reimburse health care providers on a fee-for-service basis for "reasonable" costs incurred in the treatment of beneficiaries, a system that many believe offers neither

---

[4] For additional information on Reagan's proposals, see *Congressional Quarterly Weekly Report*, Feb. 5, 1983, pp. 275-278.
[5] "The American Health System: A Survey of Leaders and Experts," March 1983. Copies of the report may be obtained from the Market Services Dept., *Prevention Magazine*, Rodale Press, Inc., 33 East Minor Street, Emmaus, Pa. 18049.

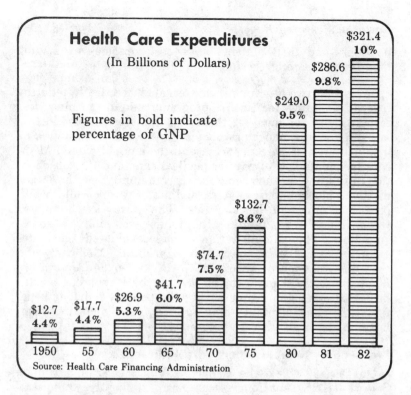

Health Care Expenditures

(In Billions of Dollars)

Figures in bold indicate
percentage of GNP

$12.7
4.4%

$17.7
4.4%

$26.9
5.3%

$41.7
6.0%

$74.7
7.5%

$132.7
8.6%

$249.0
9.5%

$286.6
9.8%

$321.4
10%

1950 55 60 65 70 75 80 81 82

Source: Health Care Financing Administration

physicians nor hospital administrators any incentive to control costs; essentially, the more they charge, the more they make.

Another factor behind rising health care costs has to do with advances in medical technology that entail expensive equipment, such as the sophisticated X-ray device called a computerized axial tomography (CAT) scanner, or complicated surgical procedures such as coronary bypass operations and organ transplants. Other innovative hospital services, such as intensive care units and kidney dialysis machines, also entail high per-patient charges. The suggestion that such services be used with greater discretion in the interest of controlling costs has stirred intense debate over the moral implications of applying "cost-benefit" analysis to decisions regarding human life.

Administration's 'Free-Market' Strategy

Throughout the 1970s, much of the debate over reform of the health care delivery system centered on various proposals for national health insurance *(see p. 102).* After the election of Ronald Reagan, however, the focus of debate shifted to the president's calls for a "pro-competitive" or "free-market" health policy.[6] The president's goal was to make health care

---

[6] For background, see "Reagan Seeks 'Competition' in U.S. Health Care System," *Congressional Quarterly Weekly Report*, Feb. 20, 1982, pp. 331-333.

providers and their patients more cost-conscious by making them more aware of the full costs of medical care.

In his first two years in office, Reagan succeeded in reducing federal spending for health programs and in turning over responsibility for many of them to the states. Cost-reduction measures in the budget reconciliation laws of 1981 and 1982 included (1) a 25 percent increase in the amount elderly Medicare recipients had to pay for medical care; and (2) consolidation of funding for such programs as community health centers, drug and alcohol abuse centers, and maternal and child health programs into four block grants. The states then assumed responsibility for allocating the funds according to federal guidelines. The administration's changes allowed the states greater flexibility in the administration of Medicaid, and according to a recent article in *The New England Journal of Medicine,* more than 30 states have cut back spending on this health care assistance program for the poor by reducing benefits, tightening eligibility standards or simply cutting reimbursements to health care programs.[7]

Prospective Reimbursement for Medicare

On Dec. 28, 1982, the Department of Health and Human Services (HHS) sent Congress a report outlining the administration's plan for replacing the existing Medicare reimbursement system, under which charges are calculated after services have been rendered, with a "prospective" system that would set prices in advance. The administration was required to come up with the plan under the terms of the 1982 tax bill, approved by Congress on Aug. 19 of that year, which also placed caps on the overall amount of Medicare reimbursement.[8]

The HHS report outlined a method of using medical and financial data to assign an average price for treating 467 specific medical conditions or combinations of conditions, known as "diagnosis related groups" or DRGs. By providing for fixed payment rates in advance, the new system would end the existing policy of paying hospitals whatever it costs them to treat beneficiaries. The idea is to encourage hospitals to minimize use of expensive procedures, equipment and personnel so that their operating costs do not exceed the set prices. Hospitals that provide treatment for less than the set amount can keep the difference.

According to President Reagan, this plan will "establish

---

[7] John K. Iglehart, "The Reagan Record on Health Care," *The New England Journal of Medicine,* Jan. 27, 1983.
[8] For details on the Medicare provisions of the 1982 tax bill, see *Congressional Quarterly Weekly Report,* Aug. 21, 1982, p. 2042.

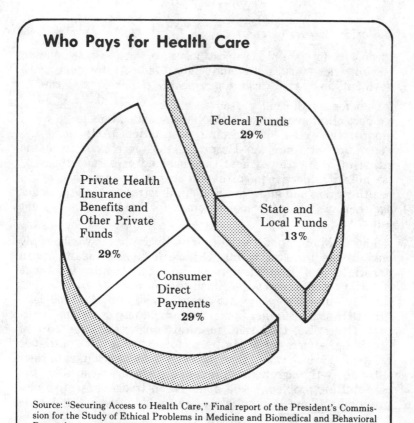

Who Pays for Health Care

Federal Funds
29%

State and
Local Funds
13%

Consumer
Direct
Payments
29%

Private Health
Insurance
Benefits and
Other Private
Funds

29%

Source: "Securing Access to Health Care," Final report of the President's Commission for the Study of Ethical Problems in Medicine and Biomedical and Behavioral Research.

Medicare as a prudent buyer of services and will ensure for both hospitals and the federal government a predictable payment for services.... Medicare traditionally paid hospitals ... whatever they spent. There were, therefore, weak incentives for hospitals to conserve costs and operate efficiently." Under the new plan, he said, " hospitals with higher costs will not be able to pass on extra costs to Medicare beneficiaries and thus will face strong incentives to make cost-effective changes in practices." [9]

The administration's plan, with some modifications, was approved by the House Ways and Means Committee on March 2. To help speed its approval, the committee attached the plan to a bill for overhauling the Social Security system. That bill was approved by Congress March 25 and sent to the president for signing.

Unlike the administration's original proposal, which called for setting one national price for each ailment, the bill approved by Congress allows for regional cost differences and differences between rural and urban hospitals. The bill also would provide

[9] Message sending his health incentives reform program to Congress, Feb. 28, 1983.

exceptions for special high-cost hospitals, such as research and teaching hospitals, and would allow Medicare to make extra payments in special cases where people required extra care.

One reason the bill passed so quickly was that it had the support of influential hospital lobbyists and two major hospital groups, the American Hospital Association (AHA) and the Federation of American Hospitals. Both preferred it to the stringent Medicare payment caps enacted as part of the 1982 tax bill. "Prospective payment will change the incentives in the health system and allow hospital administrators to better manage their payments," a spokeswoman for AHA said in a recent interview.

The main objection to the proposal was that it would apply only to Medicare payments. Critics, including the American Association of Retired Persons and the Health Insurance Association of America,[10] claimed that in order to be effective, the DRG-based prepayment system should apply to Medicaid, private health insurance plans and individuals, as well as Medicare. Otherwise, they said, hospitals might shift the cost of providing services for Medicare recipients to private insurance companies, which would then pass on the higher charges to their subscribers through higher premiums. "Until we can solve the cost-shifting problem," said John K. Kittredge, executive vice president of The Prudential Insurance Co., "we will not have cost containment."

Officials are not sure exactly how much money will be saved by the prospective reimbursement program, which will be phased in over a three-year period, but they do not expect it to solve Medicare's mounting financial problems. A recent study by the Congressional Budget Office predicted that Medicare's Hospital Insurance Trust Fund, which is part of the Social Security system, could go broke as early as 1987.[11] The main reason for the projected deficits, according to the study, is the fact that "hospital costs are growing much more rapidly than the earnings to which the Hospital Insurance tax is applied." From 1982 to 1995, costs incurred by Medicare recipients are projected to increase by an average of 13.2 percent, while covered earnings are expected to rise by an average of only 6.8 percent over the same period.

Opposition to Health Insurance Tax Plan

President Reagan's other proposals for curbing health care costs are more controversial than the Medicare reimbursement plan. Particularly controversial is his plan to tax part of em-

---

[10] Both the American Association of Retired Persons and the Health Insurance Association of America are located in Washington, D.C.
[11] Congressional Budget Office, "Prospects for Medicare's Hospital Insurance Trust Fund," February 1983.

ployer-provided health insurance benefits. The administration contends that under current law neither employees nor employers have much incentive to hold down costs. Company-sponsored benefits represent tax-free income to employees and tax-deductible business expenses to employers.

The administration wants to change this arrangement by putting a ceiling on the amount of insurance premium payments that would continue to receive preferential tax treatment. It would require employees to pay taxes on employer contributions to their health insurance in excess of $175 a month for family coverage or $70 a month for individual coverage. The administration believes this would encourage employees to pressure employers for less comprehensive insurance coverage. The average yearly income tax increase for each of the 16.5 million Americans currently receiving employer-provided health insurance benefits above the proposed ceiling would be about $140, according to administration estimates.

Reagan's proposal elicits stiff resistance from organized labor. The AFL-CIO Executive Council said the proposed tax would constitute "an unprecedented intrusion in collective bargaining" that would "turn back the clock on decades of progress by workers in winning comprehensive health care protection." [12] Organized labor is not alone in its opposition. Representatives of about 50 groups, ranging from the Chamber of Commerce of the United States and the National Association of Manufacturers to the National Council of Senior Citizens, met with Sen. Bob Packwood, R-Ore., in early January to voice their opposition to the plan. Packwood told them there was "no constituency" for the tax scheme and predicted its defeat. He said such a plan would erode the health of working Americans and set a precedent for taxes on other fringe benefits.

Controversy Over Other Reagan Proposals

Also controversial is Reagan's suggestion that Medicare beneficiaries pay more for short-term hospital stays. Under current law, Medicare recipients pay a deductible ($350 in fiscal 1984) for the first day of every hospital stay, but are fully covered by Medicare for the next 59 days. Coverage is only partial for the next 30 days, during which time the patient must pay 25 percent of the deductible ($87.50 per day). If the patient is hospitalized longer than three months, he has only 60 remaining "lifetime reserve days," for which he must pay one-half the deductible ($175 per day). Thereafter, the patient is personally liable for all hospital costs.

Under Reagan's plan the emphasis of Medicare coverage

---

[12] *AFL-CIO News,* March 5, 1983.

Recession's Impact on Access to Health Care

When workers are laid off or fired, they frequently lose more than just their jobs. They may also lose company-provided health insurance benefits. The Congressional Budget Office estimated that 10.7 million unemployed Americans and their families had no health insurance coverage last year.

As Congress debates the Reagan administration proposals for containing health care costs, support is building for some kind of health benefits program aimed at the unemployed. While business interests are opposed to extending health insurance benefits to the unemployed beyond the usual 30-day limit after layoff, the AFL-CIO has called for their extension for at least 65 weeks. Senate Finance Committee Chairman Robert Dole, R-Kan., has suggested that medical benefits for the unemployed could be financed with revenues collected through the administration's proposed tax on employer-provided group health insurance *(see p. 96)*.

would shift to long-term hospital stays. In addition to the full first-day deductible, Medicare recipients would pay 8 percent ($28 per day) through day 15, then 5 percent ($17.50 per day) through day 60, but receive full and unlimited coverage after that time. While the administration proposal would seem to satisfy previous calls for "catastrophic" insurance to cover long-term hospitalization, it would in fact save the government an estimated $2 billion a year, since most Medicare recipients would end up paying more for hospital care. Only about 200,000 of the 7 million Medicare recipients hospitalized each year stay longer than 60 days. The average stay is 11 days. If Reagan's plan is enacted, an 11-day hospital stay would cost Medicare beneficiaries almost twice as much as it does now.

Critics say Reagan's proposal violates the federal government's commitment to the elderly embodied in Medicare legislation. According to Janet Myder of the National Council of Senior Citizens,[13] it would impose "a very, very heavy burden" on the elderly "which is not going to be alleviated by [Reagan's proposal for] catastrophic protection. This is not catastrophic insurance. What is catastrophic for the elderly is the cost of a nursing home, the cost of any long-term care, the cumulative cost of all the things that Medicare doesn't pay for, like prescription drugs." Myder and other critics also fear that the proposed changes would lead private insurance companies to substantially increase premiums for "Medigap" policies, which pay the difference between public coverage and hospital

---

[13] The National Council of Senior Citizens, located at 925 15th St., N.W., Washington, D.C. 20005, represents over 4.5 million elderly people in all the states.

charges. While 60 percent of those eligible for Medicare now subscribe to private "Medigap" policies, many could no longer afford such coverage if premium prices sharply increased.

Spokesmen for groups representing the elderly also are unhappy about the administration's new interpretation of Medicaid laws, which gave states the go-ahead to require adult children of nursing home patients to pay part of the cost of their parents' care. A few states already have adopted such "family responsibility" laws, but they have delayed enforcing them awaiting federal guidelines. Rep. Henry A. Waxman, D-Calif., chairman of the House Energy and Commerce Subcommittee on Health, which has jurisdiction over Medicaid, says the administration's directive is contrary to the intent of Congress and he plans to hold hearings on the matter.

Past Approaches to Problem

THE PUBLIC and private health insurance arrangements that are partly to blame for today's health care inflation are a product of the progressive monopolization of the health care delivery system. This trend began in the latter years of the 19th century with the licensing of physicians. With fewer doctors authorized to practice medicine, fees began to rise until, by the 1920s, physicians' incomes began to far outstrip those of other workers.

Growing recognition of the impact of rising medical costs led to the formation in 1926 of the privately funded Committee on the Costs of Medical Care, which provided the first analyses of the problem in the United States and which recommended in its final reports of 1932 an increase in access to medical care for the entire population and an increase in resources to fund it. The committee's recommendations of fostering group practice and group payment for medical care were, however, condemned by the increasingly influential American Medical Association (AMA) as a dangerous challenge to the private physician's control over services provided — and fees charged — to patients. The controversy that ensued led President Franklin D. Roosevelt to exclude health care reform from the New Deal social legislation that culminated in the Social Security Act of 1935.

During the same period, both the American Hospital Association and the AMA introduced their own private insurance mechanisms, Blue Cross and Blue Shield, respectively, in response to growing demand from consumers for some form of protection from debilitating health care expenses and also to prevent single-hospital plans and prepaid group practices from weakening their monopoly of the health care delivery system. In 1934, commercial insurance companies began offering health insurance on the same fee-for-service basis, which posed few, if any, limits on the amount physicians or hospitals could charge. In this way, wrote Paul Starr, "the structure of private health plans, it seems fair to say, was basically an accommodation to provider interests." [14]

By 1958, almost two-thirds of the population was covered by hospital insurance. But while more and more Americans came under various insurance plans, only half of those aged 65 or older were covered, even though they were the most vulnerable to disease and generally the least able to pay for health care services. Awareness of the plight of the aged and poor grew throughout the 1950s and early 1960s and led to the enactment in 1965 of the Medicare and Medicaid programs.

With Medicare, all Americans, regardless of income level, are entitled upon reaching age 65 to hospital benefits as well as a voluntary supplemental policy covering 80 percent of physicians' fees. Unlike Medicare, which is funded entirely at the federal level, Medicaid was introduced as a joint state-federal program. Coverage is less uniform under this program, as the federal government may only establish standards for the types of services offered, but not the payment levels provided by the states.

Statistics indicate that Medicare and Medicaid have succeeded in greatly increasing the access of elderly and poor Americans to health care. The frequency of physician visits by people whose family incomes were below $7,000 increased by almost 50 percent between 1964 and 1980.[15] The elderly have benefited from both programs; 95 percent of them are entitled to Medicare hospital insurance, while Medicaid helps the elderly poor pay for services not covered by Medicare, such as nursing home care. In 1978, the latest year for which official statistics have been compiled, elderly Americans incurred an average annual health bill of $2,026, 63 percent of which was covered by public funds.[16]

The number of health care providers greatly increased in the 1960s, thanks largely to federal grants, scholarships and loans for medical research and education. The number of active physicians increased by 70 percent between 1965 and 1975, while the number of dentists rose by 50 percent and the number of

---

[14] Paul Starr, *The Social Transformation of American Medicine* (1982), p. 309.
[15] Department of Health and Human Services, Public Health Service, "Health, United States, 1982," p. 90.
[16] *Ibid.*, p. 152.

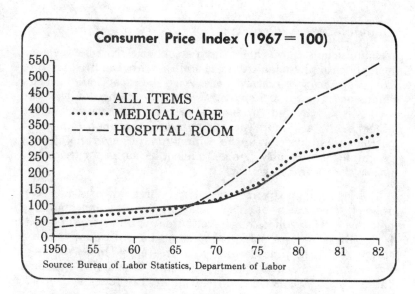

Consumer Price Index (1967=100)

ALL ITEMS
MEDICAL CARE
HOSPITAL ROOM

550
500
450
400
350
300
250
200
150
100
50
0

1950   55   60   65   70   75   80   81   82

Source: Bureau of Labor Statistics, Department of Labor

nurses doubled.[17] The same period saw a burst of hospital construction and expansion, with the help of federal funds provided through the Hill-Burton program, which began in 1946.

The portion of health care expenditures paid by third parties also increased during this period, rising from 45 percent in 1965 to 65 percent in 1970. In addition to Medicare and Medicaid, a major contributing factor to this trend was the inclusion of health insurance benefits in labor contracts. These group health insurance schemes benefited not only American workers, but also the health care industry itself, which no longer had to wait long periods for payment of fees.

'70s Health Care 'Crisis'; Turn to HMOs

Growing awareness of the medical inflation problem in the early 1970s led the Nixon administration to speak of a "crisis" in health care financing. Liberals and conservatives alike agreed on the need for reform of the health care system, but they disagreed on the best way to approach the problem. While liberals like Sen. Edward M. Kennedy, D-Mass., tended to favor some form of national health insurance, the Nixon administration lent its support to the increasingly popular prepaid group health plans, or health maintenance organizations (HMOs), which had first appeared as a radical alternative to the traditional control exercised over the industry by hospitals and private physicians.

The HMO evolved along two principal models. So-called "group models" operate their own facilities and employ their

[17] Louise B. Russell, "Medical Care," in *Setting National Priorities: Agenda for the 1980s*, ed. Joseph A. Pechman (1980), p. 175.

own physicians, nurses and other personnel. Subscribers select a primary care physician from the staff and are required to go to the group facility to receive care. With the exception of certain emergency procedures, any medical care obtained outside the facility is not covered. "Individual practice associations," on the other hand, are more decentralized. Subscribers choose a participating physician in the community, often on the basis of geographical proximity, and go to his or her office for treatment rather than to a central facility.

The HMO, by operating on a strictly prepaid basis, was seen as an effective means of encouraging physicians and hospitals to hold down costs. Since they have to work within a fixed budget, HMO physicians are unlikely to extend their patients' hospital stays beyond the time necessary for treatment. In New Jersey, for example, the average hospital stay for surgical patients enrolled in HMOs is three days, compared to four days for the general population.

Nixon's support for HMOs led to passage of a 1973 law requiring all businesses with more than 25 employees to include at least one HMO among the health benefits offered to employees. Partly as a result of this measure, the number of HMOs in the country rose from 30 in 1971 to 268 by mid-1982. The main benefit of the HMO has been a reduction in health care costs through reduced utilization of hospital services. But while effective in the communities where they exist, HMOs have yet to have a significant impact on the national health care system, as only 5 percent of the U.S. population are currently enrolled in this type of program.

National Insurance Debate; State Plans

Advocates of national health insurance were bolstered by the election of Jimmy Carter in 1976. During the presidential campaign Carter promised to introduce a "comprehensive national health insurance system with universal and mandatory coverage." But when Carter finally unveiled his plan in 1979, it turned out to be a much more limited plan to protect Americans against catastrophic medical costs. By focusing on catastrophic coverage, Carter alienated Sen. Kennedy, who was still pushing for a more comprehensive national health program similar to those available in Britain, Canada and other industrialized countries.[18]

Neither Carter's nor Kennedy's bill was approved by Congress, however, in part because of an intense lobbying campaign against them by groups representing health care providers and

---

[18] For background, see Edward M. Kennedy, *In Critical Condition: The Crisis in America's Health Care* (1972).

also because of concern in Congress over their costs. The concept of national health insurance continues to find support, particularly among organized labor and groups representing the poor and elderly. But budgetary considerations appear to have pushed this option to the back burner for the foreseeable future.

While the federal government was having trouble coming up with ways to control rising health care costs, a number of states introduced their own cost-control schemes. Some set up public agencies to review hospital budgets and/or rates, while others set up systems to regulate hospital reimbursements. Under these plans, hospitals are reimbursed prospectively in one of two ways. Either they are paid a certain rate per case of a certain type of ailment or a general budget constraint is imposed. Six states — Connecticut, Maryland, Massachusetts, New Jersey, New York and Washington — introduced prospective payment plans in 1976 or earlier. These state plans were the subject of a study that found them to be effective in containing hospital costs.[19]

It was in New Jersey that the "diagnosis-related group" (DRG) basis for calculating hospital costs was first implemented in 1980. The New Jersey plan served as the model for the new Medicare reimbursement plan recently adopted by Congress as part of the Social Security rescue bill *(see p. 94)*. Under the plan, each New Jersey hospital was required to break down all business into the 467 DRGs contained in a classification system developed at Yale University, and assign an average charge for each DRG. Patients were then billed according to their illnesses instead of the services actually received. On the basis of the hospitals' own estimates, the state of New Jersey established working annual budgets for each institution. Hospitals were encouraged to save money, as they pocketed all funds saved by working within the budget limits. But unlike the new federal program, the New Jersey plan does not just apply to Medicare, which prevents hospitals from shifting the costs incurred by some payers to other groups.

Prospects and Alternatives

CORPORATE executives are also getting more involved in attempts to hold down health care costs. In fact, according to the report prepared by Yankelovich, Skelly and White for *Prevention* magazine, "large corporations will lead the way" in

[19] Brian Biles et al., "Hospital Cost Inflation Under State Rate-Setting Programs," *The New England Journal of Medicine*, Sept. 18, 1980.

solving the problem.[20] The reason for their concern is obvious.
The corporate contribution to payments for health benefit plans
was an estimated $60 billion in 1980. "Since World War II the
employer, through negotiated benefits, has been paying more
and more of the health care costs of this country for their
employees and their dependents," Boyd Thompson, executive
vice president of the American Association of Foundations for
Medical Care, said in a recent interview. "This money was
managed by insurance companies and Blue Cross-Blue Shield
with no incentive on their part to hold down costs. The more the
premium went up, the more money they made. Now the employers, individually and collectively, are telling the insurance
companies and the Blues: 'Get out of our way, we're going to
handle this ourselves by dealing with the provider directly.' "

> *"Since World War II the employer,
> through negotiated benefits, has been pay-
> ing more and more of the health care costs
> of this country for their employees and
> their dependents."*
>
> Boyd Thompson, executive vice
> president, American Association of
> Foundations for Medical Care

In some communities corporations are banding together to
form "preferred provider organizations." Under this arrangement, groups of physicians or hospitals are enlisted by employers to provide services at competitive prices. In return, the
companies encourage their workers to use the services of the
"preferred providers." Other companies are encouraging workers to join health maintenance organizations *(see p. 101)*.
According to a newsletter published by the Group Health
Association of America, Chrysler Corp. in Detroit has taken
"the unprecedented step" of providing direct financial incentives to its workers enrolled in an HMO to sign up their
friends. Under the plan, current members of the Health Alliance
Plan of Michigan were given savings bonds of up to $250 for
signing up fellow workers in the HMO.[21]

The Business Roundtable, a group made up of the chief
executive officers of some 200 large U.S. companies, issued a
report in February 1982 on the "appropriate role for corporations in health care cost management." Among other things, it

[20] "The American Health System," *op. cit.*, p. 13.
[21] See *Group Health News*, April 1983, p. 4.

recommended greater "corporate involvement in community coalitions established to address specific local health cost management problems," as well as programs to improve employee health. Many corporate executives have already discovered that it is cheaper to keep workers healthy than to pay to treat their illnesses. Thousands of companies have set up some type of physical fitness program for employees. Often these include not only exercise facilities, but also programs on nutrition, smoking, weight-control, stress management, alcohol and drug abuse, and similiar topics.[22]

Growth of Clinics; For-Profit Hospitals

An increasingly popular alternative to traditional care in hospitals and private doctors' offices is the emergency clinic, frequently set up in suburban shopping centers. It is designed to provide quick and inexpensive service for people who are willing to pay directly for the treatment of non-life-threatening emergencies. The advantages of these "emergicenters," hundreds of which have sprung up over the past few years, include immediate service, low-cost, 24-hour access, convenient location, and no need for appointments. They are not, however, a viable substitute for the hospital emergency room, where the presence of advanced support technology is required for serious emergency situations.

Despite the rise of such alternatives, the traditional, full-service hospital remains the basic structure for delivering medical care in this country. But while the number of non-profit and public hospitals has declined in recent years, the number of for-profit hospitals has rapidly increased, often by acquiring non-profit and public facilities. According to a recent article by Teresa Riordan in *The Washington Monthly,* "the for-profit hospital industry ... grew faster during the 1970s than the computer industry." [23]

Most public and non-profit hospitals were built with the help of federal funds provided through the Hill-Burton program, which required them to admit and treat charity and "bad-debt" cases as well as insured patients. But if such facilities are acquired by a for-profit chain, such as Humana Inc., Hospital Corporation of America or National Medical Enterprises, they are freed from this requirement. Critics have accused for-profit chains of favoring privately insured patients, whose policies usually reimburse the greatest amount of hospital expenses, while dumping Medicaid and non-insured patients on public

[22] See "Physical Fitness Boom," *E.R.R.,* 1978 Vol. I, pp. 271-273.
[23] Teresa Riordan, "The Wards Are Paved With Gold," *The Washington Monthly,* February 1983, p. 41.

and non-profit institutions. "This setup drains the already anemic philanthropic resources of publics and non-profits and often forces them to close or sell out to the for-profits," Teresa Riordan wrote.

Corporations have also taken over about half of the nation's nursing homes for the elderly. One-third of the nursing homes in this country are now owned by just 20 chains, including Beverly Enterprises and ATA Services, each of which owns 250 homes around the country. Some fear this trend may discourage the development of at-home or other community-based services for those whose conditions are not serious enough to warrant institutionalization.[24]

Providing health care for the elderly is likely to be a dominant concern for many decades. It has been estimated that the number of Americans aged 65 and older will rise steadily from the current level of 11.4 percent of the population to 21.7 percent by 2050, and that the ratio of workers to non-workers will drop from 5.4-to-1 to 2.6-to-1 over the same period.[25] This "graying of America" is expected to increase the portion of the nation's wealth allocated to health care from 10 percent today to 11 or 12 percent by the end of the century.

Ethical Issues and Budgetary Constraints

While nearly everyone agrees that more must be done to hold down increases in health care costs, some fear that cost-containment initiatives may adversely affect the quality of health care in the United States. Among those expressing this concern were the members of a presidential commission on medical ethics, whose recently released final report concluded: "Efforts to contain rising health costs are important but should not focus on limiting the attainment of equitable access for the least well served portion of the public. The achievement of equitable access is an obligation of sufficient moral urgency to warrant devoting the necessary resources to it." [26]

The commission recognizes that efforts to rein in currently escalating health care costs have an ethical aspect because the call for adequate health care for all may not be heeded until such efforts are undertaken [the report continued].... But measures

[24] For background, see "Housing Options for the Elderly," *E.R.R.*, 1982 Vol. II, pp. 569-588.
[25] Jerome A. Halperin, "Forces of Change in Health Services," address delivered to the College of Pharmacy, University of Arizona at Tucson, Nov. 12, 1982. Halperin is acting director of the Office of Drugs in the Food and Drug Administration.
[26] President's Commission for the Study of Ethical Problems in Medicine and Biomedical and Behavioral Research, "Securing Access to Health Care: A Report on the Ethical Implications of Differences in the Availability of Health Services," Vol. I, March 1983, pp. 5-6. Copies of the report can be obtained, at a cost of $6, from the Government Printing Office, Washington, D.C. 20402. The 11-member commission was established by Congress in 1980. Its chairman was Morris B. Abram, former president of Brandeis University.

designed to contain health care costs that exacerbate existing inequities or impede the achievement of equity are unacceptable from a moral standpoint. Moreover, they are unlikely by themselves to be successful since they will probably lead to a shifting of costs to other entities, rather than to a reduction of total expenditures.

The report did not comment on specific legislative proposals to reduce health care expenses, but it did address some of the current controversies. For example, it was critical of proposals to charge Medicaid recipients a nominal fee for each day in the hospital or each visit to a doctor's office. "Even a small out-of-pocket charge can constitute a substantial burden for some Medicaid participants," it said. The report also came out against reductions in federal funding of Medicaid, saying this "would worsen existing inequities in the distribution of the cost of care." However, the commission did express support for the idea of reducing federal tax subsidies of health insurance, as the Reagan administration has proposed *(see p. 96)*. "If properly designed, it is unlikely that such measures would compromise access to adequate health care [nor would they have] a disproportionate impact on the most economically vulnerable people. . . ," the commission stated.

Bringing medical inflation under control without jeopardizing the quality of health care in the United States will not be an easy task. But some experts see reasons for optimism. Yankelovich, Skelly and White, in their report for *Prevention* magazine, predicted that consumers will become less deferential in dealing with physicians, challenging doctors' judgments about diagnosis, treatments, costs, etc. Not only will this help control costs, the report stated, but it could change the nature of the medical profession, since physicians will be forced to become more people-oriented. At the same time, U.S. corporations are likely to continue their efforts to hold down medical costs. "In sum," the report concluded, "all of the key actors are either poised for change or will be unable to resist the pull of change. And, given the way these groups are assessing the problems and formulating strategies, there is no reason to think that either the quality of care or the equity of its distribution will diminish. They could even improve."

Selected Bibliography

Books

Davis, Karen and Cathy Schoen, *Health and the War on Poverty: A Ten-Year Appraisal*, Brookings, 1978.

Kennedy, Edward M., *In Critical Condition: The Crisis in America's Health Care*, Simon & Schuster, 1972.

Maxwell, Robert J., *Health and Wealth*, Lexington Books, 1981.

Pechman, Joseph A., ed., *Setting National Priorities: Agenda for the 1980s*, Brookings, 1980.

Pauly, Mark V., ed., *National Health Insurance: What Now, What Later, What Never?* American Enterprise Institute, 1980.

Starr, Paul, *The Social Transformation of American Medicine*, Basic Books, 1982.

Thompson, Margaret C., ed., *Health Policy: The Legislative Agenda*, Congressional Quarterly Inc., 1980.

Articles

Keisling, Phil, "Radical Surgery: Let's Draft the Doctors," *The Washington Monthly*, February 1983.

The New England Journal of Medicine, selected issues.

Seidman, Bert, "Bad Medicine for Health Care Costs," *AFL-CIO American Federationist*, April-June 1982.

Starr, Paul, "The Laissez-Faire Elixir," *The New Republic*, April 18, 1983.

"Treating the Ailing Health Care Dollar," *Journal of American Insurance*, winter 1981-82.

Reports and Studies

Congressional Budget Office, "Prospects for Medicare's Hospital Insurance Trust Fund," February 1983.

Editorial Research Reports: "Controlling Health Costs," 1977 Vol. I, p. 61; "Health Maintenance Organizations," 1974 Vol. II, p. 601; "Health Care in Britain and America," 1973 Vol. I, p. 437; "Future of Health Insurance," 1970 Vol. I, p. 61.

President's Commission for the Study of Ethical Problems in Medicine and Biomedical and Behavioral Research, "Securing Access to Health Care," March 1983.

U.S. Department of Health and Human Services, Public Health Service, "Health, United States, 1982," 1982.

FEDERAL JOBS PROGRAMS

by

Robert Benenson

**Dec. 24
1982**

Editor's Note: Congress passed the federal gasoline tax increase just before Christmas, earmarking the funds for highway repair and other transportation projects. The higher tax went into effect April 1.

Job creation became a prime topic of the new 98th Congress, which convened in January. Reversing two years of opposition, the Reagan administration approved a $4.3 billion jobs plan that was essentially an accelerated public works program patterned after the Depression-era Public Works Administration and the Local Public Works program of the 1970s. Congress on March 21 passed a bill adding $300 million to that amount but stopped short of increasing it further for fear of a presidential veto. Reagan signed it into law three days later.

Another Depression-era idea was revived by jobs-minded representatives. The House on March 1 approved the creation of an American Conservation Corps, patterned after the Civilian Conservation Corps *(p. 118)*, to provide jobs for 100,000 youths. Senate action was awaited.

FEDERAL JOBS PROGRAMS

THE DEBATE over whether the federal government should create jobs to ease unemployment during economic downturns dominated the stormy lame-duck session of Congress. Motivated by unemployment statistics that had reached double digits for the first time since the Great Depression, congressional Democrats and many Republicans supported a variety of jobs bills introduced during the four-week special session. They even went so far as to attempt to attach a jobs bill to the continuing resolution needed to keep the government running. President Reagan's threat to veto such a resolution, which would have led to a partial shutdown of the government, caused jobs-bill advocates to back down at least until the 98th Congress convenes in January. But even the president supported passage of a 5-cent increase in the federal gasoline tax, which was touted for its job-creating potential.

In keeping with his conservative philosophy, Reagan has long been opposed to federal job-creation programs. In a Dec. 16 interview with *Washington Post* reporters Lou Cannon and David Hoffman, Reagan said: "All of our past experience shows that make-work jobs programs in the past, whatever they did in creating eventually some employment, usually it was so late that recovery had already taken place or was well under way. . . . Also, the taking of those funds from the economy to be used by government in that way resulted in uncounted unemployment in other sectors of the economy. . . . You simply shifted the jobs from one group to another."

For the first 22 months of the Reagan administration, Congress generally went along with the president's opposition to "make-work" programs. But Republican losses in the mid-term congressional elections last November, which many political analysts attributed at least in part to opposition to Reagan's economic policies, seemed to light a fire under the legislators.

The impetus for the sudden flurry of jobs programs was an unemployment situation that seemed to cry out for action. Unemployment hit 10.8 percent in November, up from 10.4 percent in October, the highest level since the Great Depression days of 1941. Michigan's unemployment rate was 17.2 percent and other Midwest industrial states were in similar depressed conditions. The December unemployment rate will be released Jan. 7, and it is expected to top 11 percent. Ironically, according to the goals of the Full Employment and Balanced Growth Act of 1978, better known as the Humphrey-Hawkins Act, unemployment was to be reduced to 4 percent by January 1983.[1]

Despite the enormous unemployment problem, conservatives moved quickly to stall the jobs program bandwagon. They claimed that past job-creating efforts had only a minor effect on short- or long-term unemployment, encouraged waste, fraud and inefficiency on the local level, and created only "dead-end, make-work jobs." But advocates of federal job-creation said a large public works program was needed not only to help the unemployed but also to repair the nation's crumbling "infrastructure" of basic public facilities.

Linking Job and Infrastructure Problems

The deterioration of America's roads, bridges, water systems and other public facilities is no secret. New York City's West Side Highway, which has been closed and razed in stages over a 10-year period, is a symbol for public works decay. As fiscal stress forced more and more cities and states to cut back on capital expenses in favor of day-to-day operations, such decay became widespread.

In early 1981, the Council of State Planning Agencies[2] published a book entitled *America in Ruins: Beyond the Public Works Pork Barrel.* According to the authors, Dr. Pat Choate and Susan Walter, "the deteriorated condition of basic facilities that underpin the economy will prove a critical bottleneck to national economic renewal during the decade unless we can find a way to finance public works." Among their suggestions were a national inventory of the nation's public works and new financing mechanisms for them. The authors also noted that "economic policy might reduce the impact of . . . a severe recession by using the nation's annual $80 billion public works investments as a counter-cyclical economic tool for providing employment in the construction, materials and equipment industries."

The book provoked some discussion, including an article in *Time* magazine entitled "Time to Repair and Restore." [3] This

---

[1] When the Humphrey-Hawkins Act, cosponsored by Sen. Hubert H. Humphrey, D-Minn., and Rep. Augustus F. Hawkins, D-Calif., was passed in October 1978, it was seen as a tribute to Humphrey, who had died the previous January. The bill originally called for the president to set meaningful, enforceable economic goals — to be achieved, if necessary, through "last resort" public service jobs for the unemployed. But conservative opposition turned Humphrey-Hawkins into a symbolic measure, with broad goals and no enforcement mechanisms. For background, see *1978 CQ Almanac*, pp. 272-279.

[2] The council, based in Washington, D.C., has been affiliated with the National Governors' Association since 1975.

[3] *Time*, April 27, 1981, p. 46.

MY UNEMPLOYMENT
INSURANCE HAS RUN
OUT... I CAN'T PAY
THE BILLS...

WE WERE FORCED TO
SELL THE HOUSE, AND
OUR KID HAD TO QUIT
COLLEGE

HEY- THINGS COULD
BE WORSE-

YOU COULD HAVE
A MAKE-WORK,
DEAD-END JOB

year, more public works experts, economists and other commentators provided their own analyses of the nation's infrastructure needs, and the topic became a news media favorite. For example, *Newsweek* ran a cover story in August on "The Decaying of America," warning that "the nation's network of roads, bridges, sewers and rails is nearing collapse." [4]

The nation's interstate highway system received much of the media's attention. Many sections of the system, which was begun over 25 years ago,[5] are reaching the end of their useful life. Heavier traffic and heavier trucks than expected have caused some interstate roads to go from uncomfortable to impassable. Choate and Walter estimated that over 8,000 miles of interstate highway, about 20 percent of the system, were in need of immediate repair. That figure did not include the thousands of state and local roads that were in serious disrepair.

Engineers are also worried about the condition of many bridges. The Department of Transportation estimated in July 1982 that 45 percent of the nation's 248,500 bridges were structurally or functionally deficient. Commuter traffic in such cities as Cleveland and Pittsburgh has had to be rerouted because of bridge closings.

Water and sewer systems in many areas are also in need of repair. Cleveland's director of public utilities, Edward Richard, told Editorial Research Reports earlier this year that the city needed $900 million to repair and renovate its sewer system. Residents of Jersey City, N.J., went without water for three days last July when an 80-year-old aqueduct ruptured. Thousands of other public facilities across the nation — including ports, railroads, mass transit systems, jails, schools and courthouses — also need repair, modernization or replacement.

Exactly how much work needs to be done is uncertain because there are no federal or state and few city inventories of public facilities and their conditions. But estimates from various sources run from the eye-popping to the apocalyptic. The Asso-

[4] *Newsweek*, Aug. 2, 1982, p. 12.
[5] See "Interstate Highway System at Twenty-Five," *E.R.R.*, 1981 Vol. II, pp. 733-752.

ciated General Contractors of America estimated that public construction costs would come to $909.9 million. Dr. Amitai Etzioni,[6] author of the recently published book *An Immodest Agenda: Rebuilding America Before the 21st Century*, calculated that America's infrastructure needs would amount to $3 trillion over 10 years — or $300 billion a year.

Many observers see the latter figure as something of a wish list. "I think we can probably rule out the $3 trillion figure as exaggerated," said Roger Vaughan, an economist who writes for the Council of State Planning Agencies. Even the smaller figure seems beyond the capacity of fiscally strapped federal, state and local governments. But public works advocates insist that something must be done. Rep. Henry S. Reuss, D-Wis., retiring chairman of the Joint Economic Committee, told Editorial Research Reports that it is "ridiculous to talk about the reindustrialization of America" without a sound infrastructure. "Merely because the need is so enormous shouldn't lull us into the position of doing nothing about it," he said.

Job-Creating Potential of Gas Tax Bill

The urgent need to do something about both the crumbling infrastructure and the unemployment problem led to the promotion of the gasoline tax increase as a jobs bill. When Transportation Secretary Drew Lewis first presented the idea to President Reagan earlier this year, it was billed simply as a much-needed boost to the Highway Trust Fund, which funds federal highway programs. Reagan shelved the idea in May, because he thought it would complicate deliberations on the deficit-reducing tax increase which was eventually passed Aug. 19. During a Sept. 28 news conference, Reagan answered a reporter who asked about further tax increases in general and the gas tax in particular by saying, "Unless there's a palace coup and I'm overtaken or overthrown, no, I don't see the necessity for that."

Lewis persisted with his pet plan, but even as late as Oct. 29, a newspaper article concerning the gas tax increase made no mention of its job-creating implications.[7] But Republican losses in the mid-term congressional elections on Nov. 2 changed all of that. Lewis began promoting an estimate that the $5.5 billion raised by the increased tax would result in 320,000 new jobs. On Nov. 22, in an unusual show of bipartisan support, House Speaker Thomas P. O'Neill Jr., D-Mass., and Senate Majority Leader Howard H. Baker Jr., R-Tenn., announced that they

---

[6] Etzioni is the first University Professor at George Washington University in Washington, D.C., and is the director of the Center for Policy Research in Bethesda, Md.
[7] *The Washington Post*, Oct. 29, 1982.

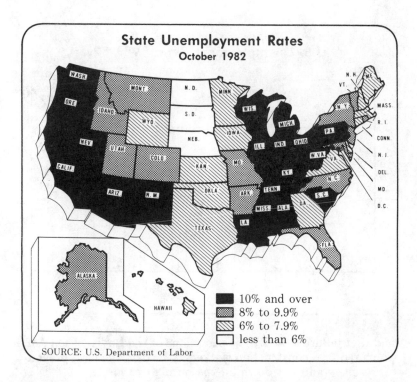

State Unemployment Rates
October 1982

Legend:
- 10% and over
- 8% to 9.9%
- 6% to 7.9%
- less than 6%

SOURCE: U.S. Department of Labor

would work together to push the highway jobs program through Congress during the lame-duck session. The next day, Reagan announced his support for the plan. In his weekly radio speech on Nov. 27, Reagan said the program would "stimulate 170,000 jobs, not in make-work projects, but in real worthwhile work in the hard-hit construction industries, and an additional 150,000 jobs in related industries."

Some economists questioned whether there would actually be a net gain of jobs through a gasoline tax increase. Martin S. Feldstein, chairman of the president's Council of Economic Advisers, said that the increased cost of gasoline would reduce consumer spending on other goods and services, and "may actually increase unemployment during the first year or two." Alice M. Rivlin, director of the Congressional Budget Office, said, "In the short term, we should expect little increase in employment."

Those who questioned the job-creation claims of the gas-tax advocates pointed out that much of the money raised by the tax would go into continuing projects, such as the completion of the interstate highway system. While this might forestall an increase in unemployment, critics said that it would not result in a net increase in jobs. They also pointed out that road-building is not particularly labor-intensive, since a large proportion of expenditures go for materials rather than wages. Conservatives

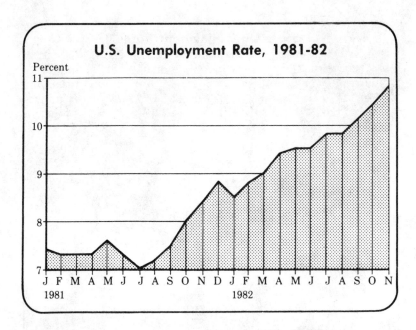

U.S. Unemployment Rate, 1981-82

Percent

said that failure to waive the provisions of the Davis-Bacon Act, which requires construction workers to be paid the local prevailing wage, would cut down on the number of jobs.

The gas tax plan was passed by the House Dec. 6, but it ran into unexpectedly stiff opposition in the Senate. Claiming that the gas tax was regressive and would fall hardest on poor and working-class people, conservatives, led by Republicans John P. East and Jesse Helms of North Carolina, staged a filibuster that threatened to scuttle the plan. The gas tax plan was finally endorsed by the Senate in the early hours of Dec. 21. House-Senate conferees agreed on a compromise version later that day. It was approved by the House, but as Congress approached adjournment it still was being debated in the Senate.

Congressional-White House Differences

Work-relief advocates were not satisfied by the gas tax proposal, some because the job claims seemed spurious, others because the predicted job creation was small compared with the dimensions of the unemployment problem. On Nov. 9, Rep. Reuss submitted a $6.8 billion plan that included infrastructure repair, "community renewal," mortgage and rental housing construction assistance, and an American Conservation Corps modeled after the Civilian Conservation Corps (CCC) of the New Deal era *(see p. 118)*. Eventually this evolved into a $5.4 billion proposal by the House Democratic leadership that included $1 billion for repair and maintenance of public facilities, $200 million for public housing modernization, $230 million in small business loans, $155 million for prison repair, $250 million for weatherization of low-income housing, $232 million for accelerated job training and relocation, $339 million for administration of unemployment services, $489 million for military housing and $50 million to be funneled through the United Way of America for emergency food and shelter for the victims of the recession.[8]

A Senate Democratic proposal submitted Dec. 7 was even more ambitious. The senators advocated spending a total of $9.7 billion: $6 billion for reconstruction of seriously impaired highway, bridge, transit and water systems; and $3.7 billion for a hodgepodge of "light" public works repairs, job retraining, employment for the elderly, reforestation, mine reclamation and public housing rehabilitation, as well as a five-week extension of unemployment benefits.

Realizing the unlikelihood that Reagan would sign a jobs bill, House Democrats attached their jobs program to the continuing resolution needed to fund federal government agencies after Dec. 17. The continuing resolution was passed by a 204-200 vote on Dec. 14. The Republican-controlled Senate, which had earlier voted to reject the $9.7 billion Senate Democratic plan, attached its own $1.2 billion jobs plan, a miniature version of the House Democratic plan, to the continuing resolution on Dec. 15. But after the president indicated that he would veto any resolution "garlanded" with jobs programs, House-Senate conferees on Dec. 19 struck out all spending for public works and other employment programs. Advocates of such programs said they would push for jobs spending early next year.

History of Jobs Programs

THE FEDERAL government has been involved in the public works area since the early days of the nation, building such things as roads, bridges and ports. Federal use of public works as a job-creating tool dates back almost as long. In 1808, the federal government turned the building of fortifications in New York City over to longshoremen and sailors who had been laid off because of the Embargo Act, which banned trade with Europe. The use of large-scale public employment programs was discussed during the periodic depressions of the late 1800s, but

[8] For background on the personal effects of the recession, see "The Charity Squeeze," *E.R.R.*, 1982 Vol. II, pp. 893-912, and "The Homeless: Growing National Problem," *E.R.R.*, 1982 Vol. II, pp. 793-812.

was never implemented. The post-World War I depression in 1920-21 spurred discussion of a counter-cyclical mechanism that would increase public works expenditures during economic downturns. President Warren Harding's Conference on Unemployment advised in 1921 that "Federal authorities, including the Federal Reserve Banks, should expedite the construction of public buildings and public works covered by existing appropriations." But the boom of the "Roaring '20s" took the urgency out of those deliberations.

In 1929, national unemployment stood at 3 percent. But in October of that year the stock market crashed, precipitating the massive economic collapse that came to be known as the Great Depression. Even as unemployment was climbing, President Herbert Hoover stuck to the traditional philosophy that the federal government should leave recovery to the private sector. "Under our political system, government is not, nor should it be, a general employer of labor," Hoover said in 1930.[9]

Hoover preferred to leave provision of relief to the states, communities and private agencies. But when joblessness soared in 1932 to 25 percent, bringing with it widespread suffering that was beyond the capacity of the traditional structures to deal with, Hoover was moved to act. He created the Reconstruction Finance Corporation (RFC), which appropriated $300 million for public construction loans. Hoover's actions were too late to save him from defeat at the hands of Franklin D. Roosevelt, but they did provide the framework for the "alphabet soup" of job-creating agencies during Roosevelt's New Deal period.[10]

CCC and Other Early New Deal Measures

One of Roosevelt's first actions was creation of the Federal Emergency Relief Agency (FERA), which provided $500 million mainly for cash relief, but also for a small number of menial jobs, such as leaf-raking and park cleaning. Roosevelt moved quickly to complement FERA with a more substantial job-creation program. Despite the modern impression of Roosevelt as the father of the "welfare state," he actually despised the idea of cash relief. "The quicker they are taken off the dole the

[9] Quotations and statistics in this section obtained from: Donald S. Howard, *The WPA and Federal Relief Policy* (1943); Arthur M. Schlesinger Jr., *The Age of Roosevelt: The Politics of Upheaval* (1960); Frank Freidel, *Franklin D. Roosevelt: Launching The New Deal* (1973); Bernard Asbell, *The F.D.R. Memoirs* (1973); William Manchester, *The Glory and the Dream* (1974).

[10] The Reconstruction Finance Corporation was continued by the Roosevelt administration. Its original role of assisting distressed businesses and localities was expanded to include such responsibilities as foreign aid and disaster relief. The RFC maintained an active role until 1954 and was disbanded in 1957. Some economists believe that the RFC concept should be revived to assist declining industries, such as automobiles and steel, and financially strapped cities and states. The most prominent RFC advocate is Felix Rohatyn, economist, investment banker and former director of the Municipal Assistance Corporation, which helped rescue New York City from default in the late 1970s.

CCC employees strung 12,000 miles of telephone line through rural areas

better it is for them during the rest of their lives," Roosevelt said shortly after taking office. "Most Americans want to give something for what they get. That something, which in this case is honest work, is the saving barrier between them and moral disintegration." Roosevelt also hoped to speed economic recovery and end the Depression by stimulating consumer spending, enhancing the nation's capital stock, and creating an atmosphere of action rather than resignation.

The first New Deal program devoted solely to job creation was the Civilian Conservation Corps (CCC). The plan to send thousands of unemployed slum youths into the country to plant trees was a product of Roosevelt's devotion to conservation and to his nostalgic notion that he could reverse the pattern of migration from rural to urban areas. There was opposition to the plan. Conservative Republicans and Southern Democrats warned that deficit spending would prevent the recovery of the private sector, and that the stimulus provided by the program would be tiny compared with an overall business recovery. The plan passed anyway, and within three months, 250,000 men were employed in 1,468 forest and park camps under Army supervision. They were paid $30 a month ($1 per day), $25 of which had to be sent home to their families.

In the nine-year existence of the CCC, over 1.5 million youths were employed in creating 65,511 new acres of wildlife refuge, 199,214 acres of national parkland, and 7,436,321 acres of national forest. The 200 million trees they planted helped prevent the kind of soil erosion that had turned the Great Plains into a "dust bowl" during the Depression. They fought forest fires, strung 12,000 miles of telephone line and built the Skyline Drive through the Shenandoah National Forest in Virginia. The CCC was said to be one of Roosevelt's proudest accomplishments.[11]

The CCC provided jobs for young men, but did not solve the dilemma of adults who were displaced by the economic collapse. Roosevelt wanted a job program that, unlike FERA, served some tangible purpose, and on Nov. 8, 1933, he created the Civil Works Administration (CWA) by taking $400 million out of a $5 billion general-purpose emergency jobs appropriation that Congress had placed at his discretion.

Roosevelt put Harry Hopkins, his relief administrator when he was governor of New York, in charge of CWA. Within two months, about 4 million people were employed on such projects as building or repairing streets, schools and airports; digging sewers; and developing parks and playgrounds. Kansas Governor Alf Landon, who would unsuccessfully challenge Roosevelt for the presidency in 1936, wrote in early 1934 that the CWA "is one of the soundest, most constructive policies of your administration and I cannot urge too strongly its continuance." But critics pointed out alleged circumstances of waste and fraud in the implementation of the program, and decried the cost when Roosevelt went back to the emergency fund for another $533 million. In 1934, Roosevelt ordered CWA shut down.

The Public Works Administration (PWA) was also established in 1933 to coordinate the construction of large public facilities, such as hospitals, schools, dams, bridges and tunnels. The PWA quickly funded a number of socially useful projects, such as the Boulder Dam on the Colorado River and the rebuilding of schools in Los Angeles following an earthquake. The agency, run meticulously by Secretary of the Interior Harold Ickes, was unmarked by scandal. But PWA provided first evi-

---

[11] Another program that aided unemployed youths was the National Youth Administration (1935-43). This program encouraged financially distressed youths to remain in high school or college by providing them with part-time jobs in school libraries and laboratories or on grounds maintenance. The average NYA monthly stipend was $15.

dence of the limited usefulness of large public works programs as counter-recessionary mechanisms.

For one thing, the programs required months or sometimes years of planning. Ickes' tight-fisted control was seen by critics as bureaucratic red tape that further hindered projects. The projects were expensive and, perhaps most damaging of all, were highly capital-intensive, with about 70 percent of expenditures going for materials, less than 30 percent for wages. Many of the projects also required skilled construction workers, and did little for either the unskilled or for unemployed white-collar workers.

In January 1935, Roosevelt sent a message to Congress that contained his intention to replace FERA once and for all with a worthwhile work-relief program. "I am not willing that the vitality of our people be further sapped by the giving of cash, of market baskets, of a few hours of weekly work cutting grass, raking leaves or picking up papers in the public parks," Roosevelt said. He outlined the requirements for a large job-creation program. Jobs must be of some value to the public, with wages larger than the dole, but not so large as to discourage return to the private sector during recovery. Projects should be labor-intensive, self-liquidating (pay for themselves with user fees), short-term and flexible enough that they could be quickly terminated during a recovery, and targeted at high unemployment areas.

WPA's Mixed Record: Boon or Boondoggle

To carry out this program, Roosevelt created the Works Progress Administration (WPA) in May 1935. The PWA hardly went out of business. Between 1933 and 1939, the Public Works Administration was responsible for 70 percent of new school construction, 65 percent of all courthouses, city halls and sewage treatment plants and 62 percent of all hospitals. The Grand Coulee, Bonneville and Fort Peck dams were built by the PWA, as were the Triborough Bridge and the Lincoln and Queens Midtown tunnels in New York City. But the PWA was so permanently eclipsed by the WPA, in both money and publicity, that many people attribute the former's accomplishments to the latter.

The WPA created thousands of programs, most of which were quick to implement, labor-intensive and inexpensive. WPA's construction funding was concentrated on levee building, street and bridge repair, tree planting, swamp drainage, flood cleanup and similar projects. WPA workers also were employed on larger-scale projects, including construction of New York's North Beach (now LaGuardia) Airport.

WPA woodwork training shop

Many teachers, researchers, professors and librarians also were hired by the WPA. Murals and sculptures by WPA artists adorn public buildings across the nation. Unemployed actors, including Orson Welles and John Houseman, were put to work in The Federal Theater, which put on a number of innovative productions until protests over its alleged leftist leanings forced Roosevelt to abolish it in 1938. The hiring of actors and intellectuals was one of the most controversial aspects of WPA, and such projects as a grant for the study of the history of the safety pin resulted in the newly popular epithet "boondoggle" being identified with the entire agency.[12]

The WPA had other problems. For one thing, it was impossible to match every unemployed worker's skills to an available job, resulting in boredom and frustration. On the other hand, means-testing and a regulation that required all WPA workers to be hired from relief rolls rather than the general labor market resulted in an over-proportion of unskilled, aged and infirm workers. Productivity suffered, and many critics accused the WPA of creating "make-work" jobs just to get people off the dole.

The "lazy" WPA worker was as pervasive a stereotype as the "welfare Cadillac" of more recent times. A popular song of the '30s went: "WPA, WPA, Lean on your shovel to pass the time

---

[12] Cowboys of the early American West used to kill time by making "boondoggles," scraps of leather braided together into ropes or belts.

away." A joke of the times told of the WPA worker who fell and broke his hip, because he had been leaning on his shovel so long that termites had eaten through it. Administration officials were angered by the inference. "[The WPA worker] has been ridiculed by thoughtless and cruel people as a loafer, and the fine works he has built or public services he has rendered have been tragically misrepresented as leaf-raking or boondoggling," WPA Deputy Administrator Aubrey Williams said in 1937.

Between 1935 and 1943, WPA employed over 8 million people. The average monthly employment was 2.1 million. The program, which began with a $5 billion appropriation, spent $11 billion before it went out of business, and it created structures and facilities that underpinned the great industrial growth of World War II and the postwar period. Some of its projects are still in use today.

Some contemporary observers credited programs like WPA with forestalling serious social turmoil. "Even if these relief workers never did anything more than dig holes and fill them up again, the WPA avoided major class riots during the Depression and kept this country out of revolution," Edmund Borgia Butler, secretary of the New York City Emergency Relief Bureau, said in 1939. Calling on Congress to extend WPA in 1938, John L. Lewis, president of the United Mine Workers and the Committee for Industrial Organization (CIO), warned of "the greatest threat to democracy, the idleness and misery of our people." And Rep. Usher L. Burdick, R-N.D. (1935-58), said, "Cut down this relief, when it cannot be done without bringing suffering to thousands of our people, and the result will be the best fertilizer communism has yet had."

The New Deal jobs programs may have reduced the magnitude of suffering and the possibility of social unrest, but it must be pointed out that work relief did not end unemployment or the Depression. As late as 1940, there were still 9 million people unemployed, in addition to the 3 million working for the WPA. An illustration of the ineffectiveness of work relief in solving the fundamental problems of the depressed economy occurred in 1938. Roosevelt, who was under pressure to balance the federal budget, cut funds for WPA and other jobs programs. Work relief employment dropped from 3.6 million in fiscal year 1937 to just over 3 million in 1938 — and the economy spun into recession, sending unemployment soaring. By fiscal year 1939, the work rolls had rebounded to 4.1 million, an all-time high.

Employment Policies After the Depression

World War II ended the need for work relief, as the manpower needs of the military and munitions industry sent unemployment plummoting to 1.6 percent. Attempts to use the Employment Act of 1946 to establish a permanent public works program that could be triggered during an economic downturn were thwarted.[13] The boom of the 1950s, which was aided by such federal programs as interstate highway construction and mortgage assistance, made such worries seem unfounded, but a recession that began in late 1960 revived interest in employment programs. President Kennedy proposed legislation in early 1962 that called for a $2 billion permanent fund that could be used to create public works jobs at the first signs of recession.

Like many of Roosevelt's programs, Kennedy's plan would have placed full control of fund distribution in the hands of the president. Congress objected to both the cost of the proposal and the presidential monopoly on the prized public works pork barrel. When the Accelerated Public Works Act finally passed in September, it contained only $900 million for a one-time, immediate public works acceleration program, with Congress controlling the distribution of funds.[14] By the time jobs were created under this law, the recession they were supposed to treat had already ended — a constant complaint about federal public works programs.

In 1965, during the heyday of the Great Society, President Johnson pushed through a pair of programs that came as close to permanent counter-recessionary mechanisms as there have been. The Public Works and Economic Development Act of 1965 created the Economic Development Administration (EDA), which was authorized to provide funds under a formula to states that were disproportionately affected by unemployment. Since its inception, the EDA has provided funds for industrial parks, sewer construction, building reconstruction, and other facilities that could assist economic growth in poor communities. The sister bill, the Appalachian Regional Development Act of 1965, has played a similar role for the high-poverty rural areas of Appalachia.

The recession of 1969-70 resulted in a different strategy by jobs program advocates. Congress passed a bill in December 1970 that would have provided $2 billion through 1974 for a "public service" jobs program to create the kind of non-construction jobs that people identified with the WPA. But President Nixon vetoed the measure, stating, "WPA-type jobs are not the answer for the men and women who have them, for

[13] The Employment Act of 1946, like the later Humphrey-Hawkins Act *(see p. 952),* was a symbolic measure that promised "useful employment opportunities" for all persons "able, willing and seeking work."
[14] See *Congress and the Nation Vol. I,* Congressional Quarterly, 1965, p. 877.

government which is less efficient as a result, or for the taxpayers who must foot the bill." In July 1971, Nixon also vetoed
an "emergency" employment bill that would have appropriated
$2 billion for public works jobs.

Nixon at the time was pushing his revenue-sharing proposal,
which would provide cash directly to cities. Nixon believed that
this was a more effective way of combatting recessions, since
local officials would know better where the money was needed
most. However, in July 1971, he relented under congressional
pressure, signing the Public Service Employment Act, providing
$2.25 billion for public service jobs, with expenditures to be
triggered when unemployment reached 4.5 percent for three
consecutive months. Then, in August 1971, Nixon signed a bill
that included emergency public works employment provisions
similar to those he had earlier vetoed. In retrospect, critics again
complained that the public works process was so slow that the
"emergency" jobs were not created until the end of the
recession.[15]

---

*"WPA-type jobs are not the answer for
the men and women who have them, for the
government which is less efficient as a result, or for the taxpayers who must foot the
bill."*

President Nixon (1970)

The jobs issue returned in 1974-75 when a recession sent
unemployment to 9.0 percent, a post-Depression record at the
time. In February 1976, the Senate sustained President Ford's
veto of a $6.1 billion public works bill. But in July, a mea-
sure that included $2 billion for public works jobs was passed
over Ford's veto.[16] The Local Public Works (LPW) program vastly expanded the role of the EDA, which adminis-
tered the program. President Carter added another $4 billion in
1977.

There is disagreement over the number of jobs created by the
Local Public Works program. An EDA study said that LPW had
created the equivalent of 96,000 year-long jobs on-site, 66,000
jobs with project suppliers and 200,000 from the economic
stimulus of the program, for a total of 350,000 jobs. However, a

---

[15] See *CQ 1971 Almanac*, pp. 181-94.
[16] See *CQ 1976 Almanac*, pp. 68-75.

1979 study by the Office of Management and Budget determined that only 30,000 jobs had actually been created.[17] The main problem in determining the number of new jobs created was the issue of "job substitution." Critics said that state and local governments used federal money to pay workers who would normally have been on their payrolls. Job substitution saves authorities money, but reduces the net impact of job creation programs. EDA assumed little substitution; OMB suggested substitution rates as high as 65 percent.

Two other issues that traditionally caused problems for public works projects resurfaced during the LPW program. For one thing, the projects were capital-intensive. According to the OMB study, only 22 percent of expenditures went for wages, and most of that went to skilled workers who had not been previously unemployed. In addition, spending on the program peaked in 1978, after the economy had begun to recover. According to Rep. William Clinger, R-Pa., who was associated with the program, "We still have, to this day, money being expended under the Local Public Works program."

During the same time that LPW was being implemented, the public service employment (PSE) program, which had been absorbed by the Comprehensive Employment and Training Administration (CETA) when it was created in 1973, was also being accelerated. In 1977, President Carter added 400,000 PSE jobs for a total of 750,000. The public service program was quickly implemented, but the program was beset by problems. Pressed by the Ford and Carter administrations to fulfill hiring quotas, local officials created numerous paper-shuffling and leaf-raking jobs that critics characterized as "make-work." Lack of tight federal supervision and regulations led to newspaper exposés of local instances of nepotism, favoritism and other kinds of fraud. Many jobs went to middle-class people instead of the hard-core, low-income unemployed for whom they were intended. Job substitution was rampant; in the early stages of the program buildup, more than two-thirds of CETA employees were moved from local or state to federal payrolls. The low unemployment trigger rate resulted in PSE employment peaking during an economic recovery, fueling inflation.

Changes in CETA's authorization in 1978 tightened standards, aiming job creation more directly at low-income unemployed and cracking down on waste, fraud and substitution. But the program never outlived the stigma it had acquired. Carter reduced CETA/PSE employment to 325,000 by the time he left office. In 1981, Reagan proposed elimination of PSE as

[17] See Harrison Donnelly, "Creating Jobs: It's Not As Easy As It Seems," *Congressional Quarterly Weekly Report*, Nov. 20, 1982, pp. 2871-74.

part of his federal austerity program, and Congress went along. By September 1981, there were no more federal public service jobs.

Current Debate in Congress

THE CURRENT debate in Congress over job-creating legislation has a familiar ring to it. In interviews with a number of experts on the subject, the arguments made both for and against the proposals were almost the same as the ones made a half-century ago about the New Deal programs. Much of the debate has centered on the "timelag" issue — the tendency of public works programs to take months or years to get geared up, providing little immediate relief for the unemployed nor stimulus for the economy.

One observer who raised the timelag issue spoke from experience. Dr. Abel Wolman, a 90-year-old professor of engineering at The Johns Hopkins University in Baltimore, was a regional administrator for the PWA and later the WPA in the 1930s. "You can't just telephone the contractors and say, 'Now, go ahead and build such or such a bridge or rebuild it or build a new water system and so on and so on,'" Wolman said, adding, "By the time you get your PWA enactments, and get into action, you are at the tail end of the recession and hopefully on the upswing."

Even some supporters of work relief agree that public works employment is not a perfect avenue for job creation. James K. Galbraith, executive director of the congressional Joint Economic Committee said, "You don't build a Hoover Dam in order to offset a six-month recession ... there's a danger that if you get too much into the highway programs as an antidote to unemployment, you will get out of sync with the business cycle."

Some observers contend that the timelag issue is irrelevant. Dr. Amitai Etzioni believes that the main criterion for any job-creation project should be whether it aids in the reindustrialization of America. "If you have something that would cost extra and takes even longer, but both reduces unemployment and [creates] something of real value, I would prefer that under the present circumstances," Etzioni said.

Critics also charge that public works programs do not really create a lot of jobs, and may actually result in a short-term loss of jobs because of the tendency of local and state governments to defer their own projects while waiting for federal government action. Roger Vaughan, who worked for two years as a public works adviser to New York Gov. Hugh L. Carey, said that when the Local Public Works program was passed in 1976 *(see p. 125)*, state and local governments cut back on their capital spending. "They were not going to commit their own funds if there was a chance that Washington was going to come in and pay 100 percent of their project costs," Vaughan said. Federal agencies have attempted to create some kind of "maintenance of effort" requirements for state and local governments, but they are difficult to enforce. "How do you measure what a state or local government would have spent in the absence of the program?" Vaughan asked.

Even during the days of the Public Works Administration *(see p. 120)*, critics said that public works programs were not labor-intensive enough to be good job-creating mechanisms. Today's skeptics note that construction work is even more machine-oriented today than 50 years ago. "Rehabilitating an aging bridge is not achieved by passing out overalls and paint to those in line for unemployment benefits and pointing them toward the crumbling edifice," Vaughan said. The repairs now going on at the Woodrow Wilson Bridge near Washington, D.C., provide a good example. In order to keep the bridge open to commuter traffic, the bridge is being repaired at night, using a new, tractor-driven, buzz saw-like machine to cut out large rectangles of bridge surface, which are then removed by crane and replaced by blocks of quick-drying concrete. Although this process is likely to save time and money, it also replaces a number of semiskilled laborers using jackhammers or picks with one skilled machine operator behind the wheel of the saw.

The most widely used alternative to public works for creating jobs is public service employment. Instead of waiting around for construction projects to get started, people are quickly hired for "service" jobs, such as working in day-care centers, providing homemaker services for the elderly or doing clerical work in government offices. Despite the advantages of easy implementation and low cost as compared to public works projects, public service employment is often stigmatized as "dead-end" and "make-work." Critics say that public service jobs rarely provide opportunities for permanent employment or advancement and do not teach workers skills that are marketable in the private sector. But advocates of public service employment say the "make-work" charge is unfair. "What we are talking about are essential services that states and localities are offering to citizens," said Sar Levitan, director of the National Council on Employment Policy in Washington, D.C.

Supporters of public service employment also claim that programs that immediately create jobs can give a much needed lift to American morale, which could have important consequences for economic recovery. "You would have a tremendous change in the perception of the way our economy's going," said James Galbraith. "People who were afraid of losing their jobs would become more confident of their prospects, they'd be more willing to go to their banks to take out a loan for a car or a house, banks would be more willing to lend to them, and it's this rounding-the-corner that this program would contribute to."

Alternatives to Traditional Job Creation

While discussion of job creation in the lame-duck session concentrated on the traditional work-relief programs, other legislative proposals also were being pushed as "job-creation" or "job-preservation" measures. Supporters credited themselves with developing imaginative alternatives to the employment problem. Cynics countered with charges of opportunism. "The unfortunate aspect is that every bill that's going to be introduced is going to have [the word] 'jobs' attached to it," said Sen. Dan Quayle, R-Ind. "So we're going to have to be a little bit selective as we try . . . to see which job stimuli and incentives are really going to work."

Last March, President Reagan presented his "enterprise zones" plan to Congress. The proposal called for granting significant tax and regulatory incentives for businesses to move into deteriorating low-income neighborhoods that have been designated as "enterprise zones" by the secretary of housing and urban development. The administration claimed that the program would create thousands of jobs in high-unemployment inner-city areas, and it received support from mayors and many urban public-interest groups. But other economists and labor union officials said that the program would result not in job-creation, but in job-shifting, with already existing businesses moving into enterprise zones just for the tax breaks. They also cited studies that show that tax breaks are ineffective as incentives for businesses to move into high-risk areas. Although Reagan called for action on enterprise zones during the lame-duck session, the plan went nowhere and will have to be reintroduced in the 98th Congress.[18]

The unions involved in industries that have been hard hit by imports, such as automobiles and steel, backed a bill introduced by Rep. Richard L. Ottinger, D-N.Y., that called for imported goods to utilize a certain percentage of "domestic content," meaning American parts and labor. The proposal used a sliding

---

[18] For background on the enterprise zones concept, see "The Charity Squeeze," *E.R.R.*, 1982 Vol. II, p. 898, and "Reagan and the Cities," *E.R.R.*, 1982 Vol. II, pp. 529-548.

scale; for example, the more cars that a Japanese automaker sought to sell in the United States, the higher the amount of "domestic content" that would have to go into it. The United Auto Workers of America (UAW) claimed the domestic content rule would result in 800,000 auto jobs created or saved. But opponents said that such protectionist measures would result in retaliation by our trading partners, resulting in thousands of lost jobs in other industries. Also, if foreign manufacturers had to pay higher costs for materials and labor, they might raise the price of the finished product, which would reduce sales and, eventually, employment. *The New York Times*, in a Dec. 14 editorial, referred to the domestic content proposal as "The Job-Killer Bill." On Dec. 15, the House passed a watered-down domestic content bill that contained an amendment that said that the bill could not violate any existing treaty or trade agreement. The Senate did not vote on the bill, however, killing it for the 97th Congress.

Another proposal that was given a jobs context was an immigration bill sponsored by Sen. Alan K. Simpson, R-Wyo., and Rep. Romano L. Mazzoli, D-Ky. The bill would have granted amnesty to many of the illegal aliens currently in the United States, but would have put stricter limits on future immigration. Although many of the jobs taken by illegal aliens, such as harsh farm labor, are rejected by most Americans, supporters of the legislation said that it would preserve as many as 100,000 jobs in the service and manufacturing industries. The bill stalled in the 97th Congress, and will have to be reintroduced next year.

There also was some support in the lame-duck session for speeding up the provisions of the Job Training Partnership Act (JTPA) of 1982. This law, budgeted for $3.9 billion, replaced the expiring CETA program. Like its predecessor, JTPA is targeted at unskilled, poor and minority workers. The new program will place more emphasis on private sector involvement and planning in training than did CETA, which gave most of the responsibility to local and county governments. Unlike CETA, there is no public service employment program in JTPA. But it does have a program to retrain "dislocated workers," those who have lost their jobs because of the decline of industries or the growth of high technology, such as computers or robots.[19] It was this provision, which was not supposed to go into effect until Oct. 1, 1983, that legislators succeeded in getting accelerated. With the efforts of Sen. Quayle, one of the cosponsors of the original legislation, $25 million for the "displaced worker" program was included in the continuing resolu-

---

[19] See "The Computer Age," *E.R.R.*, 1981 Vol. I, pp. 107-128, and "The Robot Revolution," *E.R.R.*, 1982 Vol. I, pp. 345-364.

tion passed by Congress Dec. 20. But since the duration of training programs will range between six weeks and 18 months, job training is likely to have little immediate effect on high unemployment.

Agreement on Need for Economic Recovery

There is one thing on which virtually all interested individuals agree: the unemployment problem will not really be solved until there is a strong general economic recovery. There is much disagreement, though, on how to achieve this. Most economists believe that a further decline in interest rates will be needed before the economy can recover. But there is a great deal of contention over how to go about that. Some legislators would like to see Congress maintain oversight of the Federal Reserve Board's rate-setting functions, or even set limits on interest rates. But many economists fear that this would result in political interference with economic policy which the non-partisan, objective Federal Reserve Board was created to produce. They add that the best way to reduce interest rates is to reduce the enormous federal deficit, projected for fiscal year 1983 at $150 billion to $200 billion.

But again, there is a great deal of conflict over how to reduce the federal deficit. President Reagan has been pursuing a policy of reducing federal spending for domestic programs. Other conservatives say that spending on "entitlement" programs, such as Social Security and government pensions, must be brought under control.[20] But critics of the administration blame the deficits on the big increase in defense spending pushed through Congress by President Reagan. Others say that the three-year, 25 percent tax cut passed in 1981 was excessive and too beneficial to business and upper-income individuals. They call for the closing of loopholes for business, and the elimination or limitation on tax cuts to those with earnings above $50,000.

Despite the high interest rates, the deficit and other serious problems, the administration continues to insist that recovery has begun, or will begin shortly. The administration has been making those claims since the recession started, however, and the results of November's elections were an indication that many Americans were unimpressed. If unemployment lingers at double-digit levels, public dissatisfaction will intensify pressure for jobs programs, and the new, more Democratic Congress might decide to follow the advice of Franklin Roosevelt, who told his New Dealers: "Take a method and try it. If it fails, admit it frankly and try another. But above all, try something."

---

[20] See "Social Security Options," *E.R.R.*, 1982 Vol. II, pp. 929-948.

Selected Bibliography

Books

Armstrong, Ellis L. (ed.), *History of Public Works in the United States, 1776-1976,* American Public Works Association, 1976.

Asbell, Bernard, *The F.D.R. Memoirs,* Doubleday, 1973.

Choate, Pat and Susan Walter, *America in Ruins: Beyond the Public Works Pork Barrel,* Council of State Planning Agencies, 1981.

Etzioni, Amitai, *An Immodest Agenda: Rebuilding America Before the 21st Century,* McGraw Hill, 1982.

Freidel, Frank, *Franklin D. Roosevelt: Launching the New Deal,* Little, Brown and Company, 1973.

Howard, Donald S., *The WPA and Federal Relief Policy,* Russell Sage Foundation, 1943.

Manchester, William, *The Glory and the Dream,* Bantam, 1974.

Nathan, Richard P. et al., *Public Service Employment: A Field Evaluation,* The Brookings Institution, 1981.

Schlesinger, Arthur M. Jr., *The Age of Roosevelt: The Politics of Upheaval,* Houghton Mifflin, 1960.

Articles

Anderson, Harry et al., "Jobs: Putting America Back to Work," *Newsweek,* Oct. 18, 1982.

Beck, Melinda et al., "The Decaying of America," *Newsweek,* Aug. 2, 1982.

"Controversy Over the CETA Program: Pro and Con," *Congressional Digest,* April 1981.

Friedrich, Otto, "F.D.R.'s Disputed Legacy," *Time,* Feb. 1, 1982.

"Hard Times," *The New Republic,* Aug. 9, 1982.

Levitan, Sar and Clifford M. Johnson, "The Politics of Unemployment," *The New Republic,* Sept. 20 and 27, 1982.

Noah, Timothy, "Bring Back the WPA," *The Washington Monthly,* September 1982.

Richardson, David B., "To Rebuild America — $2.5 Trillion Job," *U.S. News & World Report,* Sept. 27, 1982.

Tyler, Gus, "Those New Deal Years (1933-1938)," *The New Leader,* Dec. 28, 1981.

Reports and Studies

Editorial Research Reports: "The Charity Squeeze," 1982 Vol. II, p. 893; "The Homeless: Growing National Problem," 1982 Vol. II, p. 793; "America's Employment Outlook," 1982 Vol. I, p. 385; "Reaganomics on Trial," 1982 Vol. I, p. 1.

The National Alliance of Business, "Summary and Explanation of the Job Training Partnership Act of 1982," Oct. 6, 1982.

Cover illustration by Staff Artist Robert Redding.

THE ROBOT REVOLUTION

by

Jean Rosenblatt

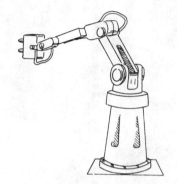

May 14
1982

THE ROBOT REVOLUTION

THEY don't call in sick, go on strike or take long lunch breaks. They can work efficiently for indefinite periods and never complain about salaries, demanding bosses or poor working conditions. "They" are industrial robots and experts see them as a way to boost this country's lagging productivity.[1] Industrial robots do hazardous, difficult and monotonous jobs that most humans would prefer not to do and they do them more reliably and, in some cases, more cheaply. Analysts estimate that robots now in use in American factories have helped boost production by 10-90 percent.

It took the first American robot manufacturer 14 years to show a profit[2] and other companies' earnings from robots are only now beginning to materialize. But the portion of corporate revenues from robots is growing significantly and interest in robotics is at an all-time high. By 1974 there were enough U.S. robot manufacturers to form a trade association, the Robot Institute of America (RIA), in Dearborn, Mich. Membership has grown to over 180 companies and corporations that supply or use industrial robots. Copies of RIA's magazine, *Robotics Today*, are so much in demand that non-subscriber copies sell out soon after printing, and attendance at trade shows has more than doubled in the last two years. The Robots VI conference, held in Detroit in March 1982, was so packed, observers noted, that the exhibition area had to be closed off to visitors for hours at a time.[3]

Many companies' robot divisions are growing at a faster rate than the rest of the organization, and new companies are entering the field just as quickly. According to Laura Conigliaro, a financial analyst with the New York investment firm Bache Halsey Stuart Shields Inc., two years ago it was difficult for small firms just starting out in robotics to attract adequate financial backing. Now, she says, venture capital firms are seeking out robot-makers rather than the other way around.

[1] Productivity is broadly defined as output per man hour. From the end of World War II through the mid-1960s, U.S. productivity increased by an average of 3.4 percent a year, but the rate of increase began declining in the 1970s. In 1981 U.S. productivity rose by only .9 percent.

[2] Unimation Inc., in Danbury, Conn., built the first U.S. industrial robot installation in 1961. The company produces about 41 percent of this country's robots.

[3] Over 27,000 people visited the exhibits at the Robot VI conference. The previous year only 6,000 people saw the exhibits. The shows are cosponsored by RIA and Robotics International, a division of the Society of Manufacturing Engineers in Dearborn, Mich.

"We're going to end up producing much of our national wealth without human interference," said Joseph Engelberger, founder and president of Unimation Inc., the nation's oldest and largest robot manufacturer. "Over the next 50 years, it will be as profound a change as the Industrial Revolution." [4] Experts predict that new developments in robotics in this decade will result in even greater productivity across a widening range of applications. "Advances are being made hourly," said George Brosseau, a project manager with the National Science Foundation in Washington, D.C. "Within the next three years, robot technology will take off like a shot."

Use of Industrial Robots in Factories

Karel Capek, the Czech playwright, novelist and essayist, wrote a play in 1921 called *R.U.R.* (Rossum's Universal Robots). Capek's satirical drama introduced the word "robot" into the English language. The playwright coined the word, which means forced labor, to describe the machines in his play that resembled people, but worked twice as hard. Until relatively recently most people pictured robots the way Capek imagined them: machinelike human look-alikes with arms and legs and personalities on the order of Artoo Deetoo in the 1977 movie *Star Wars*.

In fact, the industrial robots in today's factories look nothing like humans. They are machines with a guiding brain — a computer — and one or more mechanical arms with grippers for hands. The computer is plugged into an electrical outlet and cables transmit instructions from the computer to a control system that operates the gripper. Hydraulic pressure activates robots for heavy work.

As defined by the Robot Institute of America, a robot is "a reprogrammable multi-functional manipulator designed to move material, parts, tools, or specialized devices, through variable programmed motions for the performance of a variety of tasks." The fact that robots are reprogrammable and can perform a variety of tasks is the key to their importance. Factories have been using automated machines, such as bottle cappers, for years in mass production, but these machines can do only one task at a time. New tasks require new machines or extensive retooling of old ones, both of which are expensive and time-consuming. But robots can be reprogrammed at any time, often in a few minutes, to either switch or expand their work routines.

What allow robots to be reprogrammable are microprocessors — tiny silicon wafers about half the size of a fingernail, which

---

[4] Quoted by Stephen Solomon in "Miracle Workers," *Science Digest*, December 1981, p. 38.

Industrial robots are widely used in the automobile industry.

contain the resistors, transistors and diodes that are the brains of today's computers.[5] The steady and rapid decrease in the cost of microprocessors and related computer technology, along with skyrocketing labor costs, are responsible for the growing popularity of industrial robots.

Most of the 4,000 or so robots used in U.S. factories today work in the automobile industry, though electrical firms have also become big users. Robots do jobs like die casting, spray painting, forging, spot and arc welding, machine loading and unloading, and various types of assembling. Experts predict that by 1990 more than a third of factory assembly work will be done by robots, compared to about 5-10 percent today *(see box, p. 151)*. One system being developed can assemble a 17-piece automobile alternator in less than three minutes. Unimation already makes an assembly robot called PUMA — an acronym for "programmable universal machine for assembly" — which can pick up parts and pass them along, spray paint, weld, load and unload parts from furnaces, stamping presses and conveyors — all without supervision.

One factor making robots more feasible for assembly work is off-line programming, which increases robots' flexibility. The customary way of teaching a robot is to put it in a "learn mode" and then lead it by hand through the task it has to do. When the robot is put in an operating mode it will do exactly what it has been taught. But with off-line programming a technician can sit down at a central computer console and punch in the coordinates of a job without having literally to hold the robot's hand.

---

[5] See "The Computer Age," *E.R.R.*, 1981 Vol. I, pp. 107-128.

One of the obstacles in the development of off-line programming has been the need for a high-level computer language that can talk in geometric terms. "Some of these languages exist already, but we need better ones," George Brosseau told Editorial Research Reports. "We also need them to be standardized, so that if somebody develops a high-level control language for one robot system it can be translated into another, to avoid having to go through the whole process all over again."

Gains in Intelligence, Vision and Touch

One of the chief drawbacks of most robots is that they can do their jobs only if things are exactly where they have been programmed to find them. For example, a robot cannot tell whether a car body is in the right place on an assembly line and if not move it. To deal with such limitations, roboticists are developing senses for robots and the ability to integrate what they see and can touch with even more sophisticated electronic logic, thus enabling robots to make limited decisions.

Such intelligence — the ability to perceive and appropriately respond to changes in the environment — will allow robots to do complex assembly work without expensive human or automated supervision. "Over the next 10 years, sensors will enlarge by an order of magnitude the number of places where you can put robots in a factory," said Charles Rosen, chief scientist at the Machine Intelligence Corp. in Palo Alto, Calif.[6]

Robot vision essentially is the technique of training television or other optical receptors (such as lasers) on an object or group of objects and using that information to direct the robot's activities *(see box, p. 139)*. The television camera scans the object and transmits to a computer the thousands of dots that form the television image. The computer transforms these dots into binary code, consisting of *one,* representing the black dots, and *zero,* representing the white dots. "Now the computer is ready to 'see' the picture and make sense of it," Stephen Solomon wrote in the December 1981 issue of *Science Digest.* "Where the zeros in the picture give way to ones, the computer detects the silhouette of the object and its orientation. Instantly it calculates many of its features — an area, perimeter, diameter, and so on — and compares them with the measurement of various objects that have been programmed into its memory. When the computer discovers a similar set of parameters, it 'knows' what it is looking at." The computer then directs the robot's fingers to the edges of the object so it can pick it up.

This crude form of vision is not too useful in factories now because it requires high-contrast lighting between objects and

---

[6] Quoted by Stephen Solomon, *op. cit.,* p. 42.

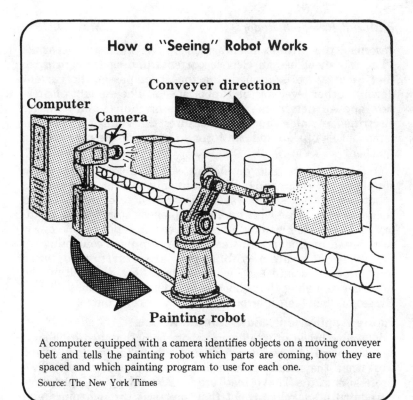

How a "Seeing" Robot Works

Conveyer direction

Computer

Camera

Painting robot

A computer equipped with a camera identifies objects on a moving conveyer belt and tells the painting robot which parts are coming, how they are spaced and which painting program to use for each one.

Source: The New York Times

their backgrounds; objects piled in a bin or moving down an assembly line rarely provide the required contrasts. But eventually, robots may be able to see even better than humans do. An electronic eye is not bound by biological limitations, and scientists could make it sensitive to infrared and ultraviolet light, which the human eye cannot perceive.

Some companies are already making and using seeing robots. International Business Machines (IBM) is test-marketing an advanced system called RS 1, designed for precision automatic assembly work. It combines sophisticated tactile and optical sensing abilities with the ability to move its arm in six directions. General Motors has developed a system called Consight, which enables a robot with an electronic camera to look at scattered parts on a conveyer belt, pick them up and move them in a specific sequence to a different work area.

Robots are also getting a rudimentary sense of touch. They can tell when a part in its gripper does not feel right and alert a human supervisor, and they can jiggle a part until it fits into place by using sensors that follow the contour of the object being worked on. Researchers at the Massachusetts Institute of Technology (MIT) have developed an artificial skin for robots consisting of sheets of rubber laced with wire. Blake M. Cornish described the process in an article in *The Futurist* magazine: "The top sheet has an electric current running through it, so that as pressure is applied, the top sheet passes the current down to other levels of the rubber sheets. The amount of pressure applied determines which sheets of rubber and wire are electrified. A microprocessor measures the voltage of the different levels of skin and can form an image of the object being touched." [7]

Researchers are also developing robots able to respond to simple voice commands. With microphones for eardrums, a robot can convert sound waves into sequences of numbers and then compare those with number sequences stored in its memory to determine meaning. Another trend in robot technology is distributed intelligence. Instead of one computer controlling an entire robot system, roboticists are starting to build microprocessors into each working part. "By distributing the intelligence among the robot's components," explained George Brosseau, "you can improve the way you can control it."

Future Applications and Domestic Robots

The new breed of intelligent robots being hatched in laboratories around the world will enable robots to do more varied work than the strictly industrial tasks they perform now. Two professors at the Tokyo Institute of Technology in Japan have developed a snakelike robot that can pass through pipes and other narrow openings to inspect and do repair work in places inaccessible to people. Unimation is designing a robot that can pluck chickens and Australian roboticists are developing robots to shear sheep.

James Albus, head of the robot division of the National Bureau of Standards in Gaithersburg, Md., predicts that during the 1990s robots will be doing construction work, such as carrying materials, lifting and positioning panels, cutting boards to size and laying bricks. Robots may also find work in mining and ocean and space exploration. By the turn of the century, Albus claims, there may be completely automated factories.

While industry will continue to be the largest market for robots, some of the most interesting developments are taking place in the medical field. Professor Hiroyasu Funakubo of Japan's Medical Precision Engineering Institute has developed a robot arm almost as flexible as a human one. These arms have been mounted in pairs on a bedside table and linked to a cart that shuttles back and forth between a storage cart and a patient's bed. The system can be activated by a keyboard, voice commands or even by whistles and gasps, for patients unable to speak.

[7] Blake M. Cornish, "The Smart Machines of Tomorrow," *The Futurist*, August 1981, p. 12.

The most advanced robot of all may be a 25-fingered breast-cancer detector being developed at Tokyo's Waseda University. Each of the fingers is equipped with a gauge hooked to a computer. As the fingers examine the breast, the computer draws a picture of the location of any lumps. Breast inspection by a robot can reduce from 200 to less than 30 the number of X-ray pictures needed to make a diagnosis.

If robots can help the economy and aid quadriplegics, can they also take out the garbage? The answer is "yes." Last Christmas Neiman-Marcus offered a $15,000 robot that could open doors, walk the dog, take out the garbage, water plants and sweep floors. So far the department store has sold only two — one to a Japanese electrical firm and the other to a Saudi Arabian. *Playboy* publisher Hugh Hefner owns a $20,000 robot that can serve drinks; it was built at Android Amusement Corp. in Monrovia, Calif.[8] Some large firms like General Electric are investigating home robots and Unimation has plans for a robot named Isaac — after science fiction writer Isaac Asimov — that will be able, among other things, to serve coffee and Danish to guests and wash the dishes afterward.

At this point it is still a lot cheaper to buy a vacuum cleaner than a robot that vacuums, but Hans Moravec, a roboticist with Carnegie-Mellon University in Pittsburgh, predicts that "home-robot technology and price will come together for the consumer in another 10 to 20 years."[9] Experts see home robots as being more entertainment centers and personal computers than household servants. But according to Gene Baley, president of Android Amusement Corp., varied "uses will be found for robots the same way they were found for airplanes."[10]

U.S.-Japanese Competition

LAST DECEMBER the investment firm Bache Halsey Stuart Shields mailed a questionnaire to selected robot vendors and users to assess trends in the robot industry. In the answers the single most-mentioned word, in contexts ranging from pricing to technology, was "Japan." Japan is the world leader in robot production and sales, producing 57 percent of the world's robots and using about three times as many robots as the United States.[11]

---

[8] These devices are more robot toys than robots, since they are manipulated by remote control. They will not graduate to robothood until they can perform chores without radio commands.

[9] Quoted in *The Christian Science Monitor*, March 31, 1982.

[10] Quoted in *The New York Times*, March 4, 1982.

[11] The United States sells 24 percent of the world's robots and Europe 19 percent. Estimates of how many robots American industry uses vary between 4,000 and 5,000; Japan has about 14,000 robots.

It was the United States, not Japan, that pioneered the building of robots in the early 1960s. U.S. technology is still thought to be the most advanced, particularly in the computer software that runs the so-called smart robots. But Japan clearly leads the United States in production and applications.

Japanese robot manufacturers tend to be bigger than their U.S. counterparts. Hitachi, for example, has 500 people working on robots, while Unimation, the U.S. leader, has only 90 robot engineers. Robotics expert Paul Aron[12] predicts that by 1985 Japan will have five times as many robots as the United States and that by then Japan will be producing about 32,000 robots a year *(see box, p. 145)*.

Like their U.S. counterparts, Japanese robot-makers have been working on advanced models with vision or tactile-sensing systems to do assembly work. By 1985 Hitachi hopes to use robots for 60 percent of its assembly operations. Last year Fujitsu Fanuc Ltd., whose president is known in Japan as the Emperor of Robots, opened a plant in which robots actually reproduce themselves — about 100 a month — though humans are still needed for the final assembly. The plant can operate around the clock with only 100 workers, one-fifth the number needed for a normal plant of the same size.

Factors Contributing to Japan's Successes

Japan's successful robot industry is partly a result of its labor practices. Employees in large Japanese corporations are guaranteed lifetime employment until age 55 or 60 and receive regular bonuses based on the company's profits. Since employees tend to identify with a company rather than a skill and are often moved from one job to another, they do not generally fear losing their jobs because of automation. They also know their bonuses will grow with the profits robots produce. In addition, companies provide retraining for workers displaced by robots, while few U.S. companies have assumed that responsibility.

The Japanese government has consistently provided incentives to the robot industry in the form of tax write-offs and subsidized loans. It also pressured 24 manufacturers and 10 insurance companies to form Japan Robot Lease, which leases welding robots to small companies for $90 a month. Not only can a round-the-clock robot provide $1,200 worth of work for $90, but employers can swap for improved versions when they become available without tying up their money in an outright purchase. The biggest government move so far is a Ministry of International Trade and Industry (MITI) program scheduled to

---

[12] Aron is executive vice president of Daiwa Securities America Inc., the U.S. subsidiary of a Japanese investment company.

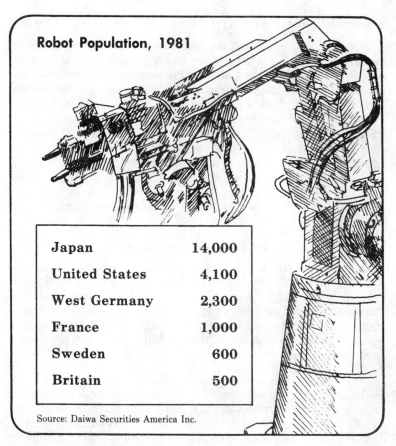

Robot Population, 1981

Japan	14,000
United States	4,100
West Germany	2,300
France	1,000
Sweden	600
Britain	500

Source: Daiwa Securities America Inc.

start in 1983 that will provide $150 million over seven years to push the development of intelligent robots.

Perhaps the most crucial element contributing to Japan's exploding robot industry is rooted in the Japanese psyche. While most Americans are unenthusiastic about the prospect of robots in their lives, the Japanese are fascinated by them and react to them in an intensely personal way. "We give them names," said Seiichiro Akiyama, a Tokyo psychologist. "We want to stroke them. We respond to them not as machines but as close-to-human beings." A common view among psychologists is that Buddhism has played an important role in the Japanese attitude. Osamu Tezuka, a cartoonist who uses robots as a theme in his work, explained: "Unlike Christian Occidentals, Japanese don't make a distinction between man, the superior creature, and the world about him. Everything is fused together, and we accept robots easily along with the wide world about us.... We have none of the doubting attitude toward robots, as pseudohumans, that you find in the West." [13]

[13] Akiyama and Tezuka were both quoted by Henry Scott Stokes in "Japan's Love Affair with the Robot," *The New York Times Magazine,* Jan. 10, 1982, pp. 26, 75.

But there are signs that Japan's love affair with robots may be faltering. This spring, under heavy pressure from Japan's biggest labor unions, the Labor Ministry began a two-year study of robots' impact on Japanese workers. Several unions, fearing loss of jobs to robots within the next five to 10 years despite Japan's lifetime employment system, have begun studies of their own. One cause for alarm is that companies that once transferred displaced workers within factories are starting to transfer them to other factories and even other cities. Although robots have not directly affected Japan's unemployment rate of 2.3 percent, some industry leaders privately admit they are slowly running out of jobs for an increasing number of workers.[14]

Big-Name Companies Entering the Market

In the years ahead, Japan's robot industry is likely to face increased competition from the United States. According to Naohide Kumagai, an executive with Tokyo's Kawasaki Heavy Industries, the Japanese realize that if Americans overcome their reluctance to use more robots and "decide to go ahead with robotization in earnest, they would easily overtake Japanese competition."[15]

Japanese robot exports have more than doubled since 1977, to $9.2 million. But exploding U.S. demand, superior Western technology in areas like software and the difficulty of servicing robots overseas could limit future growth.[16] "It's impossible for Japanese manufacturers to take over the world," said Yasuhiro Komori, general manager of the Japan Industrial Robot Association, but they still think "they are the proper parents to bring the robot baby."[17]

While U.S. industry is not happy with being a far second to Japan, it credits the Japanese with focusing world attention on robots and for broadening their applications. Industry leaders also see competition with the Japanese as positive because it has spurred U.S. vendors to increase their technological research. Although the U.S. robot industry caught on slower than Japan's, it is healthy and growing steadily. Sales have more than doubled within the last two years and are expected to reach $540 million by 1985 *(see box, p. 146)*, increasing at an average

---

[14] See "The Robot Invasion Begins to Worry Labor," *Business Week*, March 29, 1982.
[15] Quoted in "The Robots are Coming and Japan Leads the Way," *U.S. News & World Report*, Jan. 18, 1982, p. 47.
[16] Japan exports only 3 percent of its robot production, but by 1985 industry leaders expect exports to rise to 15 percent. U.S. exports have fluctuated over the last few years, reaching 15-18 percent in 1980. But according to Laura Conigliaro, Japanese and U.S. export figures are not comparable because the Japanese export "a much smaller piece of a much bigger pie."
[17] Quoted in "The Push for Dominance in Robotics Gains Momentum," *Business Week*, Dec. 14, 1981, pp. 108-109.

U.S. and Japanese Robot Production

	Units		Value (in millions of dollars)	
	U.S.	Japan	U.S.	Japan
1980	1,269	3,200	$ 100.5	$ 180
1985	5,195	31,900	441.2	2,150
1990	21,575	57,450	1,884.0	4,450

Source: Daiwa Securities America Inc.

rate of 25-35 percent annually for the rest of this decade.[18]

In just two years the number of U.S. companies selling robots has tripled to more than 50. The most significant trend has been the entry into the industry of such giants as IBM, the world's largest computer company, Westinghouse Electric Corp., Bendix Corp. and General Motors. Their participation should increase robot use in the United States and help make U.S. firms more effective competitors internationally. But to the dismay of some of the smaller U.S. robot manufacturers, many of the big-name corporations are buying robot technology from the Japanese and Europeans.

IBM made its debut into the market this year with a low-cost robot manufactured by Sankyo Seiki of Japan. General Electric announced in March a licensing agreement allowing it to produce and improve on robots by Volkswagen, Europe's largest robot manufacturer, and it has concluded similar deals with Japan's Hitachi and Italy's Digital Electronic Automation. Westinghouse will market welding robots built by two Japanese companies, and General Motors has agreed to a joint venture with Japan's Fujitsu Fanuc Ltd. to design, build and market robots in the United States; GM will buy most of the robots for its own plants. The new company, to be equally owned, will be based in southeast Michigan and will initially sell robots built in existing Japanese facilities.

Buying foreign robot technology allows companies to make a fast entry into the market, since "developing a complete robot is not done overnight," explained Jules A. Mirabal, general manager of GE's automation systems division. In the long run, however, American firms plan to develop and market their own technology. Texas Instruments and Bendix are doing so now, and some analysts think IBM only adopted a Japanese-built

[18] See Laura Conigliaro, "Bullish Days in the Robot Business," *Robotics Age*, September/October 1981.

The U.S. Robot Business

	Sales Revenues (millions of dollars)	Units Sold
1979	$ 60	1,000
1980	100	1,450
1981	155	2,100
1982	215*	3,100*
1983	280*	4,100*
1984	395*	5,900*
1985	540*	8,100*

* Estimates

Source: Bache Halsey Stuart Shields Inc.

robot after realizing it would not be able to produce its own until 1983. Industry analysts also predict that within the next few years U.S. vendors will be setting up robotics operations abroad and that more licensing agreements will flow from this country to foreign companies instead of the other way around.

Increased Competition; Recession's Impact

Increased competition in the robot industry could lead to lower prices. Last year Asea Inc., a U.S. subsidiary of the large Swedish manufacturer of the same name and the fourth largest U.S. robot manufacturer, cut its prices by 20 percent. The effects of increased competition are already being felt by the U.S. industry's two leaders, Unimation and Cincinnati Milacron, which until last year together accounted for two-thirds of American sales. Between 1980 and the end of 1982 Unimation's market share is expected to drop almost one-fifth, from 41 percent to 34 percent, while Milacron's will probably fall from 30 percent to less than 28 percent. According to Peter L. Blake, executive director of Robotics International, "There's enough business for the next two or three years, but then there will be a shakeout." [19]

Survival will tend to favor companies financially strong enough to develop and market intelligent robots and the smaller companies that have a specialization — in region, price or application. Electronics firms are likely to become the primary producers of robots because robot brains — their microprocessors, which electronics firms produce — are expected to develop much more rapidly than robot brawn — their mechanical aspects, such as manual dexterity.

[19] Quoted in "Now Everybody Wants To Get into Robots," *Business Week*, Feb. 15, 1982.

While no one predicts a major interruption in the industry's growth, analysts agree that the nation's faltering economy is limiting demand for robots. Most say that some investments have been delayed and predict that many smaller robot companies will have cash-flow problems. New business from the auto industry and related spot welding has slowed, despite overall increased sales. Even General Motors, which is committed to installing 20,000 robots by 1990 (it now has 1,400 in use or on order), has been putting only a few new robots into production at a time.

The recession's second effect on the robot industry is partly a result of the first. Vendors have been forced to market their products to a wider variety of industries and to generally step up their marketing activities. Broader marketing has not replaced the temporary order reductions from the auto industry, but has helped to educate potential users and increase product visibility. "It is our belief that this wider and more aggressive marketing approach, despite its having been forced on portions of the industry through economic circumstances, will be extremely positive for the health and sustainability of the robotics industry in the long term," said Laura Conigliaro. The entry of companies like IBM and Westinghouse into the business also will help to open up new markets, Conigliaro added, and will, along with the smaller new companies, add at least 25 percent to industry sales in 1982, partially making up for shortfalls resulting from the recession.[20]

Consequences for Society

DESPITE increased interest in robotics in this country, most U.S. companies still are approaching the new technology with caution. Although robots are cheaper than people in the long run, few companies have enough capital to invest in many at one time. But even more crucial, James Albus said in a recent interview, "We have yet to decide that robotics is good." Management resistance has been a big factor. "If you are going to automate, you are not going to get your payback for a while," said George Brosseau of the National Science Foundation. "Managers, particularly middle-managers, are very reluctant to make that decision."

Another reason for sluggish U.S. acceptance of robots has been the nation's plentiful labor supply. "Because of America's

---

[20] Laura Conigliaro, "The Current State of the Industry," *Robotics Newsletter*, Jan. 25, 1982, p. 2.

Robots in History

One of the first automatons — a wooden bird that could fly — was built by Plato's friend Archytas of Tarentum, who lived between 400 and 350 B.C. In the second century B.C., Hero of Alexandria described in his book *De Automatis* a mechanical theater with robotlike figures that danced and marched in temple ceremonies. The 13th century German philosopher Albertus Magnus was said to have built a doorkeeper out of wax, leather, glass, metal and wood that stood watch outside his monk's cell in Cologne. According to legend the young theologian Thomas Aquinas smashed it to pieces because he thought it was demonic.

Juanelo Turriano, a 16th century engineer who served Emperor Charles V, ruler of Spain and the Netherlands, entertained Charles' son and successor with small toy soldiers that fenced with swords and a shepherdess that played the lute. Even philosopher René Descartes may have experimented with robots. One legend has it that he built a female android and named her Francine. In 1637 he wrote that someone would someday construct "soulless machinery" that would behave like animals.

A French engineer, Jacques de Vaucanson (1709-1782) was elected to the Académie des Sciences for his work, which included the creation of a life-size flute-playing shepherd. He also built a mechanical duck with a thousand moving parts that could "eat" and "digest" food. The poet Goethe saw the duck years later and apparently didn't think much of it, commenting in his diary that "the duck was like a skeleton and had digestive problems."

The Germans were the first to put robots on the screen, in a chilling 1926 moving called *Metropolis*. In 1939 Electro, a walking robot, and his dog Sparko were displayed at the New York World's Fair. In the same year science fiction writer Isaac Asimov started writing robot stories.

Asimov's stories fired the imagination of a Columbia University physics student named Joseph F. Engelberger. In 1956 Engelberger had a conversation with George C. Devol, the inventor of something he called a programmed article transfer device. By the time Devol's patent application was granted in 1961, Engelberger had started Unimation Inc., which bought the rights and built developmental versions of Devol's device, now called a robot.

Since meeting Devol — who now runs a robot leasing and consulting business from his home in Fort Lauderdale, Fla. — Engelberger has been preaching the gospel of using robots to get people out of dangerous or boring jobs and to improve productivity. While American industry was slow to catch on, the Japanese were fascinated from the start. When the Japanese government invited Engelberger to lecture in 1967, an audience of over 700 executives and engineers turned out to listen.

large labor resources, we were able to postpone the robotic revolution — until approximately 1980," said Ken Susnjara, president of Thermwood Corp., a robot maker in Dale, Ind.[21] By then industry began to realize that the number of young entrants into the work force would be shrinking through the 1990s.

"In the past, whenever a new technology has been introduced, it has always generated more jobs than it displaced. But we don't know whether that's true of robot technology."

George Brosseau
National Science Foundation

Lack of understanding and technical knowledge about what robots can do and how they can solve problems also has been an inhibiting factor. Now, however, prospective users are beginning to spend millions of dollars to bring their engineers and production managers up-to-date. Companies like General Electric and Westinghouse are investing heavily in their own robot research and management training programs and industry in some cases is supplying academia with funds for their robotics programs. Five years ago there were only a few robotics training programs at colleges and universities, now there are over 30, including those at MIT and Carnegie-Mellon University in Pittsburgh. Even the lesser-known technical colleges are turning out graduates able to command starting salaries of over $30,000.[22]

Perhaps the biggest resistance to robots is people's fear of being displaced by them. In an article examining robots and the Western mind, Mark Crispin Miller of the University of Pennsylvania wrote that "the fear of robots is an apprehension of gradual displacement ... a foreboding of our own annihilation." [23] J. Timothy Heile, marketing communications manager at Cincinnati Milacron's Lebanon, Ohio, facility, told those attending the Robots VI conference last March that "The high degree of publicity about robot technology over the past several years has spawned interest, suspicion, fear, and ultimately defensive attitudes throughout society."

The Robot Institute of America and others have criticized

---

[21] Quoted by John Teresko in "Robots Come of Age," *Industry Week*, Jan. 25, 1982, p. 39.
[22] See "Filling in the Gap in Robot Training," *Business Week*, Feb. 15, 1982, p. 52H.
[23] Mark Crispin Miller, "Tools and Monsters," *The New Republic*, May 16, 1981, pp. 27, 29.

industry for not addressing these concerns and the social costs and implications of the robot revolution. As evidence of this shortsightedness they point to industry's slowness in providing retraining for workers who might be displaced by robots. "We are seeing a massive introduction of highly productive technology with little regard for the impact on individuals or the community," Dr. Harley Shaiken, a consultant to the United Auto Workers and a research associate at MIT, told a meeting of the American Management Association.[24]

Social Implications of Robot Revolution

Just about everyone agrees that the long-term impact of robots in factories and in society will be profound, though in what ways no one can predict with certainty. Thus far, the 4,000 or so robots in American factories have taken jobs that most workers do not want. Robots, therefore, are not now considered a serious threat to American workers and most labor unions have not objected to their presence on the assembly line. But the UAW estimates that assembly line labor could be cut by as much as 50 percent over the next nine years because of robots and other automation projects.

Most robotics experts believe that robots will create more jobs than they will destroy. James S. Albus of the National Bureau of Standards told Editorial Research Reports: "Robots create profits, profits create expansion in industry and expanding industries hire more people." Others are more cautious in their predictions. According to George Brosseau, "In the past, whenever a new technology has been introduced, it has always generated more jobs than it displaced. But we don't know whether that's true of robot technology. There's no question but that new jobs will be created, but will there be enough to offset the loss?"

Albus believes it is premature to worry about running out of jobs. The problem as he sees it "is in finding mechanisms by which the wealth created by robot technology can be distributed to the people who need it." [25] A solution he proposes is to make everyone stockholders in national, automated robot factories that would pay people substantial dividends. If they wanted more money people could take jobs or start their own businesses, but no one would have to.

"[T]he robot revolution," Albus wrote in *Brains, Behavior, & Robotics* (1981), "could free the human race from the regimentation and mechanization imposed by the requirement for

---

[24] Quoted by John Teresko, *op. cit.*, p. 38.
[25] James S. Albus, *Brains, Behavior, & Robotics* (1981), p. 330.

Jobs Done by Robots Now and in the Future

	Through 1981	1990
Spot welding	35-45%	3-5%
Arc welding	5-8	15-20
Materials handling, including machine loading and unloading	25-30	30-35
Paint spraying	8-12	5
Assembly	5-10	35-40
Other	8-10	7-10

Source: Bache Halsey Stuart Shields Inc.

human decision-making in factories and offices. It has the capacity to provide us all with material wealth, clean energy, and the personal freedom to enjoy what could become a golden age of mankind." The vision of robots gliding about in empty factories while people bask in robot-subsidized fulfillment seems a farfetched one. But whether we welcome robots as our saviors or fear them as our replacements, we will have to adjust to increasing numbers of them in our midst.

Selected Bibliography

Books

Albus, James S., *People's Capitalism: The Economics of the Robot Revolution,* New World Books, 1976.
___ *Brains, Behavior, & Robotics,* McGraw-Hill, 1981.
Engelberger, Joseph F., *Robotics In Practice,* Unimation Inc., 1980.
Tanner, William R., ed., *Industrial Robots,* Society of Manufacturing Engineers, 1979.

Articles

Cornish, Blake M., "The Smart Machines of Tomorrow," *The Futurist,* August 1981.
Friedrich, Otto, "The Robot Revolution," *Time,* Dec. 8, 1980.
Miller, Mark Crispin, "Tools and Monsters," *The New Republic,* May 16, 1981.
"Now Everybody Wants To Get into Robots," *Business Week,* Feb. 15, 1982.
Reed, Fred, "Can a Robot Do Your Job?" *The Washingtonian,* April 1982.
Robotics Age, selected issues (available from 175 Concord St., Peterborough, N.H. 03458).
Robotics Newsletter, selected issues (published by Bache Halsey Stuart Shields Inc.).
Robotics Today, selected issues (published by Robot Institute of America).
Schefter, Jim, "New Workers on the Assembly Line: Robots That Think," *Popular Science,* June 1980.
Stokes, Henry Scott, "Japan's Love Affair with the Robot," *The New York Times Magazine,* Jan. 10, 1982.
Teresko, John, "Robots Come of Age," *Industry Week,* Jan. 25, 1982.
"The Robots Are Coming and Japan Leads the Way," *U.S. News & World Report,* Jan. 18, 1982.

Reports and Articles

Aron, Paul, "Robots Revisited: One Year Later," Daiwa Securities America Inc. (New York), 1981.
Conigliaro, Laura, "Robotics," Bache Halsey Stuart Shields Inc., 1980.
Editorial Research Reports: "The Computer Age," 1981 Vol. I, p. 107.
Sanderson, Ronald J. and others, "Industrial Robots: A Summary and Forecast for Manufacturing Managers," Tech Tran Corp., 1982.
"Social Impacts of Robotics: Summary and Issues," Office of Technology Assessment, U.S. Congress, February 1982.

THE YOUTH UNEMPLOYMENT PUZZLE

by

Robert Benenson

Mar. 18
1 9 8 3

THE YOUTH UNEMPLOYMENT PUZZLE

A S THE school year winds down, thousands of young Americans are beginning the annual search for summer jobs. But if past years are any indication, many youths will be unable to find work this summer. Youth unemployment is more visible during the summer months, when jobless youngsters spend their daylight hours on the streets rather than in school buildings. During the rest of the year, it generally takes an event like President Reagan's proposed "subminimum wage" for youth *(see p. 160)* or House passage of a bill to create an "American Conservation Corps" to provide jobs for unemployed youth *(see box, p. 159)* to focus attention on the problem. But statistics indicate that youth unemployment is a serious year-round concern.

Joblessness for 16- to 19-year-olds peaked at 24.5 percent in December 1982, the highest for this group since such measurements began in 1948, before slipping back to 22.7 percent in January and 22.2 percent in February.[1] The overall unemployment rate in February was 10.4 percent. "We have a very serious job deficit for youth," said Sar Levitan, an economics professor at George Washington University in Washington, D.C. The dimensions of the problem are worse for minority youths. Blacks aged 16-19 had a February unemployment rate of 45.4 percent, almost two-and-one-half times higher than the rate for white teen-agers (19.7 percent).[2]

Some economists and social scientists believe these statistics underestimate the extent of the problem, especially for minority youth. Labor-force participation[3] for black youths in February was 33.5 percent, down 3.5 percent from one year earlier, and 23 percent lower than comparable figures for white youths. Because of their high unemployment and low participation rates, only 18.3 percent of all blacks aged 16 to 19 were employed in February.[4] The comparable figure for whites aged 16-19 in February was 45.4 percent.

---

[1] Figures from the Bureau of Labor Statistics, U.S. Department of Labor.
[2] In real numbers, however, there were more unemployed white youths than unemployed black youths: 1.43 million to 342,000 in February.
[3] Defined as the percentage of the total population working or looking for work.
[4] This figure, known as the "employment-population ratio," is defined as "civilian employment as a percent of the civilian noninstitutional population."

Disagreement Over Seriousness of Problem

There is hardly unanimity among economists concerning the seriousness of the youth unemployment problem. Some believe that traditional measurements of unemployment create an exaggerated impression of hardship among youth. For most teen-agers, school, not work, is the primary activity. According to the Census Bureau, in October 1981, 90.6 percent of 16- to 17-year-olds were enrolled in school. Most of these school-age youths lived with family members who supported them.

Youth unemployment is not seen as being as critical as adult joblessness, because of the "casual" nature of youth labor-force participation. Youths can move in and out of jobs and the work force with greater ease and, according to some economists, are more often working to pay for luxuries than for survival. Economists also point out that most 16- to 17-year-olds and many 18- to 19-year-olds are holding or are looking for part-time, not full-time jobs. Periods of unemployment are also shorter for youths. According to the Bureau of Labor Statistics, only 31.6 percent of youths aged 16 to 19 who were unemployed in February had been jobless for 15 or more weeks, compared with 42.4 percent for unemployed persons aged 20 or over.

Social workers like Lori Strumpf of the National Youth Work Alliance[5] call the "casual unemployment" rationale a "cop-out." She maintains there are many young people, especially from poor households, who need a job to supplement family income or, in this era of high birth rates among teen-agers, support their own families. "Everybody wishes [the average unemployed youth] was the kid that came knocking on the door during the summertime to cut the grass because he was saving money to buy a bicycle," said Strumpf. "There are kids out there who are ... helping feed their families."

The debate over the depth of the unemployment problem is more than just an academic exercise. Determining the number of youths with actual needs can have an impact on the amount of money and effort expended on public employment and training projects. The U.S. General Accounting Office, in a survey of the literature on the subject published as part of a 1982 report, found a range of need estimates from 379,000 to 3.7 million persons.[6]

[5] The National Youth Work Alliance provides technical assistance and monitors legislation for its 1,200 member agencies which deal with youth problems, including unemployment, delinquency, drug abuse and pregnancy.

[6] General Accounting Office, "Labor Market Problems of Teenagers Result Largely From Doing Poorly in School," March 29, 1982. The low estimate came from a 1979 report co-authored by Martin Feldstein, now chairman of President Reagan's Council of Economic Advisers. The high estimate came from a 1980 study by Robert Taggart, director of the Labor Department's Office of Youth Programs during the Carter administration.

Unemployment Rates for 16- to 19-Year-Olds
1973-82

	All Youths	White	Black
1973	14.5	12.6	33.0
1974	16.0	14.0	35.0
1975	19.9	17.9	39.5
1976	19.0	16.9	39.2
1977	17.8	15.4	41.1
1978	16.4	13.9	38.7
1979	16.1	14.0	36.5
1980	17.8	15.5	38.5
1981	19.6	17.3	41.4
1982	23.2	20.4	48.0

Source: U.S. Department of Labor, Bureau of Labor Statistics

Factors Contributing to Youth Unemployment

Youth unemployment affects millions of young people of all socio-economic, racial and educational backgrounds, with a wide range of reasons for being in — or out of — the work force. Virtually all experts, even those who oppose the concept of "casual" youth employment, agree that at least some percentage of joblessness is a result of young persons' greater flexibility. Youths from families with secure economic situations can afford to experiment in the job market, leaving jobs they find unsatisfactory without great financial hardship. "They do live in families that can support them, and for them it's not a critical matter," said Diane Nilsen, an economist with the Bureau of Labor Statistics.

Teen-age joblessness is also linked to some important demographic changes in the labor market. Women continue to enter the labor market in record numbers, often because of economic necessity.[7] In many cases, they are seeking employment in areas where young people have recently found jobs, such as clerical work or retail sales. "Mothers are competing with their kids, because they need a job," said Sar Levitan. "They enter the job market and then they displace the kid."

Not everyone believes this is altogether bad. John Cogan, assistant secretary of labor for policy, evaluation and research, said that when women go out and work, "the earnings of the family are higher and that generates more consumption and that itself generates more jobs." But few researchers are as sanguine about the other labor-market influx: the uncounted

[7] According to the Bureau of Labor Statistics, labor force participation by women over age 20 in February 1983 was 52.9 percent, up from 52.3 percent in February 1982 and well above the annual averages for 1980 (49.4 percent), 1970 (41.1 percent) and 1960 (35.5 percent).

thousands, if not millions, of undocumented or illegal aliens who many believe are filling the low-skilled, entry-level jobs traditionally taken by American youths.

Unemployment resulting from economic cycles or labor-force competition will be mitigated to some extent if the recession ends and an economic recovery brings about overall employment growth. But many unemployed youths will face labor-market problems even under the best conditions. Because of a combination of societal and personal handicaps, these young people have difficulty finding and keeping a job. Many of them have dropped out of school; a disproportionate number are black and residents of "inner-city" neighborhoods.

Between October 1980 and October 1981, 788,000 persons aged 16-24 dropped out of school; 65 percent were white, 21 percent black and 12 percent Hispanic. Some youths drop out because of the real or perceived necessity to find a job. But many drop out because of lack of interest or motivation. Whatever their reasons for leaving school, dropouts find rough going in the job market: 29.2 percent of whites and 71.4 percent of blacks who dropped out during the 1980-81 school year were unemployed in October 1981, according to the Bureau of Labor Statistics.

Schools have also been criticized for providing students with neither basic academic skills nor knowledge of the workings of the labor market. The decline in basic reading, writing and math skills, as measured by standardized test scores, that began in the early 1960s appears to have been slowed or reversed by the "back-to-basics" movement in many school systems.[8] But many youngsters, especially older teen-agers, remain seriously behind their grade level in skills and need remedial training. Many employers also blame the schools for failing to imbue students with "employability skills," such as job-search techniques, punctuality, dress codes and appropriate behavior on the job. "The general employer viewpoint is that the kids who come to [them], even if they have their diplomas, are seriously deficient in the basics of math, reading and certainly in the motivation department, as measured by absenteeism, tardiness and all of that," said Paul Barton, executive director of the National Institute for Work and Learning in Washington, D.C.[9]

Employment Problems Facing Minority Youth

The environment from which young people spring is seen by some experts as an important reason for their problems in the job market. Many low-income youths, especially black young-

---

[8] See "Education's Return to Basics," *E.R.R.*, 1975 Vol. II, pp. 665-684.
[9] The institute serves as a clearinghouse for information on educational and career counseling services.

American Conservation Corps

On March 1, the House, by a 301-87 margin, voted to create an "American Conservation Corps" (ACC) to provide jobs for unemployed youths. The vote came almost exactly 50 years after the creation of the Civilian Conservation Corps (CCC), the New Deal jobs program which provide the model for the ACC *(see p. 164)*.

The proposed ACC would provide $50 million in fiscal 1983 and $250 million annually in fiscal 1984-89 for conservation projects in parks, forests and Indian reservations. Supporters say the plan would create as many as 100,000 new jobs. Unemployed people aged 16 to 25 would be eligible for year-round jobs, while summer jobs would be limited to those aged 15 to 21. Hiring of the disadvantaged would be stressed.

Opponents, mainly Republicans, say the ACC would be just another make-work program that would do little to ease unemployment and much to hurt the economy. "This is a perfect symbol of the old politics of the 1930s," said Rep. Bill Frenzel, R-Minn., who said the plan would create "the most expensive jobs we've ever had." Passage of the proposal in the Republican-dominated Senate is doubtful. The program is strongly opposed by President Reagan, who in 1981 eliminated the similar Young Adult Conservation Corps that was operated under CETA.

sters from inner-city areas, come from backgrounds that provide little encouragement for educational or career attainment. "If there are no books around the home, if there are no efforts made by the parent or by the guardian to stimulate that youngster, and if their role models are basically not performing at a level which that parent might like, then that youngster is going to be cut back," said Dr. Nancy Pinson-Millburn, a psychologist who does research for various colleges in the Washington, D.C. area.

Others say that because of general high unemployment in ghetto areas, young people lack the networks that could help them obtain jobs. In better-situated families, youths are often able to get in the employment door through a relative or some other kind of contact. According to Frank Slobig, executive director of the Roosevelt Centennial Youth Project, poor black youths "don't have the contacts with adults who are working and have links to those jobs. . . . The intermediary issue is a big issue." [10]

Much has been made in recent years about the relocation of businesses and jobs from inner-city neighborhoods to downtowns and suburbs. The implication is that the poor lack the

---

[10] The Roosevelt Centennial Youth Project was established in 1982 by the Eleanor Roosevelt Institute of the Franklin Roosevelt Library in Hyde Park, N.Y. According to Slobig, its purpose is to develop access to the media and raise the level of discussion on the youth employment problem, as an antidote to the "CETA fraud-and-abuse reporting syndrome" *(see p. 166)*.

mobility to travel more than short distances to work. But Sar
Levitan referred to such reasoning as well-intentioned "racism."
"When we talk about the ghetto area of the metropolitan city,
there you have the public transportation and if you have the
jobs, the kids will find the jobs, or the black person or the
Hispanic person, will find the job," Levitan said.

But there is evidence that many employers still avoid hiring
minority youths. "Despite the progress that we may have made
in the past 30 years or so in that whole area, I think there are
still some very deep-seated, fundamental discriminatory hiring
practices that go on," said Slobig. For example, in October 1981,
the unemployment rate for 1980-81 white high-school *dropouts*
(29.2 percent) was almost half that for 1981 black high-school
graduates (50.8 percent).

Continuing Debate Over the Minimum Wage

Some people believe many unemployed youths would be able
to find jobs if it were not for the federally mandated minimum
wage. Chief among them is President Reagan, who has proposed
a subminimum wage of $2.50, 25 percent below the regular
minimum wage of $3.35. Under Reagan's plan, the lower wage
could be paid only to people 21 and younger, and only from May
1 to September 30. "This new wage will allow youngsters who
don't have any experience to make a start in the workplace,"
Reagan said in a March 5 radio address. "What we're trying to
do is get them some experience so they can move up the pay-
scale."

The minimum wage was mandated by the Fair Labor Standards Act of 1938, which also established the first comprehensive federal child labor laws. The idea behind the minimum
wage was to prevent worker exploitation, guaranteeing employed persons a decent wage. But for some supporters of the
law, including labor unions, an underlying motive was to protect
the jobs and wages of adult "breadwinners" from being undercut by young workers. Youths were protected by minimum-wage
provisions only in manufacturing industries under the original
law and only about 40 percent of youth workers were employed
in jobs that were covered by the law. But in 1955, minimum
wage coverage for youth was expanded to the fast-growing retail
and wholesale trades. Today, over 80 percent of young employees work in places that come under minimum-wage rules.

Those who believe the expanded coverage has actually resulted in a loss of job opportunities for youth cite as statistical
evidence studies such as one by the congressional Minimum
Wage Study Commission that said that a 10 percent increase in
the minimum wage would result in a decline in youth employ-

ment of between 1-2.5 percent.[11] They say that many employers, in judging what their businesses might gain by hiring a young person, cannot justify the payment of a relatively high minimum wage, especially to those who are untrained, unskilled and lacking experience. The impact, they say, has been harshest for

minority youths. "The general findings are that the minimum wage has contributed significantly to the decline in black teen-age employment and the growth in unemployment," said John Cogan of the Department of Labor.

Supporters of a subminimum wage for youth believe that employers would be more willing to hire youths and provide them with training if they could pay them a lower wage. Young workers willing to accept a lower wage in exchange for job training would be repaid by higher earnings in the long run, they say. But opponents of the subminimum wage say that its potentially harmful effects outweigh anything that might be gained from it. The most serious concern is that youths will displace older workers as employers use the subminimum wage to cut costs rather than expand employment. But according to President Reagan, his youth wage plan "will add provisions that absolutely prohibit businesses from displacing current workers by hiring young people at a lesser wage."

Others say that differential wage rates can cause conflict between employees. According to Jeffrey Newman, executive director of the National Committee on the Employment of Youth,[12] "To the degree that you had younger workers receiving lower wages than the worker, who might be only a year or two older ... standing next to him in an assembly line or fast-food restaurant, you would have enormous employee difficulties."

Many critics of the subminimum wage say that it would not actually create more youth jobs. They note that since 1961, a "student certification" program has been in effect that allows employers in the areas of retail and service trade, agriculture and higher education to pay 85 percent of the minimum wage to full-time students working part-time during the school year and

[11] Report cited by Sean Sullivan, "Youth Employment," in *Meeting Human Needs* (1982), p. 233. The Minimum Wage Study Commission was created by Congress in 1977 to study the economic and employment effects of changes in minimum wage requirements. The commission went out of existence in 1981.
[12] The committee is affiliated with the National Child Labor Committee in New York.

full-time during the summer. According to the Bureau of
Labor Statistics, 15.2 percent of all hourly workers aged
16-19 were already being paid below the minimum wage in
1982. Opponents of a universal subminimum wage say that
employers could hire many more workers under the existing waivers, but do not. Other incentive programs, such as
the Targeted Jobs Tax Credit instituted in 1978,[13] have likewise done little to enhance employment opportunities for youth,
they say.

Opponents claim that the subminimum will result only in
lower wages for youths who would have been hired anyway. "I
don't see McDonald's going out and hiring two people to do a
job that they now have one person doing . . . that's absurd," said
Newman. The idea is seen as so oriented toward large employers
of youths working part-time, such as fast-food restaurants and
amusement parks, that opponents have dubbed it the "Mc-
Donald's Windfall Gifts Amendment."

Prospects for congressional passage of the subminimum wage
are not seen as bright, especially in the Democratically controlled House, which is responsive to organized labor's strong
opposition to the proposal. The subminimum wage concept has
been floating around Congress for years, and it actually came
within one vote of House passage in 1977. Some Republicans
pressed the idea in the 97th Congress, but it never gained steam
because of Democratic opposition and the reluctance of some
Republicans, who feared that the subminimum wage might be
used as a bargaining chip by those who wanted to raise the
minimum wage for adults.

Proposed Changes in Child Labor Policies

The subminimum wage is not the only controversial proposal
concerning youth workers that the Reagan administration has
brought forth. Last July, the Labor Department created a furor
when it released proposed regulations that would have relaxed
some of the restrictive hiring and work rules concerning 14- and
15-year-olds. The regulations would have raised the maximum
hours of work for such youths from 18 to 24 hours per week,
from 3 to 4 hours a day, and would have allowed them to work
until 9 p.m. on school nights and 10 p.m. on non-school nights,
as opposed to the current 7 p.m. limits. Hiring prohibitions for
certain jobs, such as cooking, baking, laundering and clerical
work, would also have been relaxed, although hazardous work,
such as handling hot grease over an open flame, would have
been banned.

[13] The Targeted Jobs Tax Credit provides employers who hire disadvantaged youths and
cooperative education students with tax credits equal to 50 percent of the employee's first-
year wages and 25 percent of the second year's wages.

The Youth Unemployment Puzzle

Reagan administration officials say that the effort to change the child labor rules was meant only to update obsolete rules that create unnecessary impediments to employment for young teen-agers. John Cogan of the Department of Labor cited as examples regulations that allow 14- and 15-year-olds to wash cars, but not buses, trucks and vans, and rules that forbid youths in that age group from using vacuum cleaners on the insides of cars. "Maybe in 1940 it was a little dangerous for them to use vacuum cleaners in cars, but now, we don't believe it is," said Cogan. The rationale for the revised regulations, Cogan added, was that "work experience is the key to future success."

Jeffrey Newman of the National Committee on the Employment of Youth believes 14- and 15-year-olds can obtain the desired work experience in 15-18 hours per week, rather than 24 hours, which he considers too much. Claiming that the proposed rules would result in "exploitation" of children who "do not know the labor market, their rights or child labor regulations," Newman outlined five specific reasons for his opposition: 1) it would be "sadistic" to unemployed workers to open the way for 14- and 15-year-olds to take some of the few available jobs, and it could set up a confrontation between the young and older workers; 2) most of the jobs would be "dead-end," with no relation to school or employment training; 3) though prohibitions against dangerous work would stand, 14- and 15-year-olds would be allowed to work in proximity to dangerous work, tempting employers to bend the law; 4) youths working longer hours are likely to be too exhausted to do homework or take part in extracurricular school activities; and 5) young teen-agers, especially those in inner cities, would be more vulnerable to criminal attack if they worked later hours.

Protest over the proposed rules last year resulted in their withdrawal pending further examination. But Cogan, who said that the "hue and cry ... was more rhetoric than reason," told Editorial Research Reports that the Reagan administration intends to reissue the proposed regulations sometime in March.

Federal Youth Job Programs

CHILD LABOR, not unemployment, was the dominant youth issue during the early part of this century. The goal of social reformers was not to find jobs for young people, but to rescue hundreds of thousands of them from dirty and often dangerous work in coal mines, cigarette and glass factories, textile mills and other industrial locations. It was not until the Great Depression of the 1930s that youth unemployment became an overriding issue. In an economic calamity that idled a quarter of the American work force, youths had few job opportunities. By the time Franklin D. Roosevelt took office in 1933, as many as 200,000 youths were riding freight trains in a desperate search for work.

Job-creation programs were to become an important part of Roosevelt's New Deal, and the first of these provided work for young people. The Civilian Conservation Corps (CCC), established in March 1933, sent young, unmarried men to rural camps and put them to work developing park land, wildlife refuges and national forests, planting trees, fighting forest fires, and stringing telephone wire. In its nine-year existence, the CCC employed 1.5 million men.

Young people were able to avail themselves of the job placement services provided by the United States Employment Service (USES), created by the Wagner-Peyser Act of 1933. The New Deal also begat the National Youth Administration (NYA), which hired both men and women. Between 1935 and 1943, 2.7 million young people were paid small stipends by the federal government for light public-works assignments — repairing streets and public buildings, for example — or public-service assignments, such as working in libraries or offices. The NYA also encouraged students to stay in school by providing them with part-time jobs in school libraries and laboratories or in grounds maintenance.[14]

World War II brought near full employment to the United States, and the concern about youth unemployment diminished. The expanding economy continued to provide job opportunities for most youths who wanted to work. Teen-age unemployment was under 8 percent in 1954, and the employment-population ratio for black teen-agers was slightly better than that of whites (52 to 50 percent). But by the late 1950s, societal and demographic factors were changing the youth-employment picture. Automation, then in its nascent stage, was already having some impact on industrial employment. The impact was greatest on the farm, and the loss of agricultural employment hit Southern blacks the hardest. Many young blacks migrated to the cities of the South and to Northern industrial cities.

In 1961, Congress passed the Area Redevelopment Act, which provided $4.5 million a year for vocational training for un-

---

[14] See "Federal Jobs Programs," *E.R.R.*, 1982 Vol. II, pp. 949-972.

employed or "underemployed" individuals in chronically depressed areas. The next year, Congress enacted the Manpower Development and Training Act (MDTA). It was the first federal program to combine classroom training, remedial education, on-the-job training and placement services. Although the original focus of MDTA was to retrain workers whose skills had become technologically obsolete, by 1963 the emphasis had begun to shift toward training for disadvantaged workers, including unemployed, out-of-school youths.

Employment Programs During Great Society

The Economic Opportunity Act of 1964 created the first federal job-training programs aimed directly at youths: the Job Corps and the Neighborhood Youth Corps (NYC). The latter program provided part-time and summer public service employment and some job training for poor in-school and out-of-school youths. Critics complained that the NYC was little more than an income-transfer program. But more concrete results were obtained by the Job Corps program. Modeled after the Civilian Conservation Corps, the Job Corps set up residential centers in cities and training camps in rural areas, to be run by private industry. The program targeted poor youths, most of whom were black high-school dropouts. Many program participants had been in trouble with the law, or had severe personal problems, such as drug abuse.

The Job Corps turned into the most lasting of Lyndon B. Johnson's "Great Society" programs. Since 1966, nearly one million youths have entered the Job Corps program, which provides job training, remedial education and counseling services. The training is rigorous and structured, and disciplinary problems can result in removal from the program. The intensity of the program results in a high dropout rate — over 50 percent within the first 90 days — but Job Corps officials claim success with those who stay in: 80 percent employment rates for those who participated in the program for a year or more, 60 percent for those who stayed less than three months.

The Job Corps had to weather a great deal of criticism along the way, especially in its early days. The concentration on underprivileged, unskilled, often troubled youths contributed to the high dropout rate, which in turn made doubters question the effectiveness of the program. But as Sar Levitan pointed out, "The Job Corps could have been a great success from the beginning, by picking the best kids, giving them training, and then they would have had a high [job and college] placement rate . . . but they persisted, and they developed training tools for those kids."

The persistence was at a cost: the program's residential nature, the intense counseling and supervision and other necessities ran the per-trainee costs of Job Corps to well over $10,000, and detractors said that it would cost less to send a youngster to Harvard than to the Job Corps. But defenders pointed out that without the Job Corps, many participants were much more likely to go to jail than to Harvard.

Ups and Downs of the CETA Jobs Program

By the early 1970s, the proliferation of federal job-training programs under MDTA had led to complaints of inefficiency, bureaucratic red tape and program overlap. Among the most aggrieved were local officials, who said that the federal operation of the programs prevented local flexibility and often resulted in training that was irrelevant to the local labor market. President Nixon, as part of his "New Federalism" concept, backed the Comprehensive Employment and Training Act (CETA), enacted in 1973. Under CETA, the system was decentralized, with the planning and implementation of local programs given to "prime sponsors" — usually city or county governments.

Youths were eligible for many of the CETA training programs and were served by several that were targeted specifically at them. The best known were the programs created by the Youth Employment and Demonstration Projects Act (YEDPA) of 1977. The programs, established under Title IV of CETA, included: Youth Community Conservation and Improvement Projects (YCCIP), which provided jobs, mainly to dropouts, on community rehabilitation projects, with provisions for academic credit for work experience; Youth Incentive Entitlement Pilot Projects (YIEPP), which guaranteed part-time jobs during the school year and full-time jobs in the summer to potential dropouts who remained in school and met performance standards; and the Youth Employment and Training Programs (YETP), similar to the training, remedial education and placement efforts of the general CETA program, but distinguishable by a 22 percent set-aside for in-school youths.

During the 1970s, CETA developed a reputation for fraud, waste and abuse. Much of the controversy stemmed from the public service employment programs. Critics described them as "make-work" programs that provided workers, young or old, with few job skills. Local officials were accused of using CETA money to pay regular workers or to create patronage jobs for political supporters or family members. Even some members of the job-training community denounced the public service jobs element of the CETA program. "In some cities, there's no question about it, it became a political boondoggle," said Elton

Jolly, executive director of Opportunities Industrialization Centers of America *(see p. 170)*.

The training programs did not go uncriticized either. Critics said that liberal rules regarding stipends and payments for support services, such as transportation and day care, changed the role of many CETA programs from training to income support and cut down on the number of persons who could be trained. Another criticism was that lack of input from the private sector often resulted in a mismatch between skills training and available jobs. Amendments to CETA in 1978 attempted to correct this problem by creating Private Industry Councils (PICs), composed of local business leaders, but members of the business community complained that the PICs had no more than a token advisory role.

CETA is defended by many of those involved in its implementation. A 1981 study by the National Council on Employment Policy[15] reported that the rate of "social returns" on CETA classroom training was 34 percent, and was 118 percent for on-the-job training. The "social returns" measured by the study included greater employability and higher wages, reduced dependence on transfer payments and higher tax revenues.

Developing a New System

SUPPORTERS of the existing system were outflanked by its opponents; CETA had become too much of a "four-letter word" to them. YEDPA programs and public service employment were the first to go, phased out by the Reagan administration in 1981. And as CETA's authorization ran out last year, it was replaced with the Job Training Partnership Act (JTPA). A one-year transition period was set up, to end with the implementation of JTPA on October 1.

The JTPA bill was sponsored in Congress by liberal Sen. Edward M. Kennedy, D-Mass., and conservative Sen. Dan Quayle, R-Ind. The Reagan administration was at first reluctant to continue a social program that had a debatable track record, but later embraced and now extols the virtues of JTPA. While liberal legislators were happy to salvage any kind of training system, especially one with regulations that targeted the disadvantaged, conservatives were even more pleased, because they

---

[15] The council is associated with George Washington University in Washington, D.C.

rid the training programs of what they saw as some of their more objectionable features.

Chief among the changes was the larger role provided to the private sector. The PICs, rather than having a fringe advisory capacity, will play an important, if not dominant, part in the planning and implementation of local JTPA programs. "The private sector knows how to train people and what jobs to train for, so their input is critical," said John Cogan of the Labor Department. In addition, the training programs will be held to performance standards, generally meaning how many trainees are placed in unsubsidized jobs in the private sector.

Cost-effectiveness will be bolstered under JTPA, supporters say, by rules that limit the "welfare" elements of the training programs. The law states that 70 percent of JTPA funds must go for training purposes, with only 15 percent alloted for support services (stipends, day care) and 15 percent for administration. JTPA also contains no provisions for public service employment, although the summer youth employment programs have been continued at reduced funding levels.

There is also a provision mandating that 40 percent of local program efforts should be directed to people between ages 16 and 25. But there will be little federal monitoring of this rule, since almost all supervision of the program has been turned over to state and local officials. Some critics are unhappy with the control that the PICs will have over the system. According to Lori Strumpf of the National Youth Work Alliance, businesses had originally opted out of a role in CETA because they did not want to deal with hard-to-employ individuals. Strumpf also opposes limits on support services, stipends and public-service employment. "If stipends get people in training programs that will benefit them, then why not," she said.

Strumpf and others fear that such limitations, along with performance standards that reward job placement over more intangible accomplishments, such as educational and motivational upgrading, will result in the selection of only the better-educated, more motivated youths for training, a process known as "creaming." "I'm afraid that the group that really needs the training is going to get the shaft," Dan Passarella, assistant director of the CETA program in Bergen County, N.J., said at a seminar on JTPA held by the National Youth Work Alliance (NYWA) Feb. 17-18 in Washington, D.C.

Problems Finding the Programs That Work

Some youth activists are lobbying to get these provisions of JTPA changed. But others involved in job training are resigned to them. "There is limited money to put in people's pockets, we

Leading Youth Occupations
February 1983

Men 16-19

Handlers, Equipment Cleaners, Helpers and Laborers	676,000
Food Service	524,000
Sales Workers	320,000
Farming, Forestry and Fishery	198,000
Cleaning and Building Services	182,000
Machine Operators, Assemblers and Inspectors	169,000
Administrative Support, Including Clerical	143,000
Transportation and Material Moving	121,000

Women 16-19

Sales Workers	744,000
Administrative Support, Including Clerical	636,000
Food Service	547,000
Private Household Service	230,000
Health Service	106,000
Machine Operators, Assemblers and Inspectors	96,000
Personal Service	72,000
Handlers, Equipment Cleaners, Helpers and Laborers	59,000

just don't have that flexibility anymore," David Konkol, a planner in the Wisconsin Employment and Training Office, said at the NYWA seminar. "It is incumbent on us to find what's going to work."

Finding what works was on the minds of many of the training officials who attended the seminar in search of model programs that might work in their states or communities. There are thousands of training programs in existence with varying combinations of federal, state, local and private sector support, and with widely varying records of success. There are programs that have received national attention, but there is no agreement on which, if any, would be universally successful.

For example, 70001 Ltd., a Washington, D.C.-based youth employment service with programs in 17 states, has been praised in a letter from President Reagan and an Aug. 14, 1982, editorial in *The Washington Post*. The majority of 70001's clients, or "associates," are black; 99 percent are high-school dropouts; 40 percent have never held a job. The program provides intensive remedial education, attitudinal and motivational training, peer-group support and job-placement services. Corporate sponsors, which include many restaurant chains, provide information on job openings. 70001 pays no stipends to participants or subsidies to employers, but it provides counseling and other services for clients even after they have "graduated" from the program, something that many experts find lacking in other programs.

A study conducted for the Labor Department last year[16] reported that 80 percent of the young people who completed their training in the program were placed in jobs. Fourteen months after they entered the program, participants were earning an average of $24.40 more per week than a control group of non-participants. But not everyone thinks 70001 is an exemplary approach. Some observers criticize it for not providing stipends or skills training. Others say that most participants are placed in low-skilled, entry-level positions with little career advancement potential.

The programs of the Opportunities Industrialization Centers (OIC), a Philadelphia-based organization founded by Rev. Leon Sullivan in 1964, seem to overcome some of these criticisms. Along with remedial education and counseling services, the OIC programs provide underprivileged youths with concrete skills in centers such as the one visited by President Reagan in Boston Jan. 26. OIC also attempts to keep up with the changing economy; IBM has donated computer-training equipment for seven OIC centers. The organization also gets support from General Motors and General Electric. But even with private sector funding, the expense of programs like OIC that provide a broad range of services makes them reliant on public funding sources that may not be reliable in these economic times. In 1981, a 50 percent cutback in its federal funding forced OIC to close 25 of its 140 operations, with many of the surviving programs forced to retrench and to rely on volunteer personnel.

Importance of Finding Solution to Problem

With all the money and effort being spent on youth employment programs, it is appropriate to ask whether finding jobs for youths is worth all the trouble. Some economists believe that students should not be included in the unemployment statistics, since much research indicates a connection between educational attainment and long-term employment opportunities. Some school authorities worry that students who spend long hours working are too exhausted to study at the end of the day.

A study of youths in Racine, Wis., released by the Justice Department last June, said that working youths were more likely to get involved in criminal activity than non-working youths; it cited their later hours outside the home and their broader contacts in the community as reasons.[17] If true, this would explode one of America's most cherished tenets: that

---

[16] The study was conducted by Public/Private Ventures, an independent research firm in Philadelphia.
[17] Department of Justice, "Assessing the Relationship of Adult Criminal Careers to Juvenile Careers," June 1982.

work experience is a worthwhile activity for young people. But the report was criticized by many of those involved in youth employment programs. Dr. Nancy Pinson-Millburn called the evidence "purely circumstantial and coincidental."

In fact, most experts believe that youth employment is worthwhile. A 1980 study published by the Social Research Group at George Washington University found that students who worked more than 25 hours per week during their senior year had an unemployment rate 4¼ years later of 6 percent, half of that for youths who had not worked at all during their senior years.[18] "The evidence supports the value of work experience, at least from the standpoint of subsequent employment success," said Paul Barton of the Institute for Work and Learning.

A smoother transition into the work force is thought to be of special importance for disadvantaged youths. According to Diane Nilsen of the Bureau of Labor Statistics, inability to find a job or worthwhile employment can influence the attitudes of underprivileged youths. "It's telling them, 'Gee, there's not much out there, nobody likes what I can do,'" Nilsen said. "They don't tend to get a high regard for the work force, or they think it's going to let them down." Persistent unemployment can have long-term effects on a young person's attitudes and actions. "Rejection is a terrible thing," said Elton Jolly of OIC. "If you experience it enough, you get to the place where you don't apply anymore. Rejection then becomes apathy, apathy then becomes hopelessness and hopelessness becomes frustration." Many sociologists believe that such frustration contributes to destructive behavior patterns, such as crime and drug abuse.

Work experience is still widely believed to encourage habits of industry, responsibility and self-respect among young people, in addition to providing them with an introduction to the vagaries of the real world. Frank Slobig, father of five young children, said, "I don't want them growing up and waiting until they're 21 years old before they face what economic life is all about." Slobig also thinks that those who downgrade the youth unemployment problem ignore the decaying effect it could have on American economic growth and morale. "As the numbers of young people who progressively have to wait until a later age to have their first tangible experience of what it means to work increase, it has an eroding impact on a basic societal value," he said. "We're increasingly raising a generation of young people who simply don't have that basic formative experience of what it means to work."

---

[18] A. V. Harrell and P. W. Wirtz, "Social and Educational Antecedents to Youth Unemployment," Social Research Group, George Washington University, 1980.

Selected Bibliography

Books

Adams, Arvil V. and Garth L. Mangum, *The Lingering Crisis of Youth Unemployment*, The W. E. Upjohn Institute for Employment Research, 1978.

Gordon, Margaret S., *Youth Education and Unemployment Problems*, Carnegie Council on Policy Studies in Higher Education, 1979.

Meyer, Jack A. (ed.), *Meeting Human Needs: Toward a New Public Philosophy*, American Enterprise Institute, 1982.

Articles

Barton, Paul E., "Vocational Education: Federal Policies for the 1980s," *Education and Urban Society*, November 1981.

Edelman, Peter, "Child Labor Revisited," *The Nation*, Aug. 21-28, 1982.

Glover, Robert W., "Apprenticeship: A Solution to Youth Unemployment," *Transatlantic Perspectives*, July 1981.

Sheler, Jeffery L., "Black Teenagers Without Jobs: Time Bomb for the U.S.," *U.S. News & World Report*, Jan. 18, 1982.

Westcott, Diane N., "The Youngest Workers: 14- and 15-Year Olds," *Monthly Labor Review*, February 1981.

Young, Anne McDougall, "Labor Force Patterns of Students, Graduates and Dropouts, 1981," *Monthly Labor Review*, September 1982.

Reports and Studies

Bureau of Labor Statistics, "The Employment Situation: February 1983," Washington, March 1983.

Department of Labor, "Employment and Training Report of the President," Washington, 1982.

Editorial Research Reports: "Federal Jobs Programs," 1982 Vol. II, p. 949; "Pressures on Youth," 1982 Vol. I, p. 589; "America's Employment Outlook," 1982 Vol. I, p. 385; "Youth Unemployment," 1977 Vol. II, p. 765.

General Accounting Office, "Labor Market Problems of Teenagers Result Largely From Doing Poorly in School," Washington, March 1982.

National Assessment of Educational Progress, "Reading, Science & Mathematics Trends: A Closer Look," Denver, December 1982.

Public/Private Ventures, "The Impact of Pre-Employment Services on the Employment and Earnings of Disadvantaged Youth," Philadelphia, July 1982.

Welch, Finis, "Minimum Wages: Issues and Evidence," American Enterprise Institute, Washington, 1978.

Youthwork, Incorporated, "Linking School and Work," Washington, April 1981.

Business Mergers and Antitrust

by

William Sweet

Jan. 15
1982

Editor's Note: While the thrust of this Report is the trend in American business toward corporate mergers and takeovers, a counter-trend has been detected more recently. It is toward divestiture by some large companies of their acquisitions. W. T. Grimm & Co., a Chicago firm that keeps track of merger activity, counted 875 divestitures in 1982, up from 666 in 1980. The recessionary economy was considered the main reason for companies choosing to close down or sell their subsidiaries rather than retain them.

BUSINESS MERGERS AND ANTITRUST

ON JAN. 8, the Justice Department announced it was ending the two biggest antitrust actions in American history, the suits against American Telephone & Telegraph (AT&T)[1] — the world's largest company — and International Business Machines (IBM), the giant computer manufacturer. The announcements came just one day after news of the second-biggest merger in American history, U.S. Steel's takeover of Marathon Oil, and less than six months after the country's largest merger ever — the acquisition of Conoco by Du Pont. The Du Pont-Conoco takeover helped make 1981 a record year in a merger wave that began to sweep the country in the mid-1970s, and if the latest news is any indication, 1982 could end up breaking all previous highs.

Economic analysts disagree about the scope, the importance and the implications of the current merger wave, but most agree that the growing popularity of corporate takeovers is an unexpected and bewildering phenomenon. At a time when business executives and individual investors have expressed pessimism about the U.S. economy, corporations have been buying each other up as though the future could bring nothing but prosperity and profits. The nation's most prestigious brokerages and investment houses have been helping corporate executives plan acquisition campaigns, and the country's biggest commercial banks have been willing to stake billions on the outcome of merger fights.

A number of factors contribute to the takeover mania: inflation, windfall profits, changes in bank legislation, a new trend in Supreme Court decisions, certain abiding features of the U.S. tax system and some new tax breaks enacted by the Reagan administration. Not least has been a degree of uncertainty about President Reagan's antitrust policies. Eager to find out how far they would be allowed to go, corporate directors put the administration's antitrust officials to some tough tests in 1981, most notably in the two big merger battles for control of Conoco and Marathon.

---

[1] The federal judge who had been trying the AT&T case said Jan. 12 that he was "delighted that a settlement had been reached," but he refused to dismiss the case "without proper scrutiny" of the agreement.

The first fight began with a cross-border incursion last May, when Canada's Dome Petroleum made an offer to buy 22 million shares in Conoco Inc., the ninth-largest oil company in the United States. Dome's limited objective was to gain control of Conoco's Canadian oil reserves, but in the process of stripping Conoco of that particular ornament, Dome inadvertently exposed the whole company as an enticing prize.

The enthusiastic reception Dome's bid met with among Conoco's shareholders indicated that the stock market had drastically undervalued the company's other alluring assets, which include sizable oil reserves in the United States and Consolidation Coal, the second-biggest U.S. coal company. At a time of rising domestic energy prices, such features aroused wide interest, and within weeks a number of well-appointed suitors had appeared with offers to buy Conoco out.

The Conoco and Marathon Takeover Battles

In an effort to fend off an unwelcome bid from Seagram Co., the Canadian distiller, Conoco's directors opened negotiations first with Cities Service and then with E. I. du Pont de Nemours & Co. Du Pont made an initial offer for Conoco of $6.9 billion — $3 billion in cash and the rest in Du Pont stock to be exchanged for Conoco shares at a rate of 1.6 to 1. As Seagram and Du Pont escalated their bids in midsummer, Mobil Corp. took to the field with yet another offer.

Further maneuvers followed, and the participants were advised by big New York investment firms: Mobil by Merrill Lynch, Pierce, Fenner & Smith Inc.; Du Pont by First Boston Corp.; and Seagram by Lazard Freres & Co. and Shearson Loeb Rhoades Inc. Meanwhile, rumors spread that several other oil companies were arranging huge credit lines, possibly with a view of entering the battle for Conoco, or possibly with other takeover targets in mind. The suspense ended in the first week in August, when Du Pont won control of Conoco at a cost of $7.2 billion — by far the biggest takeover in U.S. history.[2]

Post-mortem accounts of why Mobil lost the fight, despite the fact that its final offer was more than $1 billion higher than Du Pont's, stressed that most investors remained deeply uncertain as to whether the Reagan administration would end up permitting a Mobil-Conoco merger. While Reagan antitrust officials had said they would not necessarily regard big business takeovers as a bad thing, it seemed unlikely for a combination of legal and political reasons that the administration could ignore a horizontal merger *(see box, p. 177)* between the country's second-largest (Mobil) and ninth-largest (Conoco) oil companies. A Du Pont merger, on the other hand, seemed to pose less

---

[2] The previous high was set in 1979, when Shell Oil Co. paid $3.65 billion for Belridge Oil.

Types of Corporate Mergers

Combinations of companies that make similar products and compete in the same market are called *horizontal mergers*. By definition, such mergers decrease the competition in a given market and make it easier for corporate directors to agree, formally or informally, to set monopolistic prices, divide markets or curtail innovation. For this reason, antitrust authorities have traditionally given proposals for horizontal mergers very close scrutiny.

Vertical mergers join concerns that are involved in different parts of the same production process: those that make different components of the same product, or manufacturers and their suppliers of raw materials. Since the individual divisions of a vertically integrated firm can be expected to remain in competition with outside suppliers of parts or materials, the effects of vertical mergers are not necessarily thought to be monopolistic.

Conglomerate mergers combine companies that are engaged in unrelated activities or that sell their products in different geographic areas, even though they market similar products. From the legal point of view, conglomerate mergers are least suspect, and they have been the most common form of merger in recent decades.

sensitive problems. Du Pont was not directly involved in the production and marketing of oil, and while it could be expected to integrate Conoco's operations into its chemical manufacturing processes, a vertical merger of this kind stood a good chance of being considered acceptable.

Business commentators perceived a number of tactical and strategic errors by Mobil. They said further that the company — famous for its assertive public relations campaigns — had set itself up for a lot of adverse publicity.[3] That did not prevent Mobil from launching a second attempt to buy a major oil company later the same year. This time, it was a fight with U.S. Steel for control of Marathon, the country's 16th-largest oil company, and this time Mobil's bid became ensnared in legal difficulties.

The Federal Trade Commission (FTC), which shares antitrust enforcement powers with the Justice Department, raised objections to the deal — though it suggested, in a highly unusual decision, that the merger might be permitted if Mobil divested itself of certain Marathon holdings. Mobil promised to sell some of Marathon's marketing and refining operations to Amerada Hess Corp., and in an apparent effort to intimidate or pressure U.S. Steel, it threatened to issue a bid to buy up 25

[3] See *The New York Times*, Aug. 7, 1981, and *The Wall Street Journal*, Aug. 6, 1981. For background on Mobil's "advocacy advertising," in which it explicitly seeks to influence "opinion leaders," see "Corporate Assertiveness," *E.R.R.*, 1978 Vol. I, pp. 467-470.

percent of the steel company's stock. All of Mobil's efforts proved unavailing, however, including a raise in its bid for Marathon to $6.5 billion. Two Ohio courts issued rulings against Mobil, and Chief Justice Warren E. Burger refused to enjoin U.S. Steel from buying Marathon shares. On Jan. 7, U.S. Steel announced it had obtained control of Marathon at a total cost of $6.2 billion.

Critical Assessment of New Merger Wave

The 1981-82 takeovers are the crest of a merger wave that began to sweep the country during the mid-1970s. Preliminary estimates put the value of companies acquired through mergers in 1981 at $82.6 billion, a record amount and 86 percent greater than the amount spent on acquisitions in 1980 *(see box, p. 195).*[4] The biggest takeovers of 1981 included, in addition to the Marathon and Conoco deals, a third major oil consolidation (the acquisition of Texasgulf by France's Elf-Aquitaine); several takeovers of mineral companies (e.g. Kennecott by Sohio and St. Joe Minerals by Fluor); and a startling number of mergers among financial and quasi-financial institutions. Major mergers also involved food and soft drink conglomerates and high technology corporations *(see box, p. 183)*

Since mid-1981, the nation's press has been filled with stories about the "new urge to merge" and the "agglomeration of America." Many writers have raised questions about the way scarce investment capital is being allocated and about the relationships between the country's largest corporations, commercial banks and investment houses. To some writers, it has seemed ironic that at a time when the government is giving business a variety of tax breaks[5] with the stated intention of stimulating corporate investment and economic productivity, many companies seem to be using their "windfall" gains not to deploy new technology or find new resources but to buy each other. "How to explain this paradox of corporate poverty in the midst of corporate riches?" one publication has asked. "How can there be a 'merger mania' involving billions of dollars in an economy supposedly starved for the money needed to invest in new plants and equipment?"[6]

Because of such concerns, Rep. Fernand J. St Germain, D-R.I., the chairman of the House Banking, Finance and Urban

---

[4] The 1981 estimate does not include the Marathon takeover, since it was consummated in 1982.

[5] In Reagan's tax bill, passed by Congress last July, business tax cuts included a simplified and accelerated depreciation system; an extension of the period over which businesses can carry forward unused tax credits; investment tax credits for research and development and the rehabilitation of old buildings; and a number of other measures. See *Congressional Quarterly Weekly Report,* Aug. 8, 1981, p. 1434.

[6] See "The Corporate Shuffle," *Dollars and Sense* (published by the Economic Affairs Bureau Inc., in Somerville, Mass.), December 1981, p. 3.

Business Mergers and Antitrust

Affairs Committee, called last July for immediate action to restrict bank credit available for multibillion-dollar acquisition campaigns. In a letter to Paul A. Volcker, chairman of the Federal Reserve Board, St Germain said that support for the Fed's policy of tight money and high interest rates "requires, at minimum, a perception that everyone is sharing in the hardship." Rep. Henry S. Reuss, D-Wis., chairman of the Joint Economic Committee, voiced support for St Germain's views.

During the Carter years, the Justice Department prepared a legislative proposal that would have banned any merger resulting in a combined company with more than $2 billion in assets or sales. President Carter did not support the proposal, but his rival for leadership of the Democrats, Sen. Edward M. Kennedy, D-Mass., proposed similar legislation in the Senate. Kennedy, together with his close collaborator in antitrust matters, Sen. Howard M. Metzenbaum, D-Ohio, also introduced a bill to bar the nation's 16 largest oil companies from acquiring any company with assets of more than $100 million.[7]

The Senate did not pass the Kennedy-Metzenbaum legislation, and after the Republicans took control of the Senate in 1981, Kennedy lost his influential position as chairman of the Judiciary Committee.[8] His successor, Sen. Strom Thurmond, R-S.C., abolished the committee's antitrust panel immediately upon taking over as chairman. Thurmond said he actually upgraded the status of antitrust, since it would now fall within the purview of the full committee, but militant critics of big business mergers strongly disagreed.

Growing Influence of Neo-Conservative Views

Not everybody agrees that the current merger wave is strange, questionable or even important. When the American Economic Association held its annual convention in Washington during the last week of December, its program of activities filled a fat little paperback book, but not one session or seminar was devoted to corporate conglomeration or antitrust policy.

Lawrence J. White, the new director of economic policy in the Justice Department's antitrust division, argues that recent mergers have not produced a greater concentration of economic power. Writing in *The Wall Street Journal*, Dec. 11, White presented statistics indicating that the share of the country's 200 largest manufacturing companies in total manufacturing increased only slightly between 1963 and 1977, and that in the economy as a whole, the largest 200 companies accounted for a

[7] See "Oil Antitrust Action," *E.R.R.*, 1978 Vol. I, pp. 101-120.
[8] Moreover, Kennedy gave up his position as ranking minority member of the committee in favor of taking the top Democratic slot on the Labor and Human Resources Committee.

decreasing share of national profits and employment through 1979.[9] Thus, White concluded, "the relative size of the country's largest corporations has not been growing, despite the merger wave and the claims to the contrary."

"The relative size of the country's largest corporations has not been growing, despite the merger wave and the claims to the contrary."

Lawrence J. White
Director of Economic Policy
U.S. Justice Department,
Antitrust Division

One reason why this is so "can be found in the substantial number of spinoffs and divestitures that have been occurring," White added. There has been a pronounced trend in recent years for conglomerates, which grew frantically in the merger wave of the 1960s, to divest themselves of unprofitable subsidiaries. Many businesses found it harder than expected to centralize control over a wide range of activities, and Wall Street investors tended to cool on conglomerates, perhaps in part because companies with diverse operations are hard to evaluate.[10] Management buy-outs, the most common form of divestiture, increased to 83 in 1981 from 49 in 1978, according to W. T. Grimm & Co., a Chicago merger brokerage firm.[11] Significant divestitures in 1981 included the sale of Winchester (guns) by Olin Corp. (chemical and metal products); Harley-Davidson (motorcycles) by AMF Corp. (industrial and leisure products); Swift by Esmark (meatpacking); and Brentano's by Macmillan (publishing).

Divestitures and mergers alike, in the view of many economists, are properly seen as a natural and healthy adjustment process in a free market economy. The neo-conservative economists associated with the "Chicago school" believe that mergers should not be viewed with any special suspicion, unless specific anti-competitive practices can be demonstrated. Robert H. Bork, one of the most influential figures associated with the

---

[9] According to White's statistics, which are based on sales minus costs of components and materials, the 200 companies accounted for 30 percent of U.S. manufacturing in 1947, 41 percent in 1963 and 44 percent in 1979.

[10] See Leslie Wayne, "Joys of Fleeing the Corporate Stable," *The New York Times*, Nov. 15, 1981, Section 3. Montgomery Ward & Co., once the nation's second-largest retail chain, dropped to sixth position after being acquired by Mobil in 1976. Its 1981 losses are estimated at over $200 million.

[11] In a management buy-out, the executives of the subsidiary purchase it from the parent, usually by offering the subsidiary's assets as security for large bank loans.

neo-conservative school, argued in a book published in 1978 that the country's antitrust laws are no longer respectable from an intellectual, legal or economic point of view.[12] Bork argued that mergers should be permitted whenever they result in better efficiency and lower costs for consumers, even when price-fixing and division of markets are involved.[13]

Changing Policies at Justice and the FTC

The neo-conservative economic philosophy has been increasingly influential in universities all over the country, and even

Thomas John Campbell

before President Reagan took office, people trained in Chicago economics were occupying middle-level government positions in growing numbers. But Reagan appointees have strengthened the ascendancy of the neo-conservatives in government. William F. Baxter, the new head of the Justice Department's antitrust division, has described himself as a "fellow traveler" of the Chicago school. Thomas John Campbell, the new head of the FTC's Bureau of Competition, is a 29-year-old prodigy who was the youngest student ever to pass the doctoral exams in economics at the University of Chicago. Milton Friedman, who was the dominant figure in the Chicago economics department for many years, was Campbell's freshman adviser and has declared himself "glad" about Campbell's appointment.

Many top Reagan officials have echoed the ideas that mergers often promote efficiency and that bigness is the just reward of sound management,[14] and this is the philosophy that is supposed to guide the administration's antitrust enforcement policies. James C. Miller 3rd, the new chairman of the FTC, has said the agency should no longer "explore the frontiers of antitrust law." Baxter has said he will take a much more lenient view toward vertical and conglomerate mergers *(see box, p. 177)* and that he will concentrate the efforts of his team at the Justice Department on enforcement of legislation barring criminal collusion to fix prices and divide markets.

---

[12] The neo-conservative economists, many of whom have worked for or been trained in the economics department at the University of Chicago, are critical of Keynesian economics and most efforts by the government to control or regulate the economy.

[13] See Robert H. Bork, *The Antitrust Paradox: A Policy at War with Itself* (1978).

[14] "Let's face it," Treasury Secretary Donald T. Regan has said, "our economy is growing, our nation is growing and the world is growing. So why shouldn't companies grow?" In a widely noted passage from a speech to the District of Columbia Bar Association, Attorney General William French Smith said last June, "Bigness in business does not necessarily mean badness," and "efficient firms should not be hobbled under the guise of antitrust enforcement."

Baxter apparently has done just what he said he would do.
Civil antitrust actions have been sharply curtailed, and at
present only one civil suit is in litiga-
tion. Baxter has terminated the department's effort to locate and break up
"shared monopolies" — industries in
which firms fix prices or divide markets
without explicit agreements.[15] Baxter is
expected to rewrite departmental
guidelines so that cases almost never
are pressed against companies that are
not direct competitors, and he is expected to go easier on companies that
exert pressure on retailers to maintain
minimum prices, deal only with one

William F. Baxter

supplier, or purchase all products offered in "package deals." In
July, Justice dropped a suit against Mack Trucks Inc., which
had been accused of conspiring with independent distributors to
fix the prices of parts.

Baxter is expected to re-evaluate the criteria for challenging
horizontal mergers, which traditionally have called for departmental action whenever a company controls more than 10
percent of a market. But Justice Department lawyers are said to
be vigorously pressing cases thought to involve criminal anti-
competitive behavior, and in one significant action last fall, they
acted to block a proposed merger between two brewers,
Heilemann and Schlitz. Baxter reportedly has introduced the
systematic use of cost-benefit analysis to determine whether the
anticipated effects of an antitrust action would justify the vast
expense of long litigation.

Dropping Action Against AT&T, IBM, Oil

The AT&T and IBM cases were not only the largest but also
two of the longest-running antitrust actions in American history. The Justice Department filed suit against IBM on Jan. 17,
1969, the last working day of the Johnson administration, and
against AT&T on Nov. 20, 1974. In both cases, the government
accused the corporate giants of exploiting their enormous assets[16] and dominant market positions to drive out weaker
competitors.

---

[15] John H. Shenefield, head of the antitrust division for three years under Carter,
launched a search for shared monopolies but was unable to find a target worthy of
prosecution. Shenefield expected to find anti-competitive practices like "price leadership"
— tacit understandings in an industry that all firms will follow the top one in setting prices
— in the older and less innovative industries, such as iron and steel, aluminum and
newsprint.

[16] AT&T, together with its local companies, has assets valued at $136 billion. IBM has
$26.7 billion in assets, according to *Fortune* magazine's latest annual listing of the 500
largest U.S. industrial companies.

Biggest Mergers in 1981*

Rank	Merging Companies		Transaction Value
1	Du Pont (chemicals)	Conoco (oil)	$7.2 billion
2	Fluor (engineering)	St. Joe Minerals	$2.3 billion
3	Standard Oil of Ohio	Kennecott (copper)	$1.8 billion
4	American Express (financial services)	Shearson Loeb Rhoades (securities)	$988.9 million
5	Nabisco (food products)	Standard Brands (food products)	$783.6 million
6	Occidental Petroleum	Iowa Beef Processors	$770.3 million
7	Penn Central (energy, real estate)	GK Technologies (wire and cable)	$699.6 million
8	GL Corp. (metals)	Trans Union (railcar leasing)	$688.2 million
9	Cooper Industries (oil)	Crouse-Hinds (electrical equipment)	$673.4 million
10	Hospital Corp. of America (hospital management)	Hospital Affiliates International (hospital management)	$650.0 million
11	Westinghouse Broadcasting	Teleprompter (cable TV)	$647.0 million
12	Sears, Roebuck (retail merchandise)	Dean Witter Reynolds (securities)	$606.9 million
13	Phibro (commodities)	Salomon Brothers (securities)	$550.0 million
14	Allegheny International (metals)	Sunbeam (appliances)	$527.9 million
15	Caterpillar Tractor (earth moving equipment)	Solar Turbines International (turbomachinery)	$505.5 million

*Excludes takeovers involving foreign companies (e.g. Texasgulf by France's Elf-Aquitaine, Santa Fe International by Kuwait Petroleum and Crocker National Bank by England's Midland Bank) and takeovers involving newly formed companies (e.g. Twentieth Century Fox Film by TCF Holdings).

Other important mergers announced in 1981 included Apex Oil-Clark Oil & Refining; General Foods-Oscar Mayer; Freeport Minerals-McMoran Oil & Gas; Tenneco-Houston Oil & Minerals; Bechtel (construction)-Dillon, Read (securities); Prudential (insurance)-Bache (securities); SmithKline-Beckman (instruments); Dr. Pepper-Canada Dry (soft drinks); and Bank of America-Charles Schwab (securities).

In explaining the Justice Department's decision to drop the suit against IBM, Baxter said he found the case to be "without merit." Department lawyers indicated that the computer industry has become much more competitive than when the suit first was filed. Numerous manufacturers of large office machines and makers of smaller personal equipment have come to be IBM rivals, and under the terms of the settlement with AT&T the telephone company is expected to become a formidable competitor in the computer and telecommunications markets.

In the proposed settlement, AT&T retains control of Bell Laboratories, its equipment manufacturer and its long-distance telephone division, but it is required to divest itself of its 22 local telephone companies. While the local companies are worth about $80 billion and account for roughly two-thirds of AT&T's assets, they have been the least profitable part of the company. As a result of their divestiture, consumers may see local telephone rates rise.

The legal transformation of AT&T from a national telephone company into a firm specializing in the processing and long-distance transmittal of information began in 1980, when the Federal Communications Commission reversed a 1956 decision that had barred AT&T from the computer market. In response to the FCC decision, AT&T was required to divide itself into two units, one regulated and one unregulated. In the negotiations that led up to the Justice Department's antitrust settlement, Baxter reportedly sought assurances that AT&T would not be allowed to subsidize its unregulated computer business out of its regulated communications operations. Now that AT&T has divested itself of the regulated operations in which it had a monopoly — the local phone companies — Baxter sees no need for special provisions to cover the problem of "cross-subsidies." Apparently, Baxter believes that the presence of competitors in the long-distance telephone market will prevent AT&T from subsidizing its telecommunications and computer operations out of long-distance rates.

In other major antitrust actions, the FTC terminated an investigation of the automobile industry last March, and in September it dropped an antitrust case against the country's eight largest oil companies.[17] The FTC staff reportedly concluded that the oil case, which was launched under pressure from congressional Democrats in 1973, had dragged on too long in the pretrial phase to warrant continuation. The FTC is under pressure to drop a suit against cereal manufacturers, in which Kellogg Co., General Mills and General Foods Corp. are charged with maintaining a shared monopoly.

New Standards in Supreme Court Decisions

Long before the Reagan administration took office, and even before the current merger wave began in the mid-1970s, the Supreme Court was beginning to adopt a more skeptical attitude toward government antitrust prosecutions. According to a review of policy on conglomerate mergers, which the American Enterprise Institute in Washington recently published,[18] the Warren Court (1954-1969) took a tough line on conglomerate

---

[17] Exxon, Mobil, Texaco, Standard of California, Gulf, Standard (Indiana), Atlantic Richfield Co. and Shell Oil Co.
[18] American Enterprise Institute, "Recent Proposals to Restrict Conglomerate Mergers" (1981), p. 12.

mergers, and "through 1972 the government won all of its anti-merger cases in the Supreme Court." Since 1973, on the other hand, there may not have been "a single unequivocal victory for either the government or private plaintiffs in Supreme Court cases challenging conglomerate mergers," the report said.

In a series of decisions in the early and mid-1960s, the Supreme Court tended to evaluate mergers primarily in terms of how market concentration would be affected by proposed combinations. In a 1963 opinion, written by Justice William J. Brennan Jr., the court ruled that a merger could be presumed illegal — subject to rebuttal — if it gave the leading company a bigger share of the market. In relatively clear-cut cases, the court said that more detailed consideration of a merger's competitive effects could be dispensed with.[19]

"Recent Supreme Court decisions on conglomerate mergers have revealed a tension between sentiment for simplified rules and a conviction that the legality or illegality of mergers should depend exclusively on their economic consequences."

In a 1964 opinion, written by Justice William O. Douglas, the court ruled that a small additional increase in market concentration was enough to invalidate a horizontal merger.[20] In a similar case the same year, in which the acquisition of a glass container company by a can company was at issue, the court again based its ruling largely on a theoretical assessment of how the changed industry structure might affect competition.[21] The court went still further in 1967, when it barred the takeover of Clorox by Procter & Gamble, on the ground that the merger would strengthen Clorox's dominant position in the liquid bleach industry by eliminating Procter & Gamble as a potential competitor.[22]

Starting in 1974, the Supreme Court began to modify its basic position, holding that a consideration of market shares alone

---

[19] See *United States v. Philadelphia National Bank*, 374 U.S. 321 (1963).

[20] *United States v. Aluminum Co. of America*, 377 U.S. 271 (1964). This decision raised the question of whether a major industrial concern would be permitted to make any acquisition, regardless of size, in its own line of business.

[21] *United States v. Continental Can Co.*, 378 U.S. 441 (1964).

[22] *FTC v. Procter & Gamble*, 386 U.S. 568 (1967). Procter & Gamble, in other words, did not produce liquid bleach but was a potential competitor.

would not suffice to invalidate a proposed merger. In *United States v. General Dynamics Corp.*, the court insisted on analysis of economic evidence in addition to theoretical considerations; the court declared that a proposed merger would no longer be held presumptively illegal just because a firm controlled a large market share.[23] In a 1977 opinion written by Justice Lewis F. Powell Jr., *Continental T.V. Inc. v. GTE Sylvania Inc.*, the court overturned a presumptive rule of illegality in the case of vertical market restrictions and insisted on demonstrable anti-competitive effects.[24]

According to the American Enterprise Institute's summary of the foregoing record, recent Supreme Court decisions on conglomerate mergers have revealed a "tension between sentiment for simplified rules" and a conviction that the legality or illegality of mergers should depend exclusively on their economic consequences. While scholars have criticized the one approach as overly simple and "too sweeping and absolute to be followed in practice," the purely economic approach has been criticized "for excluding consideration of political and social concerns," the AEI study concluded.

America's Big Merger Cycles

THE LEGAL environment always has had an important bearing on whether mergers take place, but according to an axiom amply borne out by experience, prosperity is what really breeds mergers. Typically, the instinct for agglomeration has quickened during business booms and subsided during economic slumps. The first great wave of American corporate takeovers came during the period of rapid industrialization between the Civil War and World War I, and it coincided with the construction of a national railroad system, which laid the basis for unified markets in manufactured goods and raw materials.

This was the era in which the so-called "robber barons" — entrepreneurs like John D. Rockefeller and Andrew Carnegie — created giant industrial trusts. Subsequent merger waves took place during the "Roaring '20s," in the economic boom during and after World War II, and in the 1960s, when the Kennedy and Johnson administrations sought to "get America moving again."

---

[23] 415 U.S. 486 (1974).
[24] 433 U.S. 36 (1977). The case involved territorial restrictions imposed on a dealer by a manufacturer.

The beginning of big business in America often is dated to 1882, the year the Standard Oil Trust Agreement was drawn up. The creation of the Standard Oil monopoly inspired many other industries to consolidate into similar trusts, including linseed oil, cottonseed oil, lead, distilling, matches, tobacco and rubber. The trend was partially stalled by a depression in the late 1880s and by the enactment of the Sherman Antitrust Act in 1890, which barred "every contract, combination or conspiracy in restraint of trade."[25] But the Supreme Court took an extremely relaxed position on business mergers in the 1890s, and by the end of the decade the movement toward industrial consolidation was in full swing again. Business takeovers between 1898 and 1907, the year of the "rich man's panic," involved over 15 percent of the country's manufacturing assets and gave rise to companies like General Electric and U.S. Steel — the nation's first billion-dollar corporation.

During the first decade of the 20th century, public concern about corporate power mounted sharply, partly because of the work of the "muckrakers," whose influential books included Upton Sinclair's *The Jungle* (1906) and Ida M. Tarbell's *History of the Standard Oil Company* (1904). Positions on antitrust policy became important in presidential campaigns, and the Supreme Court adopted an increasingly restrictive attitude toward mergers.

In the Northern Securities Case of 1904, the court found that two railway companies had formed an illegal combination to restrain trade, and in 1911 the court ordered the breakup of the American Tobacco Co. and Standard Oil. In 1914, Congress passed the Federal Trade Commission Act, which established the FTC, and the Clayton Antitrust Act, which prohibited price discrimination, exclusive sales contracts, interlocking directorates and the acquisition of capital stock interests in a competitor firm.

After World War I, in what was now becoming a regular cycle, the Supreme Court once again became more favorably disposed toward corporate consolidation. Weak interpretations of the Clayton Act by the court, together with increasingly frenetic speculation in stocks and bonds, helped fuel a new burst of corporate takeovers. In contrast to the first era of trust-building, when horizontal combinations predominated, there was a strong trend in the 1920s toward vertical integration and corporate diversification. Between 1920 and 1929, when the onslaught of the Great Depression put an end to the country's

[25] For a review of antitrust legislation, see Congressional Quarterly's *Guide to the U.S. Supreme Court* (1979), pp. 90-93. See also "Antitrust Action," *E.R.R.*, 1975 Vol. I, pp. 61-81.

second round of merger mania, roughly 10 percent of the manufacturing assets had been affected by takeovers.

After World War II revived the economy and, with it, the urge to merge, Congress enacted new legislation in 1950 to strengthen the Clayton Act.[26] During the next decade, government officials and the Supreme Court took a tough line on horizontal and vertical mergers. As a result, conglomerate mergers dominated business takeovers in the 1960s. Between 1965 and 1968, the year the last wave of takeovers peaked, there were roughly 7,000 mergers, and about 8 percent of American manufacturing assets were involved. According to the American Enterprise Institute, roughly 80 percent of all U.S. mergers since 1966 have been of the conglomerate kind.

Inflation and Taxes as Key Elements Today

In defiance of the time-honored principle that prosperity breeds mergers, the current takeovers have been taking place in a period of slow economic growth and low business confidence. The reasons why businesses have been rushing to acquire one another, despite pessimistic expectations about the future, are complicated, and to some extent differ from sector to sector. But the general factors at work are similar to the considerations that have prompted many individuals to invest in houses and other fixed assets. At a time when inflation has boosted the costs of investing in new plant and equipment, and prospective returns on such investments remain uncertain, many corporate directors think that buying existing assets is cheaper and safer.

According to estimates by the president's Council of Economic Advisers, the stock market value of U.S. manufacturing assets has been lagging increasingly far behind their "real" value, as measured by their replacement costs *(see box, p. 189)*. The gap between real and market values is thought to be especially large in the oil industry: On the one hand, a glut on the world petroleum market has depressed energy company stock prices; but at the same time, the decontrol of domestic oil prices has enormously increased the value of companies that possess substantial reserves in the United States.

Companies like Conoco and Marathon therefore look very attractive to prospective suitors, and among the suitors, some of the most ardent have been the large oil corporations that are flush with the "windfall profits" yielded from decontrol.[27]

[26] The Celler-Kefauver Act of 1950 prohibited mergers through acquisition of physical assets. It was sponsored by Rep. Emanuel Celler, D-N.Y., and Sen. Estes Kefauver, D-Tenn.
[27] President Carter announced he would phase out controls on domestic oil prices in April 1979, and in March 1980 Congress passed a tax on "windfall" — excessive — profits from oil, designed to raise roughly $227 billion over a decade out of about $1 trillion expected in added oil company revenues.

Tobin's q

Coincidentally, the 1981 Nobel Memorial Prize in Economic Science went to an American whose work often is cited in explanations of the 1981 merger wave. The Swedish Academy of Sciences awarded the prize to James Tobin of Yale University in recognition of his contributions to portfolio theory — the theory of how individuals and businesses "behave when they acquire different assets and incur debts," as the academy put it.

Tobin devised the "q-ratio," which measures the relationship of the market value of existing physical assets to their replacement cost. When the q-ratio is low, indicating that the stock market is undervaluing assets, companies will tend to buy up existing plant and equipment rather than invest in new technology. When the q-ratio is high, firms will tend to sell assets and make new investments.

According to statistics compiled by the president's Council of Economic Advisers, the q-ratio for American non-financial corporations has dropped drastically since the early 1970s:

1970	0.863	1976	0.740
1972	1.012	1978	0.602
1974	0.663	1980	0.526

The declining q-ratio reflects both the growing cost of plant and equipment, a result of inflation, and declining returns on stock market investment.

Mobil, the most ardent suitor of all, is reported to be acting out of a well-established corporate policy of acting aggressively, at every good opportunity, to acquire more oil reserves.[28]

For companies with huge profits, U.S. tax laws may be providing added incentives to invest in acquisitions. If a company decides to pass its profits on to its shareholders in cash dividends, the money is doubly taxed: first as corporate income, then as personal income to the shareholders. But if a company puts its profits into a sound acquisition, its investment capital is retained in full, and the value of its stock is boosted. If stockholders want to sell their stock, it is more valuable and it is taxed at a more favorable rate — as capital gains rather than as income. Frederick Scherer, an expert on industrial market structure, believes that a tax system that did not discourage cash dividends would help to curb mergers.[29]

According to a report issued by the House Committee on Small Business, "small business owners wishing to sell their

---

[28] As one of the companies created when Standard Oil was broken up in 1911, Mobil found itself without oil wells of its own. It has been the company's firm policy ever since to make up for that handicap.

[29] For Scherer's views, see Lydia Chavez, "The Agglomeration of America," *The New York Times*, July 12, 1981, Section 3. Scherer is author of *Industrial Market Structure and Economic Performance* (1970 and 1980), a standard text.

businesses are inclined to undertake tax-free stock swaps with large blue-chip companies in order to avoid the capital gains tax attendant to sales of stock for cash." [30] If the conglomerate purchases a company that has been running at a loss, the losses can be applied against the earnings of the conglomerate in certain cases.

This year, the government decided to accelerate depreciation allowances, a move that Lester C. Thurow, the economist-author, has described as a "backdoor elimination of the corporation income tax." [31] According to Thurow, capital-intensive companies in industries like steel, chemicals and petroleum will benefit most from the tax revisions, since they have the most capital to depreciate. Thurow predicts that they will end up with unused depreciation allowances, which they will put to use by purchasing labor-intensive firms. The result, Thurow believes, will be to "induce mergers between firms that would be more efficiently run separately."

Financial Sector's Current Takeover Role

A striking aspect of the current takeover wave has been the willingness of some companies to borrow billions of dollars at record-high interest rates to finance merger campaigns. One reason for this is that the acquiring corporations can deduct the interest costs of the borrowed funds as business expenses on their income taxes. Also, some corporate executives are reported to hope that they will be able to renegotiate the credit terms when interest rates drop.

Bankers apparently share the view that certain corporate assets are undervalued and will repay the high cost of their acquisition. Or perhaps, in some cases, the bankers simply believe that the giant concerns borrowing the billions can be relied on to repay their loans, regardless of whether their acquisitions pan out. David Kotz, an economist at the University of Massachusetts, contends that bankers support merger campaigns partly because they regard loans to big corporations as safe, and partly because they hope to obtain contracts for financial services with the newly combined corporations. [32] In a study Kotz prepared for the FTC on the role of banks in corporate mergers, he found that firms with strong relationships with major bank creditors are about three times more likely than

---

[30] House Committee on Small Business, "Conglomerate Mergers — Their Effects on Small Business and Local Communities," Washington, October 1980. The report, issued by the parent committee, was prepared by the subcommittee on antitrust.
[31] See Lester C. Thurow, "The Next Merger Wave," *Newsweek*, Sept. 14, 1981, p. 73. Thurow, a professor at Massachusetts Institute of Technology, is the author of *The Zero-Sum Society: Distributions and Possibilities for Economic Change*, Basic Books, 1980.
[32] Interview, Dec. 30, 1981.

other firms to merge.[33]

Quite apart from bank influence on corporate mergers, the financial sector itself has been a locus of merger activity. Because of technological innovations in banking and important changes in bank regulations, the various kinds of financial institutions — thrifts, commercial banks, insurance companies, brokerage houses and consumer finance services — have become much more competitive with one another in going after deposits and lending to business.[34] Many bank analysts expect to see the emergence of institutions that will provide every conceivable kind of financial service, and in 1981 there was indeed a remarkable number of mergers among different kinds of financial institutions: Salomon Brothers was acquired by Phibro Corp.; Shearson Loeb Rhoades Inc. by American Express; the Bache Group by Prudential; and Dean Witter by Sears, Roebuck.

Merger activity was especially hectic in the financially troubled savings and loan industry. The net worth of the nation's 3,800 federally insured S&Ls dropped by nearly $4.3 billion in the first 11 months of 1981, and the Federal Home Loan Bank Board took the unprecedented step of approving interstate mergers of thrift institutions to save ailing ones. Bank regulators have recommended legislation that would allow bank holding companies to engage in interstate banking, and Federal Reserve Chairman Paul A. Volcker has said that the Fed may allow holding companies to buy up ailing thrift institutions on an emergency basis if Congress does not enact the legislation soon.

Executives at a number of big commercial banks, led by Walter Wriston of Citibank, have been urging a faster and more comprehensive process of bank deregulation. If barriers to interstate banking and other bank restrictions are eliminated, as Wriston recommends, some estimates indicate that nearly three quarters of America's financial institutions could disappear through consolidation.[35] Currently, the U.S. bank system includes about 14,000 commercial banks, 5,000 S&Ls and 20,000 credit unions.

---

[33] Kotz found this to be true when bank creditors were represented on a manufacturing firm's board, but not when the bank relationship was confined to ownership of stock in the firm. Kotz said that his study, "Bank Influence over the Merger Activity of Large Manufacturing Companies" was approved in 1980 for publication by the FTC but later was rejected.

[34] See "Banking Deregulation," *E.R.R.*, 1981 Vol. II, pp. 573-592.

[35] See Kenneth E. Scott, "The Uncertain Course of Bank Deregulation," *Regulation*, May-June 1981, p. 45.

Competing Antitrust Philosophies

A LARGE PART of the country's banking legislation was designed to protect and preserve a system of decentralized small banks, which would remain in close touch with their home communities and use local deposits to serve local investment needs. The nation's antitrust legislation, likewise, has been based to a great extent on a Jeffersonian belief that small enterprises are intrinsically desirable not only for economic but also moral and social reasons. Lawyers, legislators and judges have tended to approach mergers with the view, enunciated by federal Judge Learned Hand in 1945, that "great industrial concentrations are inherently undesirable regardless of their economic consequences."

Departing from that fundamental belief, Reagan officials have declared that economic efficiency alone should be the test of whether big corporations are desirable or undesirable. But the House Committee on Small Business, in its report, asserted "that when a conglomerate acquires control of a mature local company, there can be adverse impacts on the local community." The report said that conglomerate mergers tended to impede communication between local business and civic leaders, alter relations between the subsidiary and other community businesses and generate a climate of economic uncertainty.

Among the witnesses who had been heard was an administrator from Hopedale, Mass., once the home of Draper Looms. According to the municipal administrator, when Rockwell International acquired Draper in 1967, the executive staff was moved immediately to Pittsburgh, the plant began to deteriorate, research and development staffs were cut, and the facility — which had employed 2,400 local people — finally was closed.

Many business analysts have said that a similar chain of events ensued after the Lykes Corp. acquired Youngstown Sheet and Tube a decade ago. Lykes has been accused of milking the steel company for profits and investing them elsewhere. After the LTV Corp. acquired Lykes in 1978, the Youngstown mills were closed down. When LTV-Vought tried to buy the Grumman Corp. in late 1981, Grumman successfully resisted the bid, charging in a media blitz that "the Texas-based conglomerate" planned to use Grumman as a cash cow.

Residents of Findlay, Ohio, the home of Marathon Oil, feared that a takeover by Mobil would result in a closing of Marathon's local headquarters. They may be resting easier now that U.S. Steel has won the battle for Marathon, but in other communities that has caused consternation. Ron Weisen, a dissident United Steelworkers leader in Homestead, Pa., has argued that the industry should be investing profits in upgrading local steel plants, not oil. In Homestead, only three blast furnaces are in operation, and the work force has been nearly halved during the last decade.

International Competitiveness of U.S. Industry

Writing in the *AFL-CIO News,* columnist Gus Tyler has suggested that U.S. Steel's purchase of Marathon is bad not only for local communities, but for the country as a whole. While it may be more profitable for U.S. Steel to produce oil than make steel, Tyler said, the fact remains that "America needs steel; it is the backbone of an industrial society." Letting the market decide how U.S. Steel should invest its profits has meant, as Tyler sees it, "that Americans prefer to buy steel from overseas so long as steel made in this country is needlessly costly because of the obsolete way in which it is made."[36]

"Great industrial concentrations are inherently undesirable regardless of their economic consequences."
Judge Learned Hand (1945)

While Tyler sees U.S. Steel's poor showing against the Japanese as a reason to oppose its conglomerate policies, many business analysts, economists and lawyers have argued that heightened foreign competition is a good reason to allow and perhaps even encourage corporate agglomeration. They argue that a large number of domestic competitors may not be needed to keep prices down in sectors where there is lively competition from foreign competitors.

In view of the fact that governments in countries like France, Japan and West Germany often encourage their industries to consolidate, so as to compete more effectively in world markets, the U.S. government may have no choice but to do the same. Thurow, who is usually identified as a liberal, has said the first thing he would do as a member of the Reagan administration

---

[36] *AFL-CIO News,* Dec. 12, 1981. According to David M. Roderick, chairman of U.S. Steel, domestic steel sales were stagnant in the first 11 months of 1981 while steel imports increased 31 percent. By the middle of the summer, Roderick said, foreign steel companies accounted for over a quarter of U.S. sales.

would be to "get out of antitrust." [37] Frederick Scherer, a leading expert on the competitive effects of concentration, has said it seems "there are genuine economies of scale to higher degrees of concentration than many of us thought before."

Many business analysts argue, though, that indiscriminate conglomerate mergers are not the way to make U.S. industry more competitive in world markets. Peter Drucker, in an interview with *Forbes,* questioned whether Marathon and U.S. Steel have anything useful to contribute to each other.[38] Surveying the current merger wave, Drucker described it as an unhealthy "inflation wave." When corporations are borrowing money at 20 percent interest to finance their acquisitions, Drucker said, they "have all invested in inflation and are endangered by monetary stability." On the other hand, Drucker expressed approval of mergers that combine companies with complementary skills.

Arthur Burck, another business consultant, asserted in an interview with *U.S. News & World Report,* that "the merger process has destroyed or weakened thousands of businesses that were star performers when they were independent." [39] "When companies get too big," Burck said, "they often lose the capacity to take risks and develop new products," and "the larger the company, the greater its stock in the status quo." Moreover, Burck said, mergers are a threat to the free enterprise system because once "the nation's economy is concentrated among a handful of large corporations, the next major step will be the takeover of giants by the government."

Matching Profit Motives and National Needs

During the latter part of the Carter administration, there was a flurry of interest in "reindustrialization," the idea that the government should adopt vigorous policies to revitalize the nation's ailing basic industries. Discussion of reindustrialization pretty much ended with Reagan's victory, which was interpreted as a mandate for policies of government deregulation and decontrol. Reagan's team has taken the position that America's industrial giants, left to themselves, will bring the country renewed prosperity.

Business leaders argue that the current merger wave represents a "redeployment of assets" — an essential precondition for adjusting the U.S. economy to changed global conditions. Allowing companies to redeploy investment funds in accordance with the dictates of projected profits may indeed be the most efficient and rational way of getting the country moving again.

---

[37] Quoted by Steve Lohr, *The New York Times,* Feb. 15, 1981, Section 3.
[38] See *Forbes,* Jan. 18, 1982, pp. 34-36.
[39] *U.S. News & World Report,* Dec. 21, 1981, p. 64.

Merger Activity: 1968-1981

	Number of corporate mergers	Dollar volume of major acquisitions (in billions)	Number of mergers and acquisitions where purchase price was $100 million or larger
1975	2,297	$11.8	14
1976	2,276	20.0	39
1977	2,224	21.9	41
1978	2,106	34.2	80
1979	2,128	43.5	83
1980	1,889	44.3	94
1981	2,861	82.6	113

Source: W. T. Grimm & Co., Chicago.

But if Americans see their basic industries deteriorate still further in the coming years, and if Reagan's policies fail to restore economic health, there may be a revival of interest in the idea that the people's elected representatives, not profits, should determine how industries are redesigned and recombined.

Selected Bibliography

Books

Bork, Robert H., *The Antitrust Paradox: A Policy at War with Itself*, Basic Books, 1978.

Fusilier, H. Lee and Jerome C. Darnell, eds., *Competition and Public Policy: Cases in Antitrust*, Prentice-Hall, 1971.

Markham, Jesse W., *et al.*, *Horizontal Divestiture and the Petroleum Industry*, Ballinger, 1977.

Neale, A. D., *The Antitrust Laws of the U.S.A.*, Cambridge University Press, 1962.

Scherer, F. M., *Industrial Market Structure and Economic Performance*, 2nd edition, Rand McNally, 1980.

Steindl, Josef, *Maturity and Stagnation in American Capitalism*, Blackwell, 1952.

Articles

Hershman, Arlene, "A New Era for Bell," *Dun's Business Month*, September 1981.

Loomis, Carol J., "The Fight for Financial Turf," *Fortune*, Dec. 28, 1981.

"New Thrust in Antitrust," *Time*, May 21, 1979.

Scherschel, Patricia M., "Battles Heat Up in Takeover Wars," *U.S. News & World Report*, Dec. 21, 1981.

Singer, James W., "Big is Back in Favor," *National Journal*, April 4, 1981.

"The Corporate Shuffle," *Dollars and Sense*, December 1981.

"The New Urge to Merge," *Newsweek*, July 27, 1981.

Uttal, Bro, "What's Ahead for AT&T's Competitors," *Fortune*, Dec. 28, 1981.

Reports and Studies

American Enterprise Institute, "Recent Proposals to Restrict Conglomerate Mergers," Washington, July 1981.

Editorial Research Reports: "Banking Deregulation," 1981 Vol. II, p. 573; "Oil Antitrust Action," 1978 Vol. I, p. 101; "Antitrust Action," 1975 Vol. I, p. 61; "Business Concentration and Antitrust Laws," 1966 Vol. I, p. 379.

Green, Mark J., *et al.*, "The Closed Enterprise System," Ralph Nader's Study Group Report on Antitrust Enforcement, Grossman Publishers, 1972.

House Committee on Small Business, "Conglomerate Mergers — Their Effects on Small Business and Local Communities," Washington, 1980.

Kotz, David, "Bank Influence on the Merger Activity of Large Manufacturing Companies," University of Massachusetts Economics Department, October 1980.

The "MacNeil-Lehrer Report," "AT&T: Unshackling the Giant," Oct. 22, 1981..

THE CHARITY SQUEEZE

by

Robert Benenson

Dec. 3
1982

Editor's Note: The American Association on Fund-Raising Counsel, a leading authority on philanthropic trends, has reported that individuals, companies and foundations gave nearly $60 billion to charity in 1982, more than ever before. Individual giving accounted for $48.7 billion of the total, an increase of 9.4 percent above the 1981 figure. However, this was below the 11.9 percent increase of the previous year.

THE CHARITY SQUEEZE

I N THE WEEKS between now and Christmas, Americans will be asked to give a little more of themselves to help others. Community fund-raising drives will be making their final appeals. Charitable and other non-profit institutions will be asking for donations in the spirit of the season. Newspapers will remind people to "remember the neediest." Salvation Army bell-ringers and sidewalk Santa Clauses will ask passersby for their dimes and quarters.

The willingness of people to pitch in to build a better society has been an American trait since the birth of the nation. But President Reagan has made it part of his administration's domestic agenda. Using the catchall phrase "private sector initiatives," Reagan has encouraged businesses, churches, voluntary organizations and individuals to become more involved in improving communities and helping individuals.

Reagan and his supporters believe that growing federal involvement in such areas as welfare, community development, health care, education and even the arts has hampered local initiative and innovation, destroyed the willingness of different sectors of society to work together, and left the fate of many communities and individuals in the hands of distant federal bureaucrats. "The truth is we've let government take away many things we once considered were really ours to do voluntarily out of the goodness of our hearts and a sense of community pride and neighborliness," Reagan said in a nationally televised address Sept. 24, 1981.

To many in the private sector, especially those involved with non-profit organizations, the symbolism of the president's call for more volunteer help was negated by the impact of recent budget cuts in social welfare, community development and similar programs. "We are trying to walk a tightrope between being supportive of an administration ... that is encouraging more giving, more volunteering, more community initiative ... and [being] one of the sharpest critics of the budget cuts, because we're in a position to see that they are already impacting the already-vulnerable," said Brian O'Connell, president of Independent Sector, an umbrella organization for non-profit groups which is based in Washington, D.C.[1]

---

[1] The group acts as a liaison between the non-profit community and governmental bodies.

Many non-profit groups rely heavily on federal funds to carry out their programs *(see box, p. 209)* and they have accused the president of pulling the rug out from under them. At the same time, the recession, which has sent unemployment soaring to double digits, and cuts in such programs as Aid to Families With Dependent Children, food stamps, housing assistance and Medicaid have greatly increased demands on social service agencies — demands that many organizations say they are incapable of meeting. Consequently, many needy people are falling into the "gap" between what government is no longer doing and what the private sector is capable of doing.

White House Task Force on Initiatives

In 1981, during the first round of federal budget cuts, President Reagan was stung by charges that his administration was unfair to the needy. To help defuse this criticism, Reagan established the Task Force on Private Sector Initiatives.[2] According to Executive Director Jerry Guth, the task force's mission is to "uncover the very best in private-sector initiative, volunteerism, partnership, philanthropy" and to "package them, explain them, articulate them, share them with a whole host of institutions."

The task force, whose one-year authorization expires at the end of December, has 44 members from the business, philanthropic, religious and political communities. It is headed by C. William Verity Jr., chairman of Armco Inc., a Middletown, Ohio, steel company known for its philanthropy and community involvement. Other well-known members include Cardinal Terence Cooke, Roman Catholic Archbishop of New York; George Romney, former governor of Michigan and chairman of the National Center for Citizen Involvement;[3] and three current Republican officeholders, Rep. Barber B. Conable Jr. of New York, Sen. David Durenberger of Minnesota and Gov. Pierre S. du Pont IV of Delaware.

Guth, who is also on loan from Armco, where he serves as a marketing executive, says the task force is not trying to find ways to make up for all of the federal budget cuts. "That was never an expectation the president or we had," Guth said in a recent interview. "Anybody who looks at the numbers knows that is absolutely impossible...." Instead, he said, the task force wants to foster greater cooperation between state and local governments, business interests, voluntary organizations and

---

[2] See Marvin N. Olasky, "Reagan's Second Thoughts on Corporate Giving," *Fortune*, Sept. 20, 1982, pp. 130-136.

[3] The center serves as a clearinghouse for information on volunteer programs and operates a network of Voluntary Action Centers which help communities and organizations coordinate and improve voluntary activities. The organization, formed in 1979 by a merger of the National Center for Voluntary Action and the National Information Center for Voluntary Action, is based in Boulder, Colo., but has a national affairs office in Washington.

Removing Impediments to Private Sector Action

The Task Force on Private Sector Initiatives has a committee on "impediments" to voluntary and other private sector activities. Chaired by Rep. Barber B. Conable Jr., R-N.Y., the committee is looking for ways to make it easier for private individuals and organizations to play a greater role in the delivery of services.

One area where the committee and other interested parties are looking is government regulation. Members of the voluntary community, especially those involved in smaller, neighborhood-oriented projects, complain that regulations often create prohibitive financial or logistical problems for them. In a recent interview, Don Underwood, a press spokesman for the task force, said he had talked to a group of black New Yorkers whose plans for a day-care center in the South Bronx were being blocked by a city regulation concerning the necessary number of toilets for such a facility. "They've been working on this project for a year or two, and they find themselves absolutely stymied," said Underwood. "It's an impediment to their financing, engineering, and it's just a small example of what an impediment is."

individuals, in line with its motto "Building Partnerships USA." "We're asking people to cross borders and do some new things," Guth said. "For most people ... that is not the most comfortable thing on earth."

Urban Partnerships That Make a Profit

One of the achievements that task force executives are proudest of is the creation of a computerized data bank containing models of successful private sector programs. As of Oct. 29, there were 2,300 "success stories" in the data bank, many of which find their way into the task force's newsletter and press releases.

Among the programs applauded by the task force is the placement of business facilities in low-income or otherwise dilapidated neighborhoods. A pioneer of this strategy was Control Data Corp., a Minneapolis-based computer manufacturing firm. In 1968, with the full support of company Chairman William C. Norris, Control Data opened a plant in a mainly black, low-income section of Minneapolis. Despite having to provide special benefits for employees, including day-care facilities, the plant, which employs over 300 workers, has turned a profit that Norris described as "a handsome one." Control Data has since opened three more plants in similar Minneapolis-St. Paul neighborhoods, and has opened facilities in the inner cities of Washington, D.C., San Antonio and Toledo.

Control Data officials emphasize the need for a profit motive to get businesses involved in such job creation and community development projects. "The magnitude of the job to be done is far beyond any potential for sheer philanthropy to fulfill,"

Control Data President Robert M. Price said.[4] To encourage other businesses to get involved, Control Data in 1978 joined a consortium of corporations and churches called City Ventures Corp. The group has been slow in starting, but Control Data has established a plant in inner-city Baltimore as part of the City Ventures project.

Baltimore is also the site of another for-profit venture that task force officials use as a model. The Inner Harbor project, a hotel, office building, shopping and entertainment complex in a formerly decaying waterfront area of downtown Baltimore, was constructed by the Rouse Corp. in the late 1970s. The company's chairman, James W. Rouse, has been active in some of the country's most successful urban renewal projects, including a similar renovation of Boston's Faneuil Hall. In developing Baltimore's inner harbor, Rouse worked closely with the city government, local business and banks, and community groups. "One of the reasons that Inner Harbor works so terribly well is that all of these key institutions ... have for the first time come together in a partnership," said Jerry Guth.

But opponents of the Reagan administration's budget policies point out that projects like City Ventures and Baltimore's inner harbor would have been impossible without federal seed money from the Urban Development Action Grant (UDAG) program.[5] The idea that federal incentives may be necessary to encourage profit-making, job-creating enterprises to move into inner cities is supported by another Reagan proposal. Last March the president submitted a plan to Congress under which businesses would receive substantial tax breaks and regulatory relief for locating in sections of inner cities designated by the secretary of housing and urban development as "enterprise zones." Although there is skepticism over the efficacy of tax incentives in luring businesses to the ghetto, many of the groups that oppose the overall thrust of Reagan's politics, including the National Urban League, support the enterprise zones plan.[6]

Debate Over Corporate Responsibilities

The most publicized endeavor of the Task Force on Private Sector Initiatives was a call last March for corporations to

[4] Price and Norris were quoted in *Newsweek*, Feb. 8, 1982, p. 69.

[5] The UDAG program provides grants for selected urban development projects. Although the grants make up only a small percentage of the projects' budgets, they do provide the credibility necessary to attract other sources of credit.

[6] The Senate Finance Committee passed the enterprise zones plan as part of an unrelated tax bill on Sept. 28, 1982, but the House has taken no action on it. Hearings have not even been held by the committees that have jurisdiction over the plan — Ways and Means, Judiciary and Banking. President Reagan made a new pitch for the plan in an address to the National League of Cities, meeting in Los Angeles on Nov. 29. But the House is still not expected to take action on enterprise zones in the lame-duck session that began Nov. 29, and the legislation probably will be resubmitted in the 98th Congress in January. For more information on the enterprise zone concept, see "Reagan and the Cities," *E.R.R.*, 1982, Vol. II, pp. 529-548.

American Philanthropy in 1981

Donors	Individuals	Bequests	Corporations	Foundations	Totals
Amount given *(in billions)*	$44.51	$3.49	$3.00	$2.62	$53.62
Percent of Total	83.0	6.5	5.6	4.9	100.0

Recipients	Religion	Education	Health and Hospitals	Social Welfare	Arts & Humanities	Other
Amount received *(in billions)*	$24.85	$7.49	$7.36	$5.32	$3.35	$5.25
Percent of Total	46.3	14.0	13.8	9.9	6.2	9.8

Source: "Giving USA," American Association of Fund-Raising Counsel, Inc., 1982 Annual Report.

double their total giving to philanthropy. Corporate philanthropy has averaged about 1 percent of pretax income. The task force called for corporations to increase that to 2 percent over the course of four years. Although the task force also called on individuals to double their giving, from an average of 2 to 4 percent of pretax income, it was the suggested corporate increase that created the greatest controversy, since it raised the whole issue of whether there was such a thing as "corporate social responsibility."

The nation has a history of corporate philanthropy that dates back at least a century, to the days when railroad industrialists funded the expansion of the Young Men's Christian Association (YMCA), which, in turn, provided good, cheap housing for workers in railroad towns. The tradition took firm root with the establishment of philanthropic foundations by such tycoons as John D. Rockefeller and Andrew Carnegie in the early part of this century.

Despite the billions of dollars invested by business in philanthropic causes, there are some businessmen and economists who are opposed to corporate philanthropy. Led by conservative economist Milton Friedman of the University of Chicago, this group believes that corporate philanthropists are playing games with other people's money. "It belongs to their workers, their employees, or their shareholders," said Friedman.[7] In fact, according to The Conference Board, a business research group in New York, only about 30 percent of American corporations contribute to philanthropy.

There are many who vehemently disagree with Friedman. The strongest protest comes from the philanthropic community. According to William Aramony, president of the United Way of America, "Friedman's in another world." Members of the White

[7] Quoted in *Fortune*, Sept. 20, 1982, p. 136.

House task force also take a strong stand in defense of their "doubling" proposal. Taking what economists would regard as a liberal view of corporate capitalism, Executive Director Guth said:

> There are those who say that the first task of business is to make a profit. That's wrong.... People organize themselves and their resources to respond to human needs and they create products and services of one kind or another to meet those needs.... The expectations of publics in communities where they have their economic life are equally valid as the whole host of other market needs that they have historically organized themselves to meet.

Others in the corporate community agree. One of the leaders in corporate philanthropy is the Minneapolis-based Dayton-Hudson Corp., which operates department stores in the Midwest. In 1947, Dayton-Hudson pledged to contribute 5 percent of its pretax income to philanthropy, and has since encouraged businesses in Minneapolis and other cities to form "5 Percent" or "2 Percent" clubs. In a speech to the Commonwealth Club in San Francisco last year, company Chairman Kenneth N. Dayton not only predicted that "increased corporate philanthropy is, indeed, an 'idea whose time has come,' " but also warned that if corporate philanthropy is not significantly increased, "we can count on a swift return to primary dependence on government for meeting all public needs, with all that implies." Dayton added, "The public's 'honeymoon' with business will come to a very abrupt end, indeed. And, given the raised expectations, the backlash could be severe enough to threaten the entire free enterprise system."

Business leaders point out that corporate philanthropy extends beyond cash donations. Some companies "lend" executives to non-profit organizations, to aid in such areas as accounting, fund raising, management and employee/volunteer training. Contributions of equipment constitute another form of corporate philanthropy and are especially popular among computer manufacturers. For example, International Business Machines Corp. (IBM), which gave $40 million in cash contributions in 1981, estimated that its contributions of equipment and loaned executives increased its philanthropic total to $80 million.[8]

Some observers credit the rise of "corporate social responsibility" to a new breed of corporate manager that has risen in recent years. "From the 1960s on, the new chief executive was much more socially conscious than we knew in the past," said Guth. However, social activists say they pressured corporations into becoming more socially responsible. "They have become

---

[8] See *The New York Times*, Sept. 22, 1982.

conscious of that because the work done by minority organizations, women's organizations, environmental organizations, public law advocacy organizations, and Nader's groups has forced
them to focus on it," said Robert O. Bothwell, executive director
of the National Committee for Responsive Philanthropy.[9]

Task Force Models of Voluntary Effort

The Reagan administration is counting on the voluntary, non-
profit sector to help some of the people affected by the recession
or the budget cuts. The task force's computer bank is full of
voluntary success stories, most of which predate the Reagan
administration's advocacy of private sector initiatives. One of
President Reagan's favorite examples of voluntary action is
Sister Falaka Fattah's House of Umoja in Philadelphia. In an
attempt to cut down on gang violence in her inner-city neighborhood, Sister Fattah began in 1968 to provide shelter and
counseling for local youths. In 14 years, she worked with over
500 boys, reclaiming most from the streets. Her efforts earned
her a meeting and a letter of praise from President Reagan.[10]

The task force gladly supplies examples of other praiseworthy
volunteer programs. Members of the United Auto Workers local
in Waterloo, Iowa, working with the Hawkeye Valley Area
Agency on Aging, formed a group several years ago called Brown
Baggers. Union workers contribute excess produce from their
gardens for distribution to the elderly and shut-ins. A New York
City organization known as J.O.B., for Just One Break, provides
free job placement for handicapped men and women. Silver Key
Senior Services provides homemaker services and meals to the
low-income elderly in Colorado Springs.

Then there are efforts that the task force does not emphasize,
but which illustrate the kinds of partnerships that the administration is advocating. In Philadelphia, for example, the
Consortium for Human Services has brought state and local
officials together with the business and voluntary communities
to plan employment and human service strategies. The city
government in Baltimore spearheads the "Blue Chip-in" campaign to raise funds from local businessmen. William Aramony
of the United Way says his organization helped set up consortiums of local businesses, foundations and voluntary agencies in
several cities.

[9] The committee, located in Washington, is a coalition of "non-traditional" non-profit
organizations, mainly those involved in minority and women's causes.
[10] Ironically, the House of Umoja was almost caught up in the Reagan budget-cutting.
During the Carter administration, Sister Fattah accepted her first federal grant in order to
create an "urban boys' town" in Philadelphia. In the first round of budget cuts in 1981, the
House of Umoja lost the equivalent of $250,000, most of it related to the loss of workers
supplied under the CETA public-service jobs program, which was terminated. However, the
loss was made up by a grant approved last summer by the U.S. Department of Health and
Human Services. According to Sister Fattah, the project will now be completed, although
her organization is one year behind in its construction schedule.

Impact of Budget Cuts

THAT WAS the good news. But according to many in the non-profit community, there is plenty of bad news for voluntary agencies and the people who depend upon them. At the same time that cuts in direct federal assistance to individuals and record-high unemployment have created a demand for voluntary relief unseen since the Great Depression, many voluntary agencies are taking deep cuts in the parts of their budgets supplied by federal grants. "It's ironic that at the time that needs are greatest, the capacity to generate resources tends to be more difficult," said Aramony.

The Reagan administration has gone to great lengths to attack the excesses of federal government programs while extolling the initiative of private sector and especially voluntary groups. However, many of these groups put much of their effort into carrying out government programs. According to an Urban Institute study,[11] non-profit groups received $40.4 billion from the federal government in 1980. That year, total philanthropic giving was $47.7 billion, and only $25.5 billion of that went to non-religious organizations. "The administration did not recognize the financial partnership and the service partnership that related government and many of these private groups," said Brian O'Connell of Independent Sector. "They assumed they were cutting public programs, when indeed much of that money was flowing to voluntary organizations."

Advocates of some of the small, minority-oriented charities paint the administration's actions in darker colors. "I think it's clear that the administration wanted to cut the budget, that it did not care about the neediest in our population," said Pablo Eisenberg, executive director of the Washington-based Center for Community Change.[12] "I don't think they gave a damn about the impact on the non-profits."

There are no exact figures on how much non-profit groups can expect to lose because Congress had completed action on only three of 13 appropriations bills before the campaign recess in October. The most quoted estimates are those in the Urban Institute study. Using the results of the fiscal year 1982 budget cuts along with President Reagan's proposals and early congressional action on the fiscal 1983 budget, authors Lester M. Salamon and Alan J. Abramson determined that the non-profit sector would lose $33 billion in federal funds between fiscal 1982

---

[11] Lester M. Salamon and Alan J. Abramson, "The Federal Budget and the Non-profit Sector," The Urban Institute, September 1982.
[12] Founded in 1968, the center provides technical assistance for its affiliate organizations, which are involved mainly in anti-poverty or community development activities.

and fiscal 1985. In addition, programs in areas in which the non-profit sector has an interest, including social welfare and community development, would lose $115 billion during that four-year period. Salamon and Abramson referred to these as "indirect cuts," since they would tend to increase demands for non-profit services.

Brian O'Connell of Independent Sector estimated that the total income for the non-profit sector over those four years would be $650 billion. Therefore, a $33 billion, or 5 percent, cut does not seem overwhelming. But as O'Connell pointed out, "The impact is not proportional. Some programs and organizations face not the 5 percent cut, but devastating slices of 50-100 percent." [13]

The hardest hit groups were the small, neighborhood organizations that were heavily dependent on federal money for their survival. But even those groups affiliated with established voluntary organizations are feeling the pinch. William Aramony of the United Way reported that United Way-affiliated organizations in large cities received an average of 47 percent of their funding from the federal government; in some cities, such as New York, the figure hit 75 percent.

The Reagan administration states optimistically that the success of the president's economic recovery program and the implementation of his "New Federalism" plan will enable worthy causes to turn to state and local governments for assistance. Advocates of some philanthropic groups, especially those in the social welfare and community development fields, are not thrilled about the prospect. "The history of increasing federal programs in the 1960s came as a direct result of the inattention of cities and states to problems of minorities and ultimately women," said Robert O. Bothwell.

Organizations Hardest Hit by Cutbacks

Although the budget cuts have pinched organizations across the voluntary spectrum, O'Connell drew a profile of the organizations most likely to be hurt. These include organizations that are most dependent on government funds, those least able to compete for block grants[14] and other government funding,

[13] "Briefing on Current Issues Impacting the Independent Sector," address presented at Independent Sector meeting, San Francisco, Oct. 25, 1982.

[14] As part of Reagan's "New Federalism" program, a number of federal programs are being combined into "block grants," with fewer regulatory strings attached for state and local governments, but with reduced funding levels. For background, see "Reagan and the Cities," *E.R.R.*, 1982 Vol. II, pp. 529-548; "Reaganomics on Trial," *E.R.R.*, 1982 Vol. I, pp. 1-20; and "Reagan's New Federalism," *E.R.R.*, 1981 Vol. I, pp. 249-268.

those least experienced at fund raising, and those that are least popular. According to James Castelli of Independent Sector, "Social welfare organizations, civic and political organizations, minority and newer organizations, and community organizations will feel the greatest impact."

The National Urban League has for years been involved in federally funded job training projects for minorities. In the fiscal year that ended last July, the Urban League funded 39 programs with a total of $34 million; in this fiscal year, $9 million will be spent on 22 projects. Other charitable organizations report similar troubles. Responding to a survey by Independent Sector, the National Council of La Raza, a Hispanic social welfare organization, said it had suffered a 40 pecent reduction in staff with a 45 percent reduction in services. Opportunities Industrialization Centers, a Philadelphia-based job training organization, lost $65 million, or 50 percent of its 1981 budget. The National Council of Churches reported that 25 domestic hunger projects with an annual average income of $142,000 in 1981 would average $72,000 in 1982.

Another problem for voluntary agencies was caused by the elimination of the Comprehensive Employment Training Administration (CETA) public service jobs program. Critics of the CETA jobs program complained that many of the jobs created were of the "makework" variety. But non-profit organizers say that CETA workers were vital to many of their functions. "Many organizations were taking advantage of the CETA program in a very useful way," said Robert O. Bothwell.

Also hindering voluntary organizations is the increase in the postal rate for non-profit groups. Last January Congress did not appropriate the full amount of an expected subsidy. As a result, the third-class bulk rate for non-profit organizations rose from 3.8 cents per piece to 5.9 cents. Although Congress restored part of the subsidy shortfall in July, the rate decreased only to 4.9 cents per piece. Since many organizations use direct mail to raise funds, or provide a magazine or newsletter to attract contributions, the increase in postal rates will cut into their capacity to provide services. O'Connell pointed out that the postal rate subsidy was one of the devices "developed by government to encourage private initiative to the public good."

Recent Increase in the Needy Population

Many social service agencies report that, as a result of the recession and federal budget cuts, they are being overwhelmed by demands for their services. In addition to requests for cash assistance to help pay rent or electricity bills, which social agencies typically receive during rough times, they have also

Reliance of Non-profit Groups on Government Funding

Proportion of total revenue provided by government grants, contracts and other programs:

Civil and Social Action	44 percent
Health Services	43 percent
Human Services	43 percent
Culture	10 percent
Education and Research	9 percent

Source: "The Fiscal Capacity of the Voluntary Sector," a study prepared by Bruce L. R. Smith of the Brookings Institution and Nelson M. Rosenbaum of the Center for Responsive Governance for a Brookings Institution conference, Dec. 9, 1981.

seen a big increase in the number of people requesting the basic necessities: food, clothing and shelter. In 1981, when President Reagan first started pressing for budget cuts, he promised to provide a "safety net" for the "truly needy." But social welfare advocates are not convinced. "I don't think that there ever was a safety net," said Father Gary Christ of the National Conference of Catholic Charities. "Someone without food or without shelter and without clothing and without the possibility of getting a job is someone who is truly needy."

Leaders of black and Hispanic organizations say that minorities are generally the most needful people in the country and have been hit the hardest by the recession. "When you get right down into the streets where we operate, it's incredible, the needless suffering in this country," said Milton Bondurant of the National Urban League. But they also point out that the problem is not exclusively a minority one. The ranks of the "truly needy" have been swelled by the "newly needy": lower-middle and middle-class Americans whose lives have been drastically changed by the recession.

Much of the demand on social agencies from the middle class is in the form of counseling services. Many people are having a hard time dealing with the psychological consequences of unemployment. Christ reported that in Buffalo, N.Y., requests for the marriage counseling services of Catholic Charities affiliates are up 20 percent over last year.

But growing numbers of middle-class people are turning to charities for the basics. Christ said that a visit to a soup kitchen would belie the stereotype of aid recipients as all welfare cases. "We're seeing people who, a couple of years ago, would have never dreamed that they'd be coming anywhere for help," Christ said. With the onset of winter, social agencies also expect an upturn in requests for shelter.[15]

[15] See "The Homeless: Growing National Problem," *E.R.R.*, 1982 Vol. II, pp. 793-812.

Cutbacks Felt in Other Non-profit Areas

While most of the national attention has been focused on these social welfare issues, other areas of the non-profit sector have also been affected by budget cuts. The Urban Institute estimated that the area of health care and financing would take $8.1 billion in direct cuts and $19.9 billion in indirect cuts. Medicaid, community mental health centers, alcohol abuse, maternal child and health and immunization are among the programs included in this area.

According to the Urban Institute, education and research will lose $5.2 billion directly and $28 billion indirectly. Programs listed in this category include student loans, school nutrition, Title I aid for disadvantaged students, Social Security payments to college students and work-study programs. Although education agencies receive a relatively small part of their funding from the federal government — 9 percent — educators worry that the budget cuts could have significant impact. For instance, there is concern that cutbacks in student aid could force many middle-class students to forgo private colleges in favor of public schools, squeezing out low-income and minority students who have traditionally found opportunity in state institutions.

Even the arts and culture communities are feeling the effect of the budget cuts. The Urban Institute found that the Reagan administration's fiscal 1983 budget proposals would result, by 1985, in more than 50 percent reductions from 1980 budget levels for the National Endowment for the Arts and the National Endowment for the Humanities, which supply grants to theater, dance and music companies, museums and other cultural institutions. The Corporation for Public Broadcasting would lose 59 percent of its funding between 1980 and 1985.

Weathering the Changes

THE REAGAN administration says it never intended to create the impression that the private sector would be able to make up for all of the budget cuts. But leaders of the non-profit community complain that Reagan's tendency to mention federal budget reductions and private sector initiatives in the same breath has raised expectations to a level that they cannot come close to meeting. "The gap is there and it's getting wider," said John J. Schwartz, president of the American Association of Fund-Raising Counsel in New York City. "Philanthropy simply can't make up the difference."

Rise in Philanthropic Giving

Year	Total Giving (billions)	Year	Total Giving (billions)
1981	$53.62	1975	$29.68
1980	47.74	1974	27.71
1979	43.31	1973	25.60
1978	39.63	1972	23.30
1977	36.02	1971	22.84
1976	32.54	1970	20.75

Source: "Giving USA," American Association of Fund-Raising Counsel, Inc., 1982 Annual Report.

Philanthropy has been growing rapidly in recent years. Last year, despite the onset of the recession, philanthropic giving scored a record increase of 12.3 percent over 1980, for a total of $53.6 billion. But according to the Urban Institute study, non-profit organizations would have to increase their income from private sources by 30-40 percent per year, or 3-4 times the all-time record increase, in order to maintain their 1980 service levels. In order to make up for all the indirect cuts, giving to voluntary agencies would have to increase by 90-100 percent per year.

Those involved in non-profit organizations cite similar statistics. Father Gary Christ said that to make up for the budget cuts in its areas of interest, Catholic Charities would have to take its best year and multiply it 4-6 times. "Anybody who really thinks that anybody can make up for the budget cuts is frankly living in a fool's paradise," he said.

Others in the non-profit community say that corporate philanthropy cannot be counted on to "fill the gap." Even after a record increase of 11.1 percent last year, corporate philanthropy still only comprised 5.6 percent of all giving. And with corporate profits plummeting in the recession, even some fund-raisers think it is unfair to ask business to dramatically increase its contributions. "When corporations are also responsible to their stockholders and a lot of our good corporate friends have names such as International Harvester and Ford Motor Co. and Montgomery Ward, is that a practical thing to ask?" said Gary Bloom of the National Urban League.

It is uncertain what the overall picture will be for philanthropy this year. William Aramony of the United Way estimated that United Way's national fund raising would increase by 6-8 percent this year, a substantial increase but less than last year's record 10.3 percent. The amount varies from locality to locality. Aramony expected Buffalo to run behind last year's pace, and Cleveland's campaign, which ended in October, raised just 0.5 percent more than last year, a result Aramony called a "miracle" considering Cleveland's depression-like condition. Some cities are running way ahead of average, including Hartford, whose United Way enjoyed a 13 percent gain over 1981. But whatever the increase, most people within the philanthropic community do not think it will be enough. "A lot of people are obviously going to be hurt, and are being hurt," said Schwartz.

Finding Fault in the Voluntary Sector

Reagan administration officials believe that too many groups were getting federal aid, that there was duplication of effort and that the time was ripe for a "sorting out." And there are those in the non-profit sector who agree. According to William Aramony, "There are some programs that should not be continued. There's nothing sacrosanct about that. What every community has to do is look at its service needs, look at its resources that are now available."

Some non-profit leaders are concerned about the reliance of some groups on federal funds. "The organizations that have done their fund-raising homework are going to raise more money," said Schwartz. "The ones that have been relying very heavily on government grants are not doing well, and they're not going to do well." But leaders of smaller, newer, neighborhood-oriented groups, many of which have poor or minority constituencies, say they lack a broad base of support and need those federal dollars. "A whole generation of organizations, some of which would have grown up to be effective forces, has been wiped out by the federal budget cuts," said Bothwell.

Brian O'Connell of Independent Sector said that there could always be streamlining, but that he gets "impatient" with critics who claim that it is time for a "shaking out." According to O'Connell, many non-profit groups have been "doing more with less" for a decade, including the YMCAs, Boys' Clubs and the National Council of La Raza.

Strategies to Deal With the Budget Cuts

The idea of stretching dollars in these hard economic times is pervasive in the non-profit community. "There is a commitment to do more with less," said Barbara J. Oliver, executive director of the National Assembly of National Voluntary Health and Social Welfare Organizations.[16] One dollar-stretching strategy being used by many voluntary organizations is the replacement of paid staff personnel with volunteers. O'Connell noted that many agencies had become addicted to the idea of professional-

---

[16] Based in New York, the assembly encourages "intercommunication" and "interaction" between the nation's large voluntary health and social welfare agencies. Its members include The United Way of America, The American Red Cross, The Salvation Army, The National Conference of Catholic Charities and the Girl Scouts of the U.S.A.

ism, and had filled many positions with professionals, such as social workers, teachers and nurses, that could just have easily been handled by volunteers. "This is one favorable aspect of the problem, there's a whole new re-emphasis on volunteers," said O'Connell.

There is also a re-emphasis on fund raising. Some established organizations are looking to new strategies to help replace lost revenues.  The National Urban League has pinpointed 300,000 likely contributors for a direct-mail campaign, has revitalized its finance committee which will conduct a two-year, 16-city fund-raising tour, and is hoping to raise $1 million from an entertainment event, the first in the organization's history. Some groups that were highly dependent on government funds are beginning to look for independent sources of revenue. O'Connell said that he tells these groups, "often to their utter consternation, that they must be prepared to devote a minimum of 25 percent of their efforts to building the kind of independent funding necessary to provide reasonable program continuity."

Some groups are either merging completely or are combining some administrative services. The Greater New York Fund/United Way published a guide earlier this year entitled "Merger: Another Path Ahead — A Guide to the Merger Process for Voluntary Human Services Agencies." Many organizations are also intensifying their public relations and lobbying efforts to try to prevent further budget cuts. Barbara Oliver said the organizations in her assembly were committed to "do something to continue to raise the consciousness of the general public and the government of their responsibility for the greater welfare."

Task Force and Reagan Policies Assessed

To the White House Task Force on Private Sector Initiatives, most of the complaints of the voluntary community and the private sector stem from a resistance to change. "For all of our talk about change, none of us accepts it very well," said Jerry Guth. "I find a lot of skepticism. . . ."

As the task force approaches its planned termination date of Dec. 31, there is also skepticism within the private sector about its role and accomplishments.[17] Some people, especially those involved with organizations that have been hard hit by the recession, see the task force as a public relations gimmick meant to divert attention from the president's budget cuts. "[Reagan] appointed a highly visible task force that could go out and talk about what the issues were and what private philanthropy ought to do with them, at the same time as he was lopping off very substantial monies to them," said Robert O. Bothwell.

"There is no responsible individual in the private, non-profit community today who will even suggest that there is a way for private giving to make up for the federal budget cuts."

Robert Bothwell, executive
director, National Committee
for Responsive Philanthropy

Pablo Eisenberg of the Center for Community Change said that the task force would have been unnecessary if it had not been for the budget cuts: "The Reagan administration and the task force talk about public-private sector partnerships, but what they're talking about is such a small drop in the bucket compared to the ... partnerships that already existed, and which the administration killed." Another problem, Eisenberg said, is that the task force is split between members who sought to be independent and others who maintained primary allegiance to the president. The task force "has never been able to get away from that tension," he said.

Others view the task force more positively. Aramony of the United Way indicated that Reagan and the task force played a useful role in encouraging more private sector activity. "[Reagan] created the climate in which corporations and individuals say, 'Uncle Sam's not there anymore, I've got to do something,' " he said. Brian O'Connell of Independent Sector praised the task force for "keeping the president focused on this area" and for putting "a new emphasis on community groups working together to solve problems." Even Bothwell was obliged to credit the task force for a "guts call" for its suggestion that corporations double their philanthropic contributions.

---

[17] Although the task force is likely to go out of business as scheduled on Dec. 31, the White House plans to continue its "Office of Private Sector Initiatives," which was established along with the task force last December. The office, which is headed by Jay Moorhead, special assistant to the president for private sector initiatives, will be in charge of carrying out the task force's recommendations to the president, which are scheduled to be submitted on Dec. 8, 1982.

There is also debate over the future direction of Reagan's economic policies. Some believe that the social programs that have already carried most of the burden of Reaganomics will continue to be victimized by budget cuts. "The meanness and the willingness to put the burden on those who can't afford it continue," said Eisenberg. However, others in the non-profit community see a trend away from the budget cuts in the administration and in Congress. "I think there's a strong sentiment against further cuts," said Aramony. Some political observers foresee greater difficulty for Reagan in pushing domestic budget cuts through a House that picked up 26 Democratic members in the recent elections.

There is one thing that virtually everyone, from the task force leadership to corporations to voluntary organizations, agrees on: whatever the incremental gains made through private sector initiatives, partnerships and belt-tightening, there is no way for the private sector to make up, dollar-for-dollar, for the federal budget cuts. How society adjusts to help the thousands of individuals and communities caught up in the transition may be the decisive issue of the next two years of Reagan's tenure.

Selected Bibliography

Books

Meyer, Jack A. (ed.), *Meeting Human Needs: Toward a New Public Philosophy,* American Enterprise Institute, 1982.

Articles

"A Spurt In Voluntarism, But Is It Enough?" *U.S. News & World Report,* Sept. 20, 1982.

"A Triple Whammy on Charities," *Business Week,* March 23, 1981.

"Can Companies Fill the Charity Gap?" *Business Week,* July 6, 1981.

Kinsley, Michael, "Waiting for Lenny," *Harper's,* March 1982.

Kirschten, Dick, "Even If Charity Does Begin at Home, Government May Still Play a Key Role," *National Journal,* May 22, 1982.

Miller, William H., "Industry Isn't Rushing Into Social Activism," *Industry Week,* Feb. 22, 1982.

Olasky, Marvin N., "Reagan's Second Thoughts on Corporate Giving," *Fortune,* Sept. 20, 1982.

Pauly, David et al., "Doing Good — at a Profit," *Newsweek,* Feb. 8, 1982.

Tuthill, Mary, "Countrywide Call for Volunteers," *Nation's Business,* March 1982.

Reports and Studies

"Analysis of the Economic Recovery Program's Direct Significance for Philanthropic and Voluntary Organizations and the People They Serve," Independent Sector, April 1982.

Editorial Research Reports: "Volunteerism in the Eighties," 1980 Vol. II, p. 905; "American Philanthropy," 1974 Vol. I, p. 21.

"Giving USA," American Association of Fund-Raising Counsel, Inc., Annual Report, 1982.

Salamon, Lester M. and Alan J. Abramson, "The Federal Budget and the Non-profit Sector," The Urban Institute Press, 1982.

Cover illustration by Staff Artist Belle Burkhart; illustrations on p. 207 and p. 213 by George Rebh.

INDEX